Diabetic Cookbook for Beginners

2 Books in 1: 3000 Days of Simple & Delicious Recipes with Inexpensive Ingredients to Manage Type 2 Diabetes and Prediabetes | 8-Week Healthy Meal Plan

By

Nathan Terrell

D1716372

Table of Contents

Book 1: Diabetic Air Fryer Cookbook

365 Days Quick and Delicious Recipes with Inexpensive Ingredients to Lower Your Blood Sugar for Type 2 Diabetes and Prediabetes | 28 Days Healthy Meal Plan

Introduction

Public health professionals would declare it a crisis if diabetes type 2 were a contagious illness that spread from person to person. Due to the rising rates of pediatric obesity, this challenging condition is now affecting an increasing number of adults as well as more and more children, particularly those belonging to certain ethnic groups. The great news is that type 2 diabetes and prediabetes may both be substantially avoided. Making lifestyle adjustments may prevent almost nine out of ten instances. The risk of acquiring heart disease and various malignancies may be decreased by making the same modifications. Five words sum up the secret to prevention, i.e. Stay active and Stay lean. If you have been diagnosed with diabetes already, advice for avoiding or reducing your risk of acquiring type 2 diabetes is also appropriate. Blood glucose regulation is enhanced by maintaining healthy body weight, eating a balanced & carbohydrate-controlled diet, and exercising often.

A healthy lifestyle for someone with diabetes entails both activity and proper diet. A balanced diet & frequent exercise can help you keep your blood glucose, commonly referred to as the sugar, within the target range, among other benefits. You should balance what you eat and drink with exercise and diabetes medicines, if you consume any, in order to regulate your blood glucose. Initially, it could seem challenging to become more active and change your drinking and eating routines. It can be easier for you to start small and ask the assistance of your family, friends, and medical professionals.

Diabetics can consume air-fried meals as part of a balanced diet. However, it's advised to restrict how often you consume such kinds of dishes each day, just as with any item that is fried in oil (little or big). Although it isn't a miraculous treatment for diabetes, it may assist those with the disease in choosing healthier alternatives to deep-fried meals. The amount of fat you consume and the number of saturated fats you consume may both be decreased using an air fryer. You may enjoy your favorite dishes in an air fryer without worrying about consuming too many calories. These little tools provide a healthier dinner with less fat and sugar by cooking food fast and uniformly. The most crucial aspect of utilizing an air fryer to prepare healthy meals is to cook them at the prescribed temperature. Not just proteins but a variety of veggies may be cooked in air fryers. They reduce the amount of oil used and the number of calories in deep-fried meals. Air fryers are beneficial for diabetes. Additionally, they let individuals eat "fried" meals without worrying about gaining weight or becoming ill from too much oil, which is particularly beneficial if you have diabetes. Food may be made more nutritious and with fewer carbs by using air fryers. Contrarily, air frying and deep frying are dangerous cooking techniques that increase the production of acrylamide, which, when ingested in excess, may lead to cancer & other health issues.

Chapter 1: Understanding Diabetes Type 2 & Benefits of an Air Fryer for Diabetics

Type 2 diabetes may be challenging to control if you are overweight or obese. Additionally, it raises the risk of high blood pressure and cholesterol, both of which are precursors to cardiovascular disease, the main killer of diabetes patients. You can better control your diabetes by leading a healthy lifestyle. Your vital health indicators, such as weight, blood pressure, blood sugar, and blood cholesterol, may also improve. Eating well and increasing your physical activity are two strategies for weight management.

It might be challenging to avoid junk food and fried foods while eating a balanced diet. When you've diabetes, fried meals are often not allowed, or they are not advised at least. However, fried meals cooked in air fryers are more suitable for a diabetic diet. You should be aware of the fact that air frying is healthier than conventional frying since it consumes fewer calories and less fat than traditional frying in oil. As a result, air-fried meals are preferable if you have diabetes and want to shed or maintain your weight, particularly if you're diabetic.

1.1 Understanding Diabetes

Diabetes occur when cells of your body are not able to absorb glucose (sugar) & utilize it as fuel. As a consequence, your bloodstream begins to accumulate additional sugar. Diabetes that is not properly managed may have catastrophic effects and harm a number of bodily organs and tissues, including the heart, kidneys, eyes, and nerves. In the United States, 34.2 million individuals of all ages, or nearly 1 in 10, have diabetes. One in five persons (approximately 7.3 million) over the age of 18 does not know they've diabetes (just below 3 percent of all adults). As individuals become older, more people are getting diabetes diagnoses. One in four persons (more than 26%) who are 65 years of age or older has diabetes.

Why it occurs:

Your body breaks the food you consume into different nutritional sources as part of the digesting process. Your body converts carbs (such as bread, rice, and pasta) you consume into sugar (glucose). When sugar is in circulation, it requires assistance—a "key"—to enter your body's cells, which make up the body's organs and tissues and are where it will be utilized. Insulin serves as this support or "key." The pancreas, an organ situated beneath the stomach, is the gland that produces the hormone insulin. Insulin is released into your bloodstream by your pancreas. The "door" in the cell wall is unlocked by insulin, allowing glucose to enter the cells of your body. The "fuel" or energy that tissues & organs need to operate effectively is provided by glucose.

Having diabetes:

- Insufficient or no insulin is produced by your pancreas.

Or

- Insulin is produced by your pancreas, but your body's cells do not react to it and cannot utilize it as they should. Your glucose level in the blood will increase if glucose cannot enter your body's cells and instead remains in circulation.

Symptoms:

Diabetes symptoms include:

- Enhanced thirst
- Weak and exhausted.
- Distorted vision
- Tingling or numbness in the feet or hands.
- Slow-healing wounds or sores.
- Unexpected weight loss
- A lot of urine.
- Frequent infections without a known cause.

- Dry mouth.

Additional signs:

- Frequently occurring urinary tract or yeast infections in women, as well as dry, itchy skin.

- Erectile dysfunction diminished muscle strength and decreased sex desire in males.

Types:

Diabetes Types include:

Type 1 (insulin-dependent) Diabetes: It's an autoimmune condition in which the body assaults itself. In this situation, your pancreas' insulin-making cells are killed. Type 1 (insulin-dependent) diabetes have its effects on up to ten percent of those who have the disease. Typically, children & young adults get the diagnosis (but anyone can get it). Diabetes was more often recognized as "juvenile" diabetes. Those who have this diabetes should take insulin daily. It is also called insulin-dependent form of diabetes for this reason.

Type 2 (adult-onset) diabetes: In this kind, either your body doesn't produce sufficient insulin, or your cells don't react to it properly. The most typical kind of diabetes is this one. This diabetes have its effect on up to ninety five percent of persons with the disease. People in their middle years and older tend to develop it. Insulin-resistant diabetes and adults-onset diabetes are two more names for Type 2.

Pre-diabetes: This condition is a precursor to diabetes Type 2. Your glucose levels in the blood are above average but not that high to get a diabetes Type 2 diagnosis.

Gestational diabetes: This kind appears in certain pregnant women. After pregnancy, the gestational diabetes often disappears. However, if you've gestational diabetes, you are more prone to eventually acquire diabetes Type 2.

It may occur in less prevalent forms like:

Monogenic diabetic syndromes: Up to 4% of all instances of diabetes are caused by these uncommon hereditary variants of the disease. Examples include young-onset diabetes with maturity and neonatal diabetes.

Diabetes associated with cystic fibrosis: This is a kind of diabetes that only affects those who have this condition.

Diabetes brought on by drugs or chemicals: Symptoms of this kind include organ transplantation, HIV/AIDS therapy, and usage of glucocorticoids.

Diabetes insipidus: Your kidneys create a lot of pee when you have diabetes insipidus, a unique, unusual illness.

Complications:

Your body's tissues & organs may sustain severe harm if your glucose level in blood is increased for a long length of time. Over the course of time, certain issues may pose a danger to life. One's complications are:

- Cardiovascular conditions such as atherosclerosis, hypertension, heart attack, high cholesterol, and chest discomfort (narrowing of arteries).

- Numbness and tingling brought on by neuropathy (nerve injury) that begins at the toes or fingers and progresses.

- Nephropathy, or damage to the kidneys, may cause renal failure and the requirement for dialysis or a kidney transplant.

- Blindness-results in eye degeneration known as retinopathy, cataracts, and glaucoma.

- The foot injury includes bad blood flow, nerve damage, and slow wound and pain healing.

- Infected skin.

- Erection problems.

- Loss of hearing.

- Depression.

- Dementia.

- Dental issues.

1.2 Type 2 Diabetes - Brief Explanation

A serious illness known as type 2 diabetes occurs when your pancreas is unable to produce enough insulin or when the insulin it does produce cannot function correctly. This indicates that your blood sugar (glucose) levels are increasing. In the UK, type 2 diabetes affects around 90% of those who have it. It is a severe ailment that may last a lifetime. If type 2 diabetes is left untreated, excessive blood sugar levels may gravely harm several body organs, such as your feet, heart, and eyes. These are referred to as diabetic complications. You may live well with diabetes type 2 and lower your chance of acquiring it, however, with the correct care and treatment.

The main cause:

To survive, you require insulin. It does a crucial task. It enables the blood glucose to feed your body by getting inside your cells. Even if you have diabetes type 2, your body continues to convert the carbohydrates in your food & drink into glucose. The pancreas subsequently releases insulin in response to this. However, since this insulin is unable to function correctly, the blood sugar levels continue to increase. More insulin is therefore released. This may gradually wear out the pancreas in certain type 2 diabetics, causing their bodies to produce less & less insulin. This puts you at risk for hyperglycemia and may result in even increased blood sugar levels. Having type 2 diabetes causes your insulin response to stop working properly. This results in the following:

- Your liver, muscles and fat (sometimes referred to as peripheral tissues) develop an inability to react to insulin, which prevents them from absorbing and using glucose.

- Your pancreas' beta cells run out of energy and are unable to make enough insulin.

Obesity:

The most common metabolic disorders are type 2 diabetes and obesity, so how you understand their matters. Despite being distinct conditions, they usually overlap. According to Caroline Apovian, MD, a specialist in nutrition and weight management, "Although lifestyle is essential for treating both obesity and diabetes, some people never become obese, and for those who do, lifestyle changes don't always work because obesity is indeed a disease & the body defends an increased body weight set point. The hormonal changes brought on by obesity might cause a patient to gain weight even after losing it. But type 2 diabetes and obesity are becoming more common. According to researchers, it's because of your surroundings. There is a greater selection of highly processed, high-fat meals available. Other "non-food things" are often present in these foods. These substances have been shown to alter how your bodies store fat & use energy by acting as endocrine disruptors. Even if there hasn't been enough research to establish a link, the majority of medical professionals and nutritionists advise against them.

Insulin resistance:

Type 2 diabetes is brought on by insulin resistance. However, it is possible to have insulin resistance while having no disease at all. Dr Chistofides says, "Diabetes is all about energy in & energy out." "There is a mishandling of how the body balances energy intake & energy demand in case of type 2 diabetes." This inefficient use of energy has an insulin resistance-causing sign of insulin insensitivity. If you consume a lot of processed meals with added sugar, your body will initially continue to release insulin as it attempts to absorb and utilise glucose. What may occur if you've prediabetes and consume too many sugary foods is as follows:

- Insulin sensitivity develops throughout time as a consequence of your peripheral tissues being less sensitive to the insulin released in excess amounts.

- Your sugar levels in the blood are still raised because your body isn't adequately absorbing and utilising glucose at this stage.

- Your pancreas' beta cells keep making and releasing insulin in an effort to control the sugar levels.

- When your beta cells are harmed and die, your body is unable to create enough insulin, which causes high blood sugar (hyperglycemia). The last sign of energy mismanagement is hyperglycemia, which is indicated by high haemoglobin A1C values and results in a type 2 diabetes diagnosis.

Diabetes type 2 symptoms:

Compared to type 1 diabetes, type 2 diabetes occurs more gradually. Many folks either don't experience any symptoms or are unaware of them. But you may observe:

- **Polydipsia:** It is an extreme case of thirst that is worse than what you experience on a hot day. You could have polydipsia if drinking doesn't satisfy it and your mouth often feels dry and cottony.

- **Hyperphagia:** In contrast to the hangry sensation you experience after missing meals, hyperphagia is an unrelenting hunger which is more bottomless. It may be hyperphagia if you've eaten a substantial, well-balanced meal (consider a dinner-sized plate), yet you still feel hungry afterwards.

- **Polyuria:** More frequent urination is referred to as polyuria. Based on your lifestyle, the drugs you're taking, & how much alcohol you consume, the frequency of toilet visits varies. However, peeing more than 7 - 8 times per day may be an indication of diabetes type 2.

- If you have diabetes type 2 and have not altered your exercise regimen or diet, weight loss may be a warning indication.

- Because blood sugar levels cause your eye lens to expand, blurred vision might appear quickly and can also come and go.

- Headaches may range in severity from mild to severe and might happen often.

- Given that yeast consumes sugar as food, having higher blood glucose levels may raise your chance of developing yeast infections.

- Extremity paresthesia, or tingling in the hands and feet, may resemble the feeling you experience when your foot "falls asleep" and may be an early indicator of diabetic neuropathy due to damage to your tiny blood vessels.

- The feeling of having a dry mouth is typically accompanied by an excessive amount of thirst.

- It takes more than being weary of being fatigued. You can be fatigued if you experience like you never get enough sleep, your body feels heavy, & even minor chores seem daunting. There may come a point when going from your room to the kitchen that seems like an Olympic sprint.

- Even the smoothest toothbrush may feel unpleasant when used to brush sore, irritated gums.

Risk factors associated with type 2 diabetes

There are certain factors that might raise your risk of developing type 2 diabetes. It's important to be mindful of these factors since

type 2 diabetes symptoms aren't usually visible. They may consist of:

- **Age.** If you are white and over 40, or if you are a Black African, African Caribbean, or South Asian and over 25, you are more in danger.

- **Ethnicity.** Black African, African Caribbean, South Asian or Chinese ancestry puts you at higher risk.

- **Family background.** For instance, if your sibling, sister, parent, or you yourself have diabetes.

- **Medical background.** For instance, if you've got a history of severe mental illness, gestational diabetes, heart attacks, or strokes.

- If you are obese or overweight.

- If you have an excessively big waist.

Diabetic Type 1 vs Type 2 Differences: There are a few key distinctions between type 1 and type 2 diabetes:

- Diabetes type 1 is an autoimmune disorder. Type 1 diabetes cannot be cured; it can only be managed. Effective treatment and a change in lifestyle may reverse type 2 diabetes.

- In diabetes type 1, the pancreas is not able to make insulin, but in diabetes type 2, you can create less insulin, and your body responds to it less effectively.

- Without their insulin medication, people with type 1 diabetes risk death. Except in cases of severe pancreatic insufficiency, type 2 diabetics should refrain from receiving insulin therapy.

1.3 Managing Diabetes Type 2

Nobody like dieting, but, as Dr Apovian notes, "Weight decreases of as low as 3-5 per cent have been demonstrated to minimise the risk of diabetes type 2 in persons who've been medically recommended to lose weight. Dietary adjustments should include more fibre, more protein, healthier fats, fewer simple carbs, and fewer processed foods, as well as a reduction in calories and a change in the amount and quality of macronutrients. When medical professionals and nutritionists speak about inflammatory diets, they mostly refer to processed foods. Yet not just food has the potential to cause inflammation. A number of lifestyle choices may also cause systemic inflammation in your body, which can impair your ability to control your blood sugar levels. The following elements encourage systemic inflammation:

- packaged food

- extra sugars

- excessive alcohol consumption

- the inadequate amount and quality of sleep

- a few autoimmune diseases

- Smoking

- Anxiety and sadness

Although controlling diabetes type 2 is a matter of personal choice, you may follow some generic advice:

- Losing weight may enhance insulin sensitivity and lower blood glucose levels if your doctor recommends it for medical reasons.

- The Dietary Approach to Stop Hypertension (DASH) diet and the Mediterranean diet have been demonstrated to be useful in treating both diabetes & cardiovascular risk, yet there is no one ideal diet.

- Exercise. If you've never exercised before, start out slowly and build up your volume & intensity as your body becomes used to it. Strength and aerobic training together are the most effective forms of exercise for managing type 2 diabetes.

- Don't eat anything processed. Eat as little packaged food as you can. You'll often find the healthiest food in the grocery store's perimeter, so shop there.

- Make an effort to obtain adequate rest.

- If medication is necessary, consult with your physician to identify the dosage that is most effective for you.

Living with Type 2 Diabetes:

It's not necessary for type 2 diabetes to be a lifelong illness. On the other hand, the moment you are diagnosed with type 2 diabetes is the perfect time to start making changes to your lifestyle for the better. According to Dr Christofides, "What you do daily may make a difference." "Park at the far corner of the parking lot. Consider using the stairs. Think about eliminating packaged goods and just purchasing fresh foods. The optimal diabetes

diet is subjective. Focus on balance and freshness. Include vegetables, whole grains, lean proteins (from meat or plants), nuts, legumes, seeds, and entire fruits in your diet.

- Be active. One of the most crucial things you really can do for your general health, including your mental well-being, is exercise. One of the greatest methods to maintain weight loss after losing it is via exercise.

- Find things you want to do and attempt to include friends and family in them. It's not necessary to exercise at a gym. Take a quick stroll in the neighborhood with a buddy, or go for a trek in the park. You'll get an added boost in health and happiness thanks to vitamin D.

1.4 Preventing Type 2 Diabetes - Role of a balanced diet

The idea of cutting up on the foods you like may feel overwhelming if you were just diagnosed with diabetes type 2 or if you were previously diagnosed with the disease but are now willing to make dietary changes. However, you may be glad to learn that maintaining a healthy diet for diabetes type 2 isn't as challenging as you might have thought, and you can still enjoy eating while managing this condition. Diabetes does not have a special diet. But the foods you consume also affect how good you feel & how much stamina you have, in addition to how you control your diabetes. An effective diabetes control strategy is built on the foundation of a balanced diet. Other pillars include managing stress, engaging in regular exercise, and taking any recommended medicines.

Balanced Diet & its Benefits:

Depending on the age, gender, level of activity, and objectives, you'll need to eat & drink

differently. However, no one meal has all the vital elements your body needs. A healthy diet thus emphasizes diversity and consuming new items from each of major food categories each day. A balanced diet entails consuming more of certain things while consuming less of others. But while our dishes and bowls have become

larger, portion sizes have increased recently. Additionally, eating bigger meals may make it harder for you to control your weight. We have additional details regarding maintaining a healthy weight for you. Below are the highlighted advantages of each food category. It's crucial for you to be aware of how certain foods may protect your heart while others have a more gradual effect on your blood sugar levels. Learn about them and how making healthy decisions may lower your chance of developing diabetic complications.

Veggies and fruits:

Diabetes does not exclude fruit consumption. Fruit and vegetables are naturally lower in calories and high in fibre, vitamins, and minerals. They also provide every meal flavour and diversity. Fresh, frozen, dry, and can all

count. To receive the most variety of vitamins and minerals, choose a rainbow of colours. Fruit juices & smoothies should be avoided since they don't include as much fibre. You may be tempted to forgo fruit and vegetables if you're attempting to reduce the number of carbohydrates you consume. But it's crucial to incorporate them daily into your diet. You may experiment with lower-care choices. Fruits and vegetables may help prevent certain malignancies, high blood pressure, heart disease, and stroke, all of which are illnesses that are more likely to affect people with diabetes.

Benefits:

- maintain the health of your gut system

- aid in preventing heart disease, strokes, and several malignancies in the body

Aim for at least five meals each day for everyone. A piece is about equal to the size of your hand's palm.

Starchy foods:

Potatoes, pasta, rice, bread, naan, chapattis, and plantains are examples of starchy foods. All of them include carbohydrates, which are converted to glucose and utilized as fuel by your cells. Some starchy meals have the drawback of rapidly raising

blood glucose levels, which might make it more difficult for you to control your diabetes. These foods have what is referred to as an increased glycemic index (GI).

There are certain starchy food alternatives that are healthier and have a more gradual impact on blood sugar levels. These include wholegrain bread, whole-wheat pasta, and basmati, brown, or wild rice, all of which have a low glycemic index (GI). Additionally, they have higher fibre, which supports healthy digestion. Therefore, if you want to reduce your carb intake, start by cutting down on foods like white bread, pasta, and rice.

Benefits:

- The fibre aids in maintaining a healthy digestive tract.
- some take longer to change your levels of blood sugar
- Whole grains safeguard your heart.

Make an effort to consume some starchy foods daily.

Foods high in protein include eggs, meat, fish, beans, almonds, and lentils:

Protein-rich foods like meat and fish help to maintain the health of your muscles. Less red & processed meat is necessary for a healthy diet since these meats have been connected to heart disease and cancer. Omega-3 oil, which is abundant in oily fish like salmon, mackerel, and sardines, may aid in protecting the heart.

Benefits:

- Keeps your muscles in good condition.
- Fish oil protects your heart.

Try to eat something from this category of food each day. Particularly, consume 1 or 2 servings of oily fish per week. You do not, however, have to consume meat every day.

Dairy products and substitutes:

Calcium and protein are abundant in milk, cheese, and yoghurt, which are wonderful for your bones, teeth, and muscles. However, certain dairy products are heavy in fat,

especially saturated fat, so pick lower-fat substitutes.

In low-fat versions of dairy products like yoghurt, look for added sugar. If you need it sweeter, it's best to use unsweetened yoghurt & add some berries. If you prefer soy milk as a dairy substitute, choose one that is calcium-fortified and unsweetened.

Benefits:

- good for the teeth and bones
- prevents muscle deterioration

Every day, you need some calcium.

Oils & spreads:

While less saturated fat is necessary, you still

need some fat in your diet. This is so that the risk of heart disease and stroke might be increased. Some saturated fats could raise blood cholesterol levels. Butter, palm nut oil, and coconut oil are some of these less healthful alternatives. Foods like vegetable oil, olive oil, rapeseed oil, spread prepared from these oils, & nut butter is examples of healthier saturated fats.

Benefits:

- Unsaturated fats support heart health.

1.5 Diabetic Diet

Simply keeping to regular mealtimes and consuming healthy foods in moderation constitutes a diabetic diet. A diabetic diet is a balanced, calorie- and fat-free eating regimen that is naturally high in nutrients. Fruits, vegetables, and whole grains are essential components. In actuality, a diabetic diet is the healthiest diet for the majority of people.

Creating a diabetic diet:

Your doctor will probably suggest that you see a nutritionist assist you in creating a healthy eating plan if you've diabetes or prediabetes. The plan assists you in managing your weight, controlling the risk factors of heart disease, including high blood pressure & blood fat levels, and controlling your blood glucose (sugar) levels. Extra calories & fat cause your blood sugar to spike, which is not

what you want. If blood glucose levels aren't controlled, it may cause major issues, including high blood sugar (hyperglycemia), which, if it persists, may result in long-term concerns like nerve, kidney, and heart damage.

Making smart meal selections and keeping track of your eating patterns will help you maintain your blood glucose levels within a safe range. Weight reduction has a variety of additional health advantages, as well as making blood glucose management simpler for most persons with type 2 diabetes. A diabetic diet offers a well-planned, nourishing strategy to safely attain your goal if you want to reduce weight.

A diabetic diet is composed of:

- Eating 3 meals one day at regular intervals is the foundation of a diabetic diet. This improves how well you utilise the insulin your body makes or receives from a medicine.

- You may create a diet focused on your health objectives, preferences, and lifestyle with the assistance of a trained dietitian. Additionally, he or she may advise you on how to change your eating patterns, such as by picking portions that are appropriate for your size & level of exercise.

Suggested foods:

Use these nutrient-dense meals to make your calories count. Pick wholesome carbs and meals high in fibre, seafood, and "good" fats.

Nutritious carbs:

Simple carbohydrates like sugars and complex carbs like starches are broken down during digestion to produce blood glucose. Concentrate on wholesome carbs, like:

- Vegetables

- Fruits

- whole grains

- Beans, peas, and other legumes

- dairy goods with low fat, including milk & cheese

- Don't consume meals and beverages with extra fats, sweets, or salt, as well as less healthful carbs.

Foods high in fibre:

All plant food components that your body cannot digest or absorb are considered to be dietary fibre. Your body's digestion is moderated by fibre, which also helps to regulate blood sugar levels. Fibre-rich foods include:

- Vegetables

- Fruits

- Nuts

- Beans, peas, and other legumes

- whole grains

Heart-healthy fish

Eat seafood that is good for your heart at least 2 times a week. Omega-3 fatty acids, which are abundant in fish like salmon, tuna, mackerel, and sardines, may reduce heart disease.

Healthy fats:

Monounsaturated & polyunsaturated fatty acid-rich foods may aid in lowering your cholesterol levels. These consist of:

- Avocados
- Nuts
- Olive, peanut, and canola oils
- Don't go overboard, however, since fats all contain a lot of calories.

Foods to avoid:

Diabetes accelerates the formation of blocked & hardened arteries, increasing the risk of heart disease & stroke. The following ingredients may be detrimental to your efforts to maintain a healthy diet for your heart.

Saturated fats. Animal proteins, including butter, hot dogs, beef, sausage, & bacon, should be avoided, as should high-fat dairy products. Also, keep palm kernel and coconut oils to a minimum.

Tran's fats. Don't consume Trans fats, which are included in stick margarine, shortening, baked products, and processed snacks.

Cholesterol. Dairy products having high fat content, animal high-fat proteins, liver, egg yolks, & any other organ meat are all sources of cholesterol. Aim to consume not more than 200 mg of cholesterol every day.

Sodium. Limit your daily salt intake to 2,300 milligram or less. If you've high blood pressure, your doctor could advise you to set your sights even lower.

Putting everything together creates a strategy.

To assist you in maintaining a normal blood glucose level, you may develop a diabetic diet using a number of different strategies. You could discover that 1 or a combination of the following strategies works for you with the assistance of a dietitian:

1. The plate approach.

The ADA (Americans Diabetes Association) provides a straightforward meal-planning approach. Basically, it emphasizes eating more veggies. Take the following actions to prepare your plate:

- Nonstarchy veggies, such as carrots, spinach, and tomatoes, should make up half of your meal.
- Give a protein, like a lean pork, tuna, or chicken, a quarter of the dish.
- Add whole grains, like brown rice, or starchy vegetable, like green peas, to the final part of the plate.
- Include "healthy" fats in moderation, such as those found in avocados or nuts.
- Include a dish of dairy or fruit along with a glass of water, coffee or unsweetened tea.

2. Counting carbs.

Carbohydrates have the most effect on the blood glucose level since they break down into glucose. You may want to learn how to calculate the number of carbs you consume so that you can change the insulin dosage to assist in regulating your blood sugar. It's critical to monitor the carbohydrate content of each meal and snack.

You can learn portion control techniques from a nutritionist, who can also help you become a knowledgeable label reader. Additionally, you may learn from him or her how to pay close attention to portion size & carbohydrate content. A nutritionist may show you how to calculate the number of carbs in each meal and snack if you are taking insulin and how to change your insulin dosage appropriately.

3. Select your meals.

To assist you in making meal and snack plans, a nutritionist may suggest that you choose a certain food. A variety of foods are available for selection from lists that include sections for carbs, proteins, and fats.

"Choice" refers to one serving within a category. Serving each other item in that category contains about the same number of calories, protein, carbs, and fat as that meal option, as well as the same impact on blood sugar levels. For instance, selections on the starch, fruit, and milk list range from 12 - 15 grams of carbs.

4. Glucose index.

The glycemic index is used by some diabetics to choose meals, particularly carbs. This system places foods high in carbohydrates in order how affect blood sugar levels. Ask your dietician whether you think this approach would be effective for you.

Outcomes of a diabetic diet:

The easiest method to maintain control over your glucose level and avoid diabetic problems is to stick to your healthy eating plan. Additionally, you may modify it to meet your own objectives if you want to reduce weight.

A diabetic diet has additional advantages outside only helping you control your blood sugar. Following a diabetic diet is believed to lower the risk of cardiovascular illnesses and some forms of cancer since it suggests eating plenty of fruits, vegetables, and fibre. Additionally, eating low-fat dairy products

may lower your future chance of having poor bone mass.

1.6 Antidiabetic Lifestyle

People who are more likely to develop diabetes & those who have already received a type 2 diagnosis are often urged to make lifestyle adjustments to assist in controlling their condition.

- Two and a half hours of moderate-intensity exercise or one hour and fifteen mins. of high-intensity exercise per week are the suggested lifestyle interventions.
- Progressive weight loss to reach a healthy BMI (body mass index).
- increasing consumption of vegetables & other meals rich in nutritional fibre, swapping refined carbs for whole-grain options
- lowering the consumption of saturated fat

Physical exercise: It is advised to engage yourself in either 2 and 1/2 hours of exercise of moderate intensity or 1 and 1/4 hours of vigorous exercise. Physical exercise with a moderate intensity includes:

- Rapid walking
- Cycling over a mostly level surface
- Aquatic exercise
- Hiking
- Rollerblading
- using a hand lawnmower

Among the vigorous physical activities are:

- Jogging
- swimming
- cycling at high speed or on an incline
- Football
- Gymnastics
- Skipping

It may be possible to refer certain patients for supervised or organized exercise sessions.

Loss of weight:

Overweight people should attempt to reduce weight gradually until they reach a healthy BMI. A healthy BMI is between:

- Ranging from 18.5 to 24.9
- Alternatively, for those of South Asian ancestry, between 18.5 & 22.9

Striving for progressive weight reduction with a goal of losing 5 to 10% of body weight over the course of a year is advised for those whose BMI is over the recommended limit. Losing weight may assist persons who already have type 2 diabetes or pre-diabetes better regulate their blood sugar levels and lower their chance of acquiring diabetes. Your doctor may recommend that you participate in an organized weight reduction program if your BMI is higher than 30. Orlistat is a weight reduction medication that may be recommended to those who are unable to lose weight via lifestyle modifications.

Stress:

It has been shown that stress increases the risk of type 2 diabetes. An individual's body triggers the threat response when they are under stress. Stress hormones are produced, raising blood pressure and blood sugar levels and activating the immune system, among other changes in the human body.

- Digestion, development, and other non-essential body processes are reduced so that energy may be utilized to combat or escape the danger that is triggering the threat response.

- Controlling blood sugar levels may be exceedingly challenging when someone is under constant stress, especially if they are unaware of their stress levels.

A straightforward, non-toxic method to regulate stress-related fluctuations in blood sugar is to use stress management strategies like mindfulness. The likelihood of acquiring complications associated with diabetes, like stroke, heart disease, hypertension, and

mental health issues, including depression and anxiety, is also decreased by lowering stress levels.

1.7 Using an Air-Fryer - Diabetes-Friendly Cooking Equipment

The air fryer does not really fry the food; instead, it more closely resembles a countertop convection oven that has been improved. (However, keep in mind that baking and air-frying are two distinct processes.) This little appliance boldly asserts that it can simulate the results of deep-frying with just hot air and little or no oil at all. The popularity of this technology has increased over the past few years. Numerous meals, such as freshly baked cookies, roasted vegetables, homemade French fries, & frozen chicken wings, can be air-fried.

How an Air-fryer works:

The top part of the air fryer houses the heating element and fan. Hot air travels down and around the food you have put in the basket of the fryer when it is turned on. The food has a crisp texture akin to deep-frying without using oil because to the rapid circulation.

How to operate the air-fryer:

Put the food into the basket.

The basket's capacity may range from 2-10 quarts, depending on the size of your air fryer. To make the dish lovely and crispy, you usually need to add one to two tablespoons of the oil. To speed up cleaning, if you're pressed for time, use foil in the air fryer.

Establish the time & temperature.

Based on the thing you are preparing, air fryer cooking times & temperatures may vary from 5-25 mins at 350°-400°F.

Allow food to cook.

To ensure equal crisping, you can sometimes need to turn or flip the food midway while

cooking. It's important to clean the equipment when you have finished cooking. Type-2 diabetes can be averted with the use of an air fryer. The cooking method used by air fryers is known as "air frying," and it doesn't utilize oil which is absorbed in the food. When an item is

cooked in the air fryer, this may lower the fat level by up to 80%.

Using an Air-fryer to make a meal for a diabetic patient.

Air fryers are hailed as the healthy alternative to deep frying, & they are in many ways significantly healthier than deep fryers & many other methods of cooking. The main reason for this is that the air fryer can reduce the amount of fat in food by up to 80 percent by not using oil, and it also does a great job of preserving nutrients while cooking. You should monitor the amount of salt and fat you consume each day since too much of either may increase your risk of heart disease, high blood pressure, cholesterol, and blood sugar swings. A diabetic would thus profit from cooking in an air fryer since the amount of fat and salt may be reduced. Prepare dishes with the air fryer that are high in protein & vitamins.

You can prepare vegetables, beef, fowl, fish, nuts, soups, and more using an air fryer. In fact, many who choose to follow low-carb, "keto," & blood sugar diets have found the air fryer to be a useful tool. For making crispy French fries, whether frozen or freshly cooked potato cut fries, both air fryers & deep fryers are often utilized. However, you may get comparable effects using vegetables, more specifically: jimaca, celeriac, rutabaga, and zucchini, in place of French potato fries, which are high in carbs. Obesity and overweight have been demonstrated to raise the risk of diabetes type-2 and a wide range of other metabolic disorders. One must cut down on daily calorie consumption to stop the development of such disorders. An air fryer is a terrific tool for this project.

Foods that are deep fried have a high-fat content because they are cooked in hot oil, which is then absorbed into the meal throughout the cooking process. Less than half as many calories are included in each gram of fat (9 calories per gram compared to 4 calories for each gram of carbohydrate or protein). In certain situations, the air fryer may reduce food fat by up to 80%. Every meal prepared in an air fryer would have much fewer calories if the fat level were drastically reduced. Air-fried

chicken wings have more protein than deep-fried chicken wings do. Except when it's deep-fried when it's truly fairly fat, chicken flesh is pretty lean meat. With this in your mind, you may be able to see how using an air fryer might be advantageous for anybody attempting to get in shape or eat better, both of which are excellent strategies to stave against illnesses like type-2 diabetes.

Using the oil in an Air-fryer:

For diabetics, air fryers offer a contemporary substitute for conventional cooking techniques. Foods that are air-fried tend to be healthier since they cook rapidly and with little to no oil. An excellent technique to cook with fewer fat and calories is to use an air fryer. You can cook excellent food without fearing it drying out or burning on the base of the pan, thanks to its ability to distribute heat evenly.

One oil is known as rice bran oil. It is a good option for diabetics since it is high in monosaturated fatty acids, which lower

cholesterol. Canola oil can be a wise option for diabetics, according to another study. The risk of cardiovascular illnesses has been shown to be lower when these oils are consumed. Other options are olive oil, coconut oil, avocado oil, and sunflower oil if you can't locate either of these. Olive oil's reputation as 1 of the healthiest oils for diabetics is another factor.

1.8 Overall Health Benefits of Using an Air fryer

When used correctly, air fryers provide a number of health advantages:

Losing weight may be aided by using air fryers.

Increased consumption of fried meals is directly linked to an increased risk of obesity. This is due to the fact that meals that are deep-fried often include a lot of fat and calories. Weight reduction is aided by converting to air-fried meals from deep-fried meals & by taking lesser harmful oils on a daily basis.

Air Fryer Reduces Calories.

Since they use a lot less oil than conventional fryers, air fryers also save calories. For instance, dishes that are air-fried may just need

one tsp. of oil, which only contributes 40 calories. In comparison, using only one tbsp. of oil during deep-frying increases calorie content by roughly 120. So, switching from deep-fried to air-fried items may aid in weight control.

Compared to deep frying, air frying might be safer.

Foods are deep-fried by heating a big container of hot oil. This might be dangerous. Although air fryers do become hot, there's no chance of splashing, spilling, or unintentionally touching boiling oil. To guarantee safety, users should use frying appliances carefully and according to instructions.

The danger of hazardous acrylamide production is decreased by air fryers.

Food frying in oil may lead to the development of hazardous substances like acrylamide. When meals are cooked at high heat, such as when deep frying, this chemical develops in some of the foods. Acrylamide may be related to the emergence of several malignancies, including ovarian, endometrial, breast, pancreatic, and esophageal cancer, as per the International Agency for the Research on Cancer. Although the findings are inconclusive, Trusted Sources have also shown a connection between dietary acrylamide & ovarian, endometrial, or kidney

malignancies. People may reduce their risk of eating food containing acrylamide by shifting to air frying.

Reducing consumption of fried foods lowers illness risk.

Numerous harmful health issues have been linked too frequently using oil in cooking and eating traditional fried dishes. One may lessen their chance of developing these issues by using alternate cooking techniques for deep frying.

Chapter 2: Air Fried Diabetic Diet ~ Appetizers & Side Recipes

1. Coconut Shrimp

Ready in: 20 mins.

Serves: 4

Difficulty: easy

Ingredients:

- 2 beaten egg whites
- 1 lb. of (peeled & deveined) raw shrimp (large), 20 to 30 shrimp
- 1 tbsp. of water
- 1/4 cup of coconut flakes, unsweetened
- 1/2 cup of panko bread crumbs (whole-wheat)
- 1/2 tsp. of ground cumin
- 1/2 tsp. of ground coriander
- 1/2 tsp. of turmeric
- 1 cooking spray (nonstick)
- 1/8 tsp. of salt

Directions:

- Make use of paper towels to pat the shrimp dry. In a small bowl, mix the water and egg whites by whisking.
- In a separate small bowl, mix the coconut, panko bread crumbs, cumin, coriander, turmeric, and salt.
- The shrimp should be coated in the mixture of panko after being dipped in the egg mixture, letting any excess fall back into the bowl. The coated shrimp should be put on a wire rack. Repeat with all of the shrimp.
- Put the shrimp into the air fryer basket in a single layer. Spray nonstick cooking spray on the shrimp for two seconds. Air fried for 4 minutes at 205°C. Overturn the shrimp. Shrimp should be air-fried for two to four minutes or until golden brown. Serve hot.

Nutritional values per serving:

Total Calories: 180 kcal, **Fats:** 4.5 g, **Carbohydrates:** 9 g, **Protein:** 28 g

2. Fried Spicy Green Beans

Ready in: 20 mins.

Serves: 4

Difficulty: easy

Ingredients:

- 1 tbsp. of olive oil
- 1/2 oz. of green beans, fresh (trimmed)
- 1 tsp. of chilli garlic paste (Thai-style)
- 1/4 tsp. of salt
- 1 tbsp. of panko bread crumbs (whole-wheat)

Directions:

- Put green beans into a medium bowl and season with salt, panko bread crumbs, chile-garlic paste, and olive oil.
- Fill air fryer basket with the green beans. Set temperature up to 205°C & air fry for 3-4 minutes. Shake the basket of the air fryer. Add another 5-7 minutes to the air fryer. Serve hot

Nutritional values per serving:

Total Calories: 60 kcal, **Fats:** 4 g, **Carbohydrates:** 7 g, **Protein:** 2 g.

3. Sweet Potato Nachos

Ready in: 30 mins.

Serves: 4

Difficulty: medium

Ingredients:

- 1 sweet potato, medium (sliced in chips, 1/8-inch thick)
- 1 & 1/2 cup of the pepper-&-onion blend, frozen (partially thawed & drained)
- 1 cooking spray, nonstick
- 1 jalapeño pepper (cut lengthwise & seeded)
- 1/4 cup of salsa
- 1/4 cup of reduced-fat Mexican-style or cheddar cheese, shredded
- 2/3 cup of thinly sliced radishes
- 1/2 cup of romaine lettuce, shredded
- 4 cherry tomatoes (in fourths)
- 1 tbsp. of fresh cilantro, minced
- 2 tbsp. of light sour cream

Directions:

- Spread out the slices of sweet potato into the air fryer basket. Spray for one second with nonstick cooking spray. Over the potatoes, distribute the frozen veggies equally. Over the veggies, place the jalapeno skin side up. Spray for one second with nonstick cooking spray.

- Air-fried the potatoes for 20 mins, or until they are done, at a temperature of 190°C. They need to be crisp and delicate, not squishy. Jalapenos should be removed and placed in a bowl. Loosely cover with a kitchen towel, and let it stand for five minutes.

- Over the veggies, equally, distribute the cheese. Till the cheese is melted, air fried the food for two minutes.

- Remove the charred or browned peel off the jalapeno pepper with the point of a sharp knife. Peel and mince the pepper.

- Lift potatoes and veggies out of the air fryer basket using a spatula then spread them out evenly on a serving tray. The veggies should be covered with chopped jalapeno. Add the lettuce, tomatoes, radishes, and salsa on top. Add some cilantro and a spoonful of sour cream. Serve right away.

Nutritional values per serving:

Total Calories: 100 kcal, **Fats:** 3 g, **Carbohydrates:** 17 g, **Protein:** 4 g

4. Rosemary-Garlic Brussels sprouts

Ready in: 30 mins.

Serves: 4

Difficulty: medium

Ingredients:

- 2 minced garlic cloves
- 3 tbsp. of olive oil
- 1/2 tsp. of salt
- 1 pound of Brussels sprouts (halved), trimmed
- 1/4 tsp. of pepper
- 1-1/2 tsp. of fresh rosemary, minced
- 1/2 cup of panko bread crumbs

Directions:

- Set the air fryer up to 176°C. In a medium microwave-safe bowl, combine the first four ingredients. Microwave on high for 30 seconds.

- Add 2 tablespoons of the oil mixture and toss the Brussels sprouts. Place the Brussels sprouts onto a tray and cook for 4–5 minutes in an air fryer basket. Mix the sprouts. About 8 more minutes of simmering are needed to get the sprouts close to the desired level of softness. Stirring halfway during the cooking period.

- Toss remaining oil mixture, rosemary, & bread crumbs; sprinkle over sprouts. Cook for a further 3-5 minutes, or until the sprouts are tender and the crumbs are browned. Serve right away.

Nutritional values per serving:

Total Calories: 164 kcal, **Fats:** 11 g, Carbohydrates: 15 g, **Protein:** 5 g

5. Red Potatoes

Ready in: 20 mins.

Serves: 8

Difficulty: easy

Ingredients:

- 2 tbsp. of olive oil
- 2 pounds of small red potatoes (unpeeled), cut in wedges
- 1 tbsp. of minced rosemary (fresh) or 1 tsp. of dried crushed rosemary
- 1/2 tsp. of salt
- 2 cloves of garlic, minced
- 1/4 tsp. of pepper

Directions:

- Set air fryer up to 205°C. Put some oil on the potatoes. Toss lightly to coat after adding salt, rosemary, pepper, and garlic.
- Place in an air-fryer basket on an ungreased tray. Cook potatoes for 10 to 12 minutes, tossing once until they are golden brown & soft.

Nutritional values per serving:

Total Calories: 113 kcal, **Fats:** 1 g, Carbohydrates: 18g, **Protein:** 2 g.

6. Delicious Radishes

Ready in: 25 mins.

Serves: 6

Difficulty: easy

Ingredients:

- 3 tbsp. of olive oil
- 2-1/4 pounds of radishes, trimmed & quartered (about almost 6 cups)
- 1 tbsp. of fresh oregano (minced) or 1 tsp. of dried oregano
- 1/8 tsp. of pepper
- 1/4 tsp. of salt

Directions:

- Set air fryer up to 190°C. Toss the remaining ingredients with the radishes.
- Put the radishes in the air fryer basket on an oiled tray. Cook for 12 to 15 minutes, stirring periodically, until crisp-tender.

Nutritional values per serving:

Total Calories: 88 kcal, **Fats:** 7 g, Carbohydrates: 6 g, **Protein:** 1 g.

7. Breaded Summer Squash

Ready in: 25 mins.

Serves: 4

Difficulty: medium

Ingredients:

- 3 tbsp. of olive oil
- 4 cups of yellow summer squash, thinly sliced (3 medium)
- 1/2 tsp. of salt
- 1/8 tsp. of cayenne pepper
- 1/2 tsp. of pepper
- 3/4 cup of Parmesan cheese, grated
- 3/4 cup of panko bread crumbs

Directions:

- Set air fryer up to 176°C. Squash should be put in a big bowl. Season with oil and add; toss to coat.

- Combine cheese and bread crumbs in a small bowl. Squash should be dipped into the mixture of crumbs and patted to help the coating adhere. Squash should be arranged in one single layer in the air fryer basket on a tray in batches. Cook for approximately 10 minutes, or until the squash is soft and the coating is golden brown.

Nutritional values per serving:

Total Calories: 203 kcal, **Fats:** 14 g, Carbohydrates: 13 g, **Protein:** 6 g

8. Herb & Lemon Cauliflower

Ready in: 20 mins.

Serves: 4

Difficulty: easy

Ingredients:

- 4 tbsp. of olive oil, divided

- 1 head of cauliflower (medium), cut in florets (about almost 6 cups)

- 1/4 cup of fresh parsley, minced

- 1 tbsp. of fresh thyme, minced

- 1 tbsp. of fresh rosemary, minced

- 1 tsp. of lemon zest, grated

- 1/2 tsp. of salt

- 2 tbsp. of lemon juice

- 1/4 tsp. of red pepper flakes, crushed

Directions:

- Set the air fryer up to 176°C. Cauliflower & 2 tbsp. of olive oil are combined in a large bowl and coated. Cauliflower should be placed in one single layer in the air fryer basket on a tray in batches. Cook for 8 to 10 mins, stirring halfway through, or until

the edges are browned, and the florets are soft. Add the remaining ingredients and 2 tablespoons of oil to a small bowl. Transferring the cauliflower to a big bowl, add the herb mixture and mix well.

Nutritional values per serving:

Total Calories: 161 kcal, **Fats:** 3 g, Carbohydrates: 14g, **Protein:** 8g

9. Air-Fried Asparagus

Ready in: 20 mins.

Serves: 4

Difficulty: easy

Ingredients:

- 4 tsp. of olive oil

- 1/4 cup of mayonnaise

- 1-1/2 tsp. of lemon zest, grated

- 1/2 tsp. of pepper

- 1 clove of garlic, minced

- 1/4 tsp. of seasoned salt

- 2 tbsp. of Parmesan cheese, shredded

- 1 pound of asparagus (fresh), trimmed

- Lemon wedges, optional

Directions:

- Set the air fryer up to 190°C. Combine the 1st 6 ingredients in a large bowl. Asparagus is added; toss to coat. Place in one single layer on the oiled tray in the air fryer basket while working in batches.

- Cook for 4-6 minutes, or until tender and gently browned. Sprinkle with some Parmesan cheese after transferring to a serving plate. Serve with lemon slices, if preferred.

Nutritional values per serving:

Total Calories: 156 kcal, **Fats:** 15 g, Carbohydrates: 3g, **Protein:** 2g

10. Green Tomato Stacks

Ready in: 35 mins.

Serves: 4

Difficulty: medium

Ingredients:

- 1/4 tsp. of lime zest, grated
- 1/4 cup of mayonnaise, fat-free
- 2 tbsp. of lime juice
- 1/2 tsp. of pepper, divided
- 1 tsp. of minced thyme (fresh) or 1/4 tsp. of dried thyme
- 1/4 cup of all-purpose flour
- 3/4 cup of cornmeal
- 2 egg whites (large), lightly beaten
- 1/4 tsp. of salt
- 2 red tomatoes (medium)
- 2 green tomatoes (medium)
- Cooking spray
- 8 slices of Canadian bacon, warmed

Directions:

- Set the air fryer up to 190°C. Refrigerate until serving. Combine lime zest, mayonnaise and juice, thyme, and 1/4 teaspoon pepper. Egg whites should be in a separate shallow bowl from the flour. Mix cornmeal, salt, and the last 1/4 teaspoon of pepper in a third bowl.

- Make four crosswise slices out of each tomato. Sprinkle some flour on each slice and shake off the excess. Toss in the cornmeal mixture, then dip in the egg whites.

- In the air-fryer basket, arrange tomatoes on a greased tray in batches and spritz with some cooking spray. Cook for 4-6 minutes, or until golden brown. Toss with cooking spray and turn. Cook for another 4-6 minutes, or until golden brown.

- Place 1 slice of each green tomato, bacon, and red tomato on top of each other for each serving. Eat with sauce.

Nutritional values per serving:

Total Calories: 114 kcal, **Fats:** 2 g, Carbohydrates: 18 g, **Protein:** 6 g

11. Air-Fried Roasted Green Beans

Ready in: 35 mins.

Serves: 6

Difficulty: medium

Ingredients:

- 1/2 pound of fresh mushrooms, sliced
- 1 pound of green beans (fresh), cut into pieces (2 inches)
- 1 red onion (small), halved & thinly sliced
- 1 tsp. of Italian seasoning
- 2 tbsp. of olive oil
- 1/8 tsp. of pepper
- 1/4 tsp. of salt

Directions:

- Set the air fryer up to 190°C. All ingredients should be combined and coated in a big bowl.

- Arrange the veggies in the air fryer basket on the oiled tray. Cook for 8–10 minutes, or until barely tender. Cook for a further 8 to 10 minutes, tossing to distribute until browned.

Nutritional values per serving:

Total Calories: 76 kcal, **Fats:** 5 g, Carbohydrates: 8g, **Protein:** 3g

12. Crispy bacon

Ready in: 8 mins.

Serves: 5

Difficulty: easy

Ingredients:

- 5 strips of bacon

Directions:

- Add bacon to the air fryer basket that has been heated to 190°C. Make an effort to layer it.
- Cook for 6-8 minutes, monitoring every few minutes to ensure the required amount of crispiness is reached.
- Add eggs if desired!

Nutritional values per serving:

Total Calories: 91 kcal, **Fats:** 8 g, Carbohydrates: 0 g, **Protein:** 2g

13. Air Fried Vegetables

Ready in: 30 mins.

Serves: 8

Difficulty: medium

Ingredients:

- 1 cup of broccoli florets
- 1/2 cup of baby carrots
- 1 cup of cauliflower florets
- 1/2 cup of sliced yellow squash
- 1/2 cup of sliced mushrooms
- 1/2 cup of sliced baby zucchini
- 1 small sliced onion
- 1 tbsp. of olive oil
- 1/4 cup of balsamic vinegar
- 1 tbsp. of minced garlic
- 1 tsp. of black pepper
- 1 tsp. of sea salt
- 1/4 cup of parmesan cheese
- 1 tsp. of red pepper flakes

Directions:

- Set the Air Fryer for three minutes at 200°C. Olive oil, garlic, salt, balsamic vinegar, pepper, & red pepper flakes should all be combined in a big bowl.
- Blend well. Vegetables are added; mix to combine. Fill the Air Fryer basket with veggies. For 8 minutes, cook.
- Cook veggies for a further 6 to 8 minutes after shaking them. Bake for 1 to 2 minutes after adding cheese.

Nutritional values per serving:

Total Calories: 61 kcal, **Fats:** 2 g, Carbohydrates: 7 g, **Protein:** 3 g

14. CrispyGarlic Croutons

Ready in: 20 mins.

Serves: 10

Difficulty: easy

Ingredients:

- 2 cups of Bread, half of loaf (200g)
- 2 tbsp. of Olive Oil
- 1 tbsp. of Marjoram
- 1/2 tbsp. of Garlic Powder

Directions:

- Ensure that the bread has cooled. Slice it into squares, then the same-sized slices. Put all the croutons in a large bowl large enough to include all of the herbs & oil.
- Add marjoram, dry garlic, and oil. Completely combine all the croutons using a large spatula. Ensure sure the oil & herbs are distributed evenly.
- Put as many of your Croutons as your Air Fryer will hold. If you add more than one layer, they won't crisp up completely.
- Turn on the air fryer. Since you previously covered your Croutons with oil, you don't need to add any more.

- You must use the temperature settings you're used to for your Air fryer.
- The Crunchy Croutons are set to be served after 10 minutes. Serve them warm or hot, or allow them to cool. Everything depends on how you want to utilize them.

Nutritional values per serving:

Total Calories: 50 kcal, **Fats:** 4g, **Carbohydrates:** 1 g, **Protein:** 2g

15. Air Fried Cabbage

Ready in: 15 mins.

Serves: 4

Difficulty: easy

Ingredients:

- 1 head of cabbage
- 1 tsp. of sea salt
- 2 tbsp. of olive oil
- 1 tbsp. of Old Bay Garlic and Herb seasoning
- 1 tsp. of ground pepper (fresh)

Directions:

- Divide the cabbage into quarters, then insert the pie-shaped pieces into the air fryer.
- Sprinkle olive oil all over the cabbage segments. On the cabbage, season with salt, pepper, and Old Bay.
- Do 5 minutes of air frying at 190°C. Use tongs to toss the cabbage; the pieces will separate into big bits.
- Do 3–4 extra minutes of air frying

Nutritional values per serving:

Total Calories: 105 kcal, **Fats:** 7 g, Carbohydrates: 10g, **Protein:** 2g

16. Jalapeño Bacon Wrapped Poppers

Ready in: 25 mins.

Serves: 6

Difficulty: easy

Ingredients:

- 6 jalapeño peppers
- 12 uncured bacon slices, not thick cut
- 4 ounces cream cheese, at normal temperature
- ⅓ cup of shredded cheddar cheese
- Ranch Dressing to dip, (Optional)
- ½ tsp. of garlic powder

Directions:

- Remove the seeds & ribs by lengthwise slicing each jalapeno pepper in half. Wash the hands before continuing.
- Garlic powder, shredded cheddar, and cream cheese should all be mixed together in a bowl.
- To make things simpler, use a little silicone spatula to spoon the filling into each side of the jalapeno pepper.
- Take 1/2 to 3/4 of a bacon slice and tie it around each pepper, according to the size of the peppers. To enable you to tuck the ends in, start at the bottom. Make sure you have lots of bacon rolled around and terminating beneath the pepper and that you wrap them pretty tightly. By doing this, the filling won't be exposed, and the bacon won't shrivel up and seep out.
- Place them on the air fryer's wire racks; use six per rack and bake them at 185°C for 15 minutes. Bake for a further 3 to 4 minutes, or till the bacon is crisp, at 200°C.
- Present them warm, with the option of dipping them in ranch dressing.

Nutritional values per serving:

Total Calories: 125 kcal, **Fats:** 9 g, Carbohydrates: 2g, **Protein:** 5 g

17. Air-Fried Okra

Ready in: 35 mins.

Serves: 8

Difficulty: medium

Ingredients:

- ½ cup of all-purpose flour
- 1 tsp. of garlic powder
- ¼ cup of cornmeal
- 2 eggs (large), lightly beaten
- 8 ounces of okra pods (fresh), halved lengthwise
- 1 tbsp. of water
- Cooking spray
- ½ tsp. of Cajun seasoning (Optional)
- ½ tsp. of kosher salt, divided
- ½ cup of mayonnaise
- 2 tbsp. of ketchup
- 2 tbsp. of fresh chives, chopped
- 1 tsp. of Worcestershire sauce
- 1 tsp. of hot sauce

Directions:

- Set the air fryer up to 200°C and wait five minutes. Garlic powder, cornmeal, and flour are combined on a small plate. In one separate shallow dish, combine the eggs and water. Okra is dipped in the egg mixture, then dredged in the mixture of flour, and the excess is shaken off.

- Spread a good amount of frying spray over the okra and place half of it evenly in the fryer basket. Cook for about 10 mins, shaking the container halfway through, then coat with cooking spray

once more. Place the salt on a dish once you've transferred the okra there with the rest of the okra & 1/4 tsp. Salt, repeat the process. If desired, evenly distribute Cajun spice over the okra.

- In the meanwhile, mix the mayonnaise, chives, Worcestershire, ketchup, and spicy sauce into a small bowl. Serve the sauce beside the okra.

Nutritional values per serving:

Total Calories: 150 kcal, **Fats:** 11 g, Carbohydrates: 11 g, **Protein:** 2 g

18. Crispy Chickpeas

Ready in: 20 mins.

Serves: 4

Difficulty: medium

Ingredients:

- 1 can of unsalted chickpeas (15 ounces), rinsed & drained
- ¼ tsp. of smoked paprika
- 1 ½ tbsp. of toasted sesame oil
- ¼ tsp. of crushed red pepper
- Cooking spray
- ⅛ tsp. of salt
- 2 wedges of lime

Directions:

- Cover several layers of the paper towels with chickpeas. Roll the chickpeas beneath the paper towels for drying them on all sides, then add additional paper towels on top and pat until extremely dry.

- In a medium bowl, combine chickpeas & oil. Salt, crushed red pepper, and paprika should be added. Pour into a cooking spray-coated air fryer basket. Cook for 12 to 14 minutes at 205°C, shaking the basket regularly until very nicely browned. Serve the chickpeas with lime wedges on top.

Nutritional values per serving:

Total Calories: 132 kcal, **Fats:** 5.4g, Carbohydrates: 14 g, **Protein:** 4.7 g

19. Air-Fried Zucchini

Ready in: 30 mins.

Serves: 4

Difficulty: medium

Ingredients:

- 2 tbsp. of Parmesan cheese, grated
- ½ tsp. of dried oregano
- 1 tbsp. of extra-virgin olive oil
- ½ tsp. of salt
- ¼ tsp. of onion powder
- ¼ tsp. of garlic powder
- ¼ tsp. of ground pepper
- 2 large zucchini (8-ounce), sliced into 1/4-inch thick pieces
- ⅛ tsp. of crushed red pepper
- Lemon wedges, to serve
- 2 tsp. of lemon juice

Directions:

- Set the air fryer up to 205°C and wait five minutes. In a medium bowl, combine the Parmesan, oregano, oil, salt, pepper, onion powder, garlic powder, and crushed red pepper. Add the zucchini and combine.

- Place the slices of zucchini in one single layer into the fryer basket, working in batches if required. Cook for 10 to 12 minutes, turning once, until golden brown. Lemon wedges should be served with lemon juice.

Nutritional values per serving:

Total Calories: 64 kcal, **Fats:** 5 g, Carbohydrates: 5 g, **Protein:** 2 g

20. Air-Fried Plantains

Ready in: 55 mins.

Serves: 4

Difficulty: medium

Ingredients:

- 2 ripe plantains, medium (about 1 and 1/4 pounds), peeled & sliced (1/2 inch)
- ¼ tsp. of salt
- 2 tbsp. of avocado oil, divided

Directions:

- For 10 minutes, preheat the air fryer to 182°C. Spray frying oil on the fryer basket liberally. In a medium dish, combine plantains with 1 tbsp. Oil. Place the plantains into the fryer basket in a single layer, working in batches if required. Cook for 5 minutes, then turn the plantains and cook for an additional 6 to 8 minutes, or until they are well-browned and crispy. Transfer plantains with caution to a chopping board.

- Flatten each slice of plantain into a disk approximately 1/4-inch thick using the flat base of a small dish or pan; transfer to a larger bowl. Mix the remaining 1 tbsp. oil with the mashed plantains. Return the plantains to the fryer basket in a single layer, working in batches if required. Cook for 5 to 7 minutes, until certain areas are crisp. Serve right after adding salt.

Nutritional values per serving:

Total Calories: 171 kcal, **Fats:** 7 g, Carbohydrates: 29 g, **Protein:** 1g

21. Air-Fried Carrots

Ready in: 20 mins.

Serves: 6

Difficulty: easy

Ingredients:

- 1 pound of carrots (small), peeled & cut lengthwise in half

- 1 tbsp. of olive oil
- 2 tbsp. of Parmesan cheese, grated
- 2 tsp. of brown sugar
- ½ tsp. of smoked paprika
- 1 tsp. of dried tarragon
- ¼ tsp. of ground pepper
- ½ tsp. of salt

Directions:

- Set the air fryer up to 205°C and wait five minutes. Spray some cooking spray on the frying basket lightly.

- In a medium bowl, combine the carrots, oil, Parmesan, brown sugar, paprika, tarragon, salt, and pepper; toss to combine. Add carrots to the basket of the fryer and cook for 6 minutes; if required, work in batches. For a further 6 minutes, sauté the carrots on the other side until they are soft and golden.

Nutritional values per serving:

Total Calories: 68 kcal, **Fats:** 3 g, Carbohydrates: 9 g, **Protein:** 1 g

22. Air-Fried Eggplant

Ready in: 50 mins.

Serves: 8

Difficulty: easy

Ingredients:

- 2 eggplants (small), sliced in 1/4-inch thick
- ¼ cup of all-purpose flour
- ½ tsp. of salt
- 2 eggs (large), lightly beaten
- ¼ cup of Parmesan cheese (grated), plus some more for garnish
- ½ cup of panko breadcrumbs, whole-wheat
- 1 ½ tsp. of Italian seasoning

- 1 tbsp. of chopped fresh parsley
- Cooking spray, Olive oil

Directions:

- Salt the slices of eggplant equally, then set aside for 10 minutes. With a paper towel, dry the eggplant slices.

- Cover a shallow dish with flour. Put the eggs in a separate, small dish. In a third shallow dish, mix the panko, Parmesan, and Italian seasoning together. Slices of eggplant should be dredged in flour, then dipped in egg, excess shaken off, and finally dredged in panko mixture.

- Set the air fryer up to 182°C. Spread frying spray liberally over the eggplant slices and arrange half of them in an equal layer in the fryer basket. Cook for 5 to 6 minutes, or until brown and crispy on one side. Cook the eggplant slices for 5 to 6 minutes, flipping them halfway through until they are golden and crispy. Place on a platter. With the remaining slices of eggplant, repeat the process. Add some parsley and more Parmesan for garnish, if preferred.

Nutritional values per serving:

Total Calories: 53 kcal, **Fats:** 2 g, Carbohydrates: 8 g, **Protein:** 3 g

23. Blooming Onions

Ready in: 35 mins.

Serves: 8

Difficulty: medium

Ingredients:

- Cooking spray
- 2 eggs (large)
- 2 large sweet onions (12-ounce)
- ½ cup of low-fat milk
- 1 tsp. of paprika, divided
- ¼ cup of whole-wheat flour
- ½ tsp. of garlic powder

- ½ tsp. of salt, divided
- ½ tsp. of onion powder
- 1 cup of panko breadcrumbs
- ¼ tsp. of cayenne pepper, divided
- 2 tbsp. of cocktail sauce
- ½ cup of mayonnaise

Directions:

- For five minutes, preheat the air fryer to 190°C. Spray cooking spray on the fryer basket.
- Remove the onion's stem end and peel it. On a cutting board, arrange the onions root-side down. Make 16 slices by cutting through each of the onions, stopping 1/4 inch just above the roots.
- In a medium bowl, combine the eggs, flour, milk, and 1/2 tsp. Paprika, 1/4 tsp. Salt, 1/8 tsp. Cayenne, garlic and onion powders. In another medium dish, add the breadcrumbs.
- Dredge each onion into the breadcrumbs to fully coat it after dipping it in the batter and letting the excess drip off. (During the dredging operation, pull onion "petals" apart frequently to ensure that batter and breadcrumbs are entering every crevice.) After spraying the basket with cooking spray, add the onions. Cook for 20-25 minutes or until crispy. Finish by adding the last 1/4 tsp. of salt.
- In the meanwhile, combine the remaining 1/2 tsp. Paprika, 1/8 tsp. Cayenne, cocktail sauce, and mayonnaise in a small dish. Along with the dipping sauce, serve the onions.

Nutritional values per serving:

Total Calories: 170 kcal, Fats: 11g, Carbohydrates: 15g, Protein: 3 g

24. Air-Fried Broccoli

Ready in: 25 mins.

Serves: 4

Difficulty: medium

Ingredients:

- 1 medium head of broccoli (14-ounce), trimmed & cut into bite-size florets
- 2 tbsp. of olive oil
- ¼ cup of Parmesan cheese, grated
- 1 tsp. of garlic powder
- 1 lemon wedge
- ¼ tsp. of ground pepper

Directions:

- For five minutes, preheat the air fryer to 190°C. In a large bowl, combine the broccoli, oil, Parmesan, garlic powder, and pepper. Stir to combine.
- Place the broccoli into the fryer basket in a single layer, working in batches if required. Cook for 5 to 7 minutes, or until crisp and tender. Before serving, transfer to the serving dish & squeeze a lemon slice over the top.

Nutritional values per serving:

Total Calories: 105 kcal, Fats: 9 g, Carbohydrates: 5 g, Protein: 4 g

25. Air-Fried Spaghetti Squash

Ready in: 25 mins.

Serves: 4

Difficulty: easy

Ingredients:

- 1 tbsp. of olive oil
- ½ tsp. of kosher salt
- 1 spaghetti squash, small (2 pounds), halved & seeded
- ¼ tsp. of ground pepper

Directions:

- For five minutes, preheat the air fryer to 190°C.
- Apply oil to the squash's flesh and season it with salt & pepper. Place the squash into the fryer basket with the skin side down and cook for approximately 18 minutes, working in batches if required.
- Squash should be taken out of the air fryer. With a fork, shred the flesh & transfer it to a serving plate.

Nutritional values per serving:

Total Calories: 82 kcal, **Fats:** 4 g, **Carbohydrates:** 11 g, **Protein:** 1 g

Chapter 3: Air Fried Diabetic Diet - Beef Recipes

1. Italian-Style Beef Meatballs

Ready in: 45 mins.

Serves: 12

Difficulty: medium

Ingredients:

- 1 shallot (medium), minced (almost about two tbsp.)
- 2 tbsp. of olive oil
- 3 cloves of garlic, minced (almost about 1 tbsp.)
- 2 tbsp. of whole milk
- 1/4 cup of panko crumbs (whole-wheat)
- 2/3 pound of lean ground beef
- 1 egg (large), lightly beaten
- 1/3 pound of bulk turkey sausage
- 1/4 cup of flat-leaf parsley, fresh (finely chopped)
- 1 tbsp. of fresh thyme, finely chopped
- 1 tbsp. of fresh rosemary, finely chopped
- 1 tbsp. of Dijon mustard
- 1/2 tsp. of kosher salt

Directions:

- Set the air fryer up to 200°C. Over medium-high heat, preheat the oil into a medium nonstick pan. Add the shallot and sauté for 1 to 2 minutes, or until soft. Add the garlic and simmer for approximately one minute, until fragrant. Remove from heat.

- Combine panko & milk in a big bowl. Allow standing for five minutes.

- Combine panko mixture with meat, turkey sausage, parsley, egg, rosemary, mustard, thyme, salt, and sautéed shallot and garlic. Gently blend by stirring.

- Form the mixture into 1 & 1/2-inch balls with care. Put the formed balls in the air fryer basket in a single layer. Half the meatballs should be cooked for 10 to 11 minutes at 200°C until they are just barely browned and done. Get rid of it and stay warm. The remaining meatballs, and repeat.

- You may serve the warm meatballs with the toothpicks as an appetizer or as a main meal with rice, pasta, or spiralized zoodles.

Nutritional values per serving:

Total Calories: 122 kcal, **Fats:** 8 g, **Carbohydrates:** 0 g, **Protein:** 10 g

2. Air Fried Meatloaf

Ready in: 45 mins.

Serves: 6

Difficulty: easy

Ingredients:

- 2 eggs (large)
- 2 pounds of ground beef (80/20)
- 1/4 cup of milk
- 1 packet of meatloaf seasoning (1.5 ounces)

- 2/3 cup of Italian breadcrumbs
- 1 tbsp. of Worcestershire sauce

For topping:

- 1/2 cup of light brown sugar
- 1 cup of ketchup
- 1/2 tbsp. of Worcestershire sauce
- 1 tbsp. Of Dijon mustard

Directions:

- Set your air fryer's thermostat to 182°C.
- In a large bowl, mix together the eggs, beef, milk, meatloaf seasoning, bread crumbs, and Worcestershire sauce. You may just use your hands or a large spoon.
- Shape it into a loaf, then set it into the air fryer.
- It needs 25 minutes to cook.
- Combine the brown sugar, ketchup, Dijon mustard, & Worcestershire sauce into a small bowl while the meatloaf cooks.
- Place 1/4 cup of topping mix on the meatloaf after 25 minutes. It should reach 67°C after 5-10 minutes of further cooking in the air fryer.
- Take the meatloaf out of the air fryer, put more ketchup mixture on top, and serve.

Nutritional values per serving:

Total Calories: 189 kcal, **Fats:** 9 g, Carbohydrates: 13g, Protein: 14 g

3. Cheeseburger Pockets

Ready in: 12 mins.

Serves: 4

Difficulty: easy

Ingredients:

- 1 lb. of Beef (Ground), Cooked and Drained
- 1 can of Biscuit dough (8 Count)
- Sharp Shredded Cheddar Cheese

Directions:

- Take the biscuits out from the can & roll or flatten the dough with your hands to make it as thin as possible.
- Four of the flattened biscuits should be topped with a piece of ground meat and shredded cheddar cheese.
- Top the biscuit with the meat and cheese with another biscuit that hasn't been topped. Pull the dough into a pocket until it is completely enclosed.
- Seal the edges by pressing a fork down on edge.
- As many pockets as will fit should be placed in oiled air fryer baskets.
- Once inside the air fryer, if preferred, coat with the olive oil cooking spray before air frying for 4-5 minutes at 185°C.
- After the timer sounds, gently flip the pockets over.
- Air Fry for 4-5 more minutes at 185°C. Given that every air fryer heats differently check on them after three to four minutes.
- When finished, they will become well browned.

Nutritional values per serving:

Total Calories: 382 kcal, **Fats:** 24g, Carbohydrates: 7 g, **Protein:** 33 g

4. Air Fried Hamburgers

Ready in: 23 mins.

Serves: 4

Difficulty: medium

Ingredients:

- ½ tsp. of salt
- 1 pound of ground beef (lean), 80/20
- ½ tsp. of onion powder
- ½ tsp. of pepper
- ¼ cup of barbecue sauce, optional
- ¼ tsp. of garlic powder

For serving:

- 4 buns of hamburger
- Toppings, as desired

Directions:

- In a medium bowl, combine the meat, pepper, salt, onion powder, & garlic powder.
- Make 4 patties that are approximately 1/2" thick. With your thumb, press a tiny hole into the centre of the patties. If using barbecue sauce, brush it on the patties.
- Set the air fryer's temperature to 187°C. Add patties to the basket in a single layer.
- Cook for six minutes. When the meat reaches 67°C, flip the burger over & cook for an additional 3–5 minutes.
- Cook for another minute after adding cheese, if using. Put on buns.

Nutritional values per serving:

Total Calories: 365 kcal, **Fats:** 19 g, Carbohydrates: 22 g, **Protein:** 25 g

5. Crispy Empanadas

Ready in: 27 mins.

Serves: 8

Difficulty: easy

Ingredients:

- 1 bell pepper, diced
- 1 lb. of ground beef
- 1 packet (1 oz.) of taco seasoning
- 1 package of pie crusts, refrigerated (2 crusts total), at room temperature
- 1/4 cup of water or beef broth
- 1/2 cup of cheese shredded
- 1 whisked egg
- 1/2 diced onion

Directions:

- Cook the ground beef, green and red peppers, & onions in a medium skillet over medium heat until the ground beef gets browned and the onions are translucent.
- Add water and taco seasoning; stir. Take the food off the stove and let it cool.
- Lay out the pie crust on a surface that won't stick. Take one of the pie crusts, and using a round cup or bowl (one with a 5-inch diameter works great), cut out 3 circles from it.
- Combine the leftover dough and roll it out to a thickness that is comparable to the original crust. Circle-cut a fourth one. The second pie crust should be processed similarly for a total of 8 pieces.
- Spoon a couple of teaspoons of the beef mixture over each circle after it has cooled, then top with cheese. Each dough circle should be folded in half, and the edges should be sealed with a little water. Edges may be pressed using a fork.
- Brush each empanada with the beaten egg. Four at a time, place empanadas in the oiled air fryer basket. Heat the air fryer to 182°C for five minutes.
- Cook for 5-7 minutes at 182°C or until the tops are as browned as you want. Serve with your preferred toppings, such as lettuce, sour cream, tomatoes, salsa, and guacamole.

Nutritional values per serving:

Total Calories: 189 kcal, **Fats:** 14 g, Carbohydrates: 2g, **Protein:** 13 g

6. Taco Pie

Ready in: 30 mins.

Serves: 4

Difficulty: medium

Ingredients:

- 1 onion, diced
- 1 tbsp. of oil
- 8 oz. of protein, ground (vegetarian, ground beef substitute etc.)
- ½ cup of corn kernels
- 1 tbsp. of taco seasoning
- ½ cup of Bisquick
- 2 eggs
- 1 cup of milk
- 1 cup of chopped lettuce
- 1 cup of cheddar cheese, shredded
- 1.5 cup of tomatoes (fresh), diced

Directions:

- Heat the oil in a pan over medium heat, add the onion, & sauté for 3 minutes more before adding the protein and cooking it through.
- Corn and spices may then be added. To blend, stir.
- Whisk the Bisquick, milk, and eggs in a small bowl. Add to the pan mixture.
- Fill the air fryer pot that is oiled with the whole skillet mixture. For 16-minute air fry at 190°C. At the ten-minute mark, stir.
- Add cheese and continue to air fry for 3 minutes.
- Add lettuce and chopped tomatoes on top. Enjoy!

Nutritional values per serving:

Total Calories: 403 kcal, **Fats:** 22g, Carbohydrates: 28g, **Protein:** 25 g

7. Beef & Bean Taquitos

Ready in: 25 mins.

Serves: 20

Difficulty: easy

Ingredients:

- 1 Package of Regular or Gluten-Free Taco Seasoning
- 1 Pound of Ground Beef
- 1 can of Refried Beans
- 20 Tortillas (White Corn)
- 1 Cup of Sharp Cheddar, Shredded

Directions:

- If the ground beef hasn't been prepared yet, start by doing so.
- According to the directions on the box, brown the meat over medium-high heat before adding the taco seasoning.
- When you are through with the meat, microwave the tortillas for approximately 30 seconds to soften them.
- Spray non-stick cooking spray on a layer of foil or add it to the air fryer basket.
- Each tortilla should be topped with cheese, beans, and ground meat.
- Wrap them firmly and put them into the air fryer seam side down.
- Add a little mist of oil spray, preferably one containing olive oil.
- Cook for 12 minutes at 200°C. Repeat with any extra tortillas.

Nutritional values per serving:

Total Calories: 181 kcal, **Fats:** 9 g, Carbohydrates: 14g, **Protein:** 11 g

8. Lamb Meatball Kebabs

Ready in: 35 mins.

Serves: 8

Difficulty: medium

Ingredients:

- 1 pound of ground lamb
- 1 pound of ground beef
- 1 onion (small), diced finely
- 1/4 cup of parsley (fresh), chopped
- 2 cloves of garlic, minced
- 2 tsp. of cumin
- 1 tsp. of allspice
- 1 1/2 tsp. of salt
- 1/2 tsp. of paprika
- 1/2 tsp. of nutmeg
- 1/4 tsp. of black pepper
- 1/4 tsp. of cinnamon

Directions:

- In a food processor, combine all the ingredients and process until smooth.
- Form the beef mixture into kebab-like patties by dividing it into equal parts (or any other shape you like).
- Fill the basket of the air fryer with kebabs. Avoid overlapping. Based on the size of the air fryer, you may have to cook the meatballs in batches.
- Cook for 12 minutes at 195°C, rotating once.

Nutritional values per serving:

Total Calories: 238 kcal, **Fats:** 6 g, **Carbohydrates:** 1g, **Protein:** 22 g

9. Zucchini Filled With Hamburger

Ready in: 22 mins.

Serves: 6

Difficulty: easy

Ingredients:

- 1 pound of ground beef
- 3 Zucchinis
- 1 cup of tomato sauce
- 1 tbsp. of Italian Seasoning, in half
- Salt & black Pepper
- 1 tbsp. of Garlic, minced
- Olive Oil Cooking Spray
- 1 Cup of Mozzarella, grated

Directions:

- Wash and pat dry zucchini gently.
- Remove the zucchini's stem, then cut each one in half lengthwise.
- To form a boat-shaped container for the ground beef, use a spoon to scoop out the inside of the zucchini seeds.
- Season the zucchini well with salt & pepper. Add a half-teaspoon of Italian seasoning next.
- Spray the small casserole dish that is appropriate for air frying inside and out. As an alternative, air fry the zucchini on foil.
- In a skillet over medium heat, brown the beef with the garlic, 1/2 tsp. Italian seasoning, and salt and pepper. Tomato sauce should be added when the steak begins to brown.
- After thoroughly combining, simmer the meat for a further 3 minutes to fully integrate the sauce.
- Pour the ground beef into the prepped zucchini boats at that point.

- Sprinkle freshly grated mozzarella over the ground meat.

- Insert a casserole dish or the basket of air fryer basket into which the zucchini boats will fit. There could be a need for two batches, based on the size of your air fryer.

- The zucchini boats are air-fried for 10 minutes at 182°C.

- Serve warm.

Nutritional values per serving:

Total Calories: 312 kcal, **Fats:** 20 g, **Carbohydrates:** 7 g, **Protein:** 26 g

10. Beef Meatball Wraps

Ready in: 35 mins.

Serves: 8

Difficulty: medium

Ingredients:

- ¼ cup of mint (fresh), finely chopped

- 1 ½ cups of plain Greek yoghurt.

- 3 tbsp. of lemon juice, freshly squeezed

- ½ tsp. of salt divided

- 3 minced cloves of garlic, divided

- ½ tsp. of pepper divided

- 1 lb. of ground lamb

- 1 lb. of lean beef (ground), 92% lean

- ¾ cup of English cucumber seeded & shredded

- ½ cup of thinly sliced red onion

- 1 tomato (large), sliced

- 8 Greek flatbreads

- 3 cups of shredded lettuce

Directions:

- Peel, slice and use a spoon to remove the cucumber's seeds. Cucumber should be finely chopped and put into a dish or sieve. While you make the sauce, set them aside.

- Combine yoghurt, mint, 2 minced cloves of garlic, lemon juice, 1/4 teaspoon salt, and 1/4 tsp. Pepper in a medium bowl.

- While assembling the meatballs, divide 1/3 cup of the yoghurt mixture, cover the remaining sauce, and chill.

- Combine the ground beef, lamb, 1 minced clove of garlic, remaining salt, pepper, and 1/3 cup yoghurt mixture into a large mixing dish. Knead the ingredients with your hands until it is well blended. To properly operate the mixture and combine it.

- Using a food scale, divide the mixture into eight 4-ounce balls, which you should then form into 5-inch cylinders. Place the meatballs on the rack of the air fryer, spacing them apart to allow for optimum air circulation, and coat the basket with nonstick spray. You may have to do this in 2 batches if you've got a small appliance.

- Preheat the air fryer to 205°C. Cook for 7-8 minutes, turn and cook for an additional 4-6 minutes, or until cooked through and lightly browned. The internal temperature of the meat should be 67°C.

- Combine the Greek yoghurt sauce with the strained, finely chopped cucumber.

- Top the meatball with tomato, lettuce, red onion, and yoghurt sauce on the Greek flatbread.

Nutritional values per serving:

Total Calories: 277 kcal, **Fats:** 16 g, **Carbohydrates:** 5 g, **Protein:** 26 g

11. Manwich Air-Fried Sloppy Joe Bombs

Ready in: 40 mins.

Serves: 16

Difficulty: medium

Ingredients:

- 1 can of Manwich
- 1 lb. of ground beef
- 1 can of flakey biscuits
- 1 egg
- 1 cup of mozzarella cheese

Directions:

- Brown the ground meat in a medium skillet.
- After draining the fat, add the Manwich can and stir. Let the meat cool fully. For leftovers, try this recipe.
- Use a rolling pin or your hands to press the biscuit dough into a flat surface.
- Place around 2 tbsp. of cheese in the dough's middle. Mix cheese by hand into the dough
- Meanwhile, sprinkle 1/4 cup or so of the mixture of meat over the mozzarella.
- Close the sides by pinching them together, taking care not to get sauce on the dough.
- After that, roll a little in your palm before putting it in the basket or on the sprayed Air Fryer tray.
- Apply the egg wash by brushing.
- After flipping, cook for a further 8 minutes in an air fryer that has been prepared to 190°C.
- Perform one last flip, then cook for an additional 4 minutes, or till golden brown & the inside is no longer doughy.
- Give it five minutes to settle and cool before serving.

Nutritional values per serving:

Total Calories: 118 kcal, **Fats:** 7 g, Carbohydrates: 2 g, **Protein:** 10 g

12. Cheeseburger Dumplings

Ready in: 30 mins.

Serves: 24

Difficulty: medium

Ingredients:

- 2 tbsp. of vegetable oil (30 ml)
- 1 pound of beef (454 g)
- 1/2 onion (small), minced
- 1 tbsp. of Worcestershire sauce (15 ml)
- 1 tsp. of garlic powder (5 ml)
- 1/2 tsp. of kosher salt (2.5 ml), or to taste
- 1 1/2 cups of grated cheese (170 g), Cheddar, blue cheese, Swiss, whatever you like etc.
- Black pepper, freshly grated
- 10 slices of pickles, diced (optional)
- 24 to 30 dumpling wrappers
- water for sealing wrappers

Directions:

- To prepare the filling, heat a skillet to a medium-high temperature. After adding the oil, add the onion. Cook until softened for around 1-2 minutes. Add the Worcestershire sauce, salt, black pepper, garlic powder, and ground meat. Cook the meat for 3 to 4 minutes, or until it is well cooked and browned. Take the food off the stove and let it cool.
- The cheese & optional chopped pickles should be added to the filling after the meat has cooled.
- Place around 2 tablespoons of filling in the centre of each dumpling wrapper. Spread over the edge of the wrapper

after dipping your finger in the water. To seal the dumpling, gently fold it in half and press the sides together. As you close the dumpling, gently push out any extra air and flatten it.

- After beginning to roll the dumpling, wet the top edge of the wrapper to assist in sealing the end. Repeat with the remaining dumplings. Spray or brush on oil to coat.

- Arrange the dumplings in a single layer into the air fryer basket. If feasible, try to avoid having them overlap or touch.

- Air fry for 8 to 10 minutes at 182°C, flipping halfway through. Cook the wrapper until it becomes golden and crispy. In order to prevent the layers from becoming tough and chewy, if you use the bigger wrapper, cook the food for a bit longer.

- Provide warm ketchup, mustard, and barbecue sauce for dipping.

Nutritional values per serving:

Total Calories: 68 kcal, **Fats:** 4 g, **Carbohydrates:** 1 g, **Protein:** 7 g

13. Beef Tenderloin

Ready in: 47 mins.

Serves: 8

Difficulty: easy

Ingredients:

- 1 tbsp. of vegetable oil

- 2 pounds of beef tenderloin at normal temperature

- 1 tsp. of dried oregano

- ½ tsp. of cracked black pepper

- 1 tsp. of salt

Directions:

- Set the air fryer's temperature to 200°C. With paper towels, pat the beef tenderloin dry.

- The tenderloin should be put on a platter. Sprinkle oregano, salt, & pepper over the steak and drizzle the oil all over it. Incorporate oil and spices into the meat. Folding the roast to fit into the air fryer basket is necessary. Put the basket away.

- Lower the heat to 198°C. Do 22 minutes for air frying. Again turn down the heat to 182°C. Cook for a further ten minutes. The medium setting on an instant-read thermometer should read 57°C.

- The tenderloin should be taken out of the basket and placed on a platter. Before serving, let sit undisturbed for 10 minutes at least.

Nutritional values per serving:

Total Calories: 238 kcal, **Fats:** 10 g, **Carbohydrates:** 0.2 g, **Protein:** 32g

14. Steak Fajitas

Ready in: 30 mins.

Serves: 6

Difficulty: easy

Ingredients:

- 1/2 cup of diced red onion

- 2 tomatoes (large), seeded & chopped

- 1/4 cup of lime juice

- 3 tbsp. of minced cilantro (fresh)

- 1 seeded jalapeno pepper, minced

- 2 tsp. of cumin (ground), divided

- 1 beef (about 1 & 1/2 pounds) flank steak

- 3/4 tsp. of salt, divided

- 1 onion (large), halved & sliced

- Avocado slices & lime wedges optional

- 6 warmed tortillas, whole-wheat (8 inches)

Directions:

- To make salsa, combine the first five ingredients into a small dish; then, season with 1/4 tsp. Salt and 1 tsp. Cumin. Let it stand till serving.

- Set the air fryer up to 200°C. Add salt and leftover cumin to the steak. In the air-fryer basket, place it on a greased surface. Cook for 6 to 8 minutes on each side or until the meat is the desired doneness (a thermometer should, for medium-rare, register 57°C; for medium, 60°C; and for medium-well, 70°C). Take out of a basket, then stand for five minutes.

- In the meanwhile, put one onion in the air fryer basket on a tray. Cook for 2-3 minutes, stirring once, until crisp-tender. Serve steak in tortillas with salsa & onion after thinly slicing it against the grain. Serve with slices of lime and avocado, if preferred.

Nutritional values per serving:

Total Calories: 309 kcal, **Fats:** 9 g, Carbohydrates: 29 g, **Protein:** 27g

15. Steak Bites

Ready in: 10 mins.

Serves: 4

Difficulty: easy

Ingredients:

- 1 tbsp. of soy sauce

- ½ tbsp. of olive oil

- 16 oz. of striploin steaks in 1-inch cubes

- 1 tsp. of chilli powder

- ⅛ tsp. of salt

- ½ tsp. of black pepper

- ½ tsp. of onion powder

- ½ tsp. of garlic powder

- 1 tsp. of chilli pepper flakes

- ½ tbsp. of brown sugar

Directions:

- Set the air fryer at 200°C.

- Place the cubed steak in a mixing bowl and add the olive oil & soy sauce. Mix well till coated.

- Combine the dry ingredients in a separate small dish before adding them to the bigger bowl containing the steak cubes.

- Place the beef cubes in the basket of the air fryer and cook for 5 minutes at 200°C or till desired doneness.

- Take out of air fryer. Serve with some garlic butter on the side for dipping, garnished with chopped parsley (Optional).

Nutritional values per serving:

Total Calories: 243 kcal, **Fats:** 13 g, Carbohydrates: 1 g, **Protein:** 20 g

Chapter 4: Air Fried Diabetic Diet ~ Pork Recipes

1. Bacon Hot Dogs

Ready in: 15 mins.

Serves: 4

Difficulty: easy

Ingredients:

- 4 slices of bacon

- 4 hot dogs

- 4 buns of hot dog

- **For serving:** mustard, ketchup, BBQ sauce, jalapeños, pickles, onions, etc.

Directions:

- Tightly encircle hot dogs with strips of bacon.

- To hold the bacon securely to the hot dog, if desired, use a toothpick. Make sure the hot dogs' tips are covered with bacon. Put in the air fryer's tray or basket.

- Depending on your chosen texture, the size of the hot dogs, and how do you want your bacon, air fry for 8 to 10 minutes at 193°C. During the second half of cooking, flip the hot dogs. If you're using toothpicks, take them out before serving!

- Cook your hot dogs and bacon a bit hotter if you want them extra crispy.

Follow these guidelines instead: Air fry for 6 to 8 minutes at 204°C. During the second half of cooking, flip the hot dogs. If you're using toothpicks, take them out before serving!

- Place bacon-wrapped hot dogs inside the buns & air fry for a further minute, or till the bread is warm, for warm crispy hot dog buns. Serve with your preferred garnishes.

Nutritional values per serving:

Total Calories: 321kcal, **Fats:** 17g, **Carbohydrates:** 30g, **Protein:** 12g

2. Bacon Zucchini Fries

Ready in: 25 mins.

Serves: 8

Difficulty: medium

Ingredients:

- 8 slices of bacon or as much as needed (in half lengthwise)

- 1 lb. (2 small to medium) of zucchini (454 g)

- oil spray

- Some black pepper

- 2 tsp. of garlic powder salt (10 ml), or to taste

Directions:

- Slice the zucchinis lengthwise, then into wedges that are 1-inch (2.5 cm) wide at the base (often quartered for small to medium-sized zucchini). Spray some oil on the zucchini lightly. Garlic powder, salt, & pepper are used to season all dishes.

- After adding bacon, add black pepper to the wrap (optional). Put the zucchini into the air fryer basket or tray after tooth-picking the bacon into it to keep it in place.

- Air Fry it at 193°C for 10 to 16 minutes, or till the bacon is as crispy as you want.

- Halfway through cooking, turn the zucchini. Prior to serving, let the food cool for a few minutes (zucchini would be very hot). Before eating, take out any toothpicks.

Nutritional values per serving:

Total Calories: 119kcal, Fats: 10g, Carbohydrates: 3g, Protein: 4g

3. Pork Belly Bites & Bbq Sauce

Ready in: 30 mins.

Serves: 4

Difficulty: medium

Ingredients:

- 1 tsp. of soy sauce or Worcestershire sauce (5 ml)

- 1 lb. of pork belly (454 g), rinsed and patted dry

- 1/2 tsp. of garlic powder (2.5 ml)

- Black pepper & salt

- 1/4 cup of BBQ sauce, sugar-free (optional)

Directions:

- Heat your Air Fryer for 4 minutes at 205°F. The pork bits will get a pretty excellent sear as a result.

- If necessary, peel the pork belly's skin. The pork belly should be cut into 3/4" cubes and put in a bowl. Worcestershire sauce, salt, garlic powder, and pepper are used to season. In the air fryer basket, distribute pork belly into a uniform layer.

- Air-fried the pork belly for 10 to 18 minutes at 205°C, shaking and rotating it twice throughout the cooking duration.

- Cook it for a further 2 to 5 minutes if you need it more done. To determine how well done the pork belly is cooked, check it.

- If preferred, season with more salt and pepper. In order to bring the tastes out, it requires a substantial quantity of spice. Add optional barbecue sauce and drizzle as desired. Serve hot.

Nutritional values per serving:

Total Calories: 590 kcal, Fats: 60g, Carbohydrates: 1g, Protein: 11g

4. Pork Egg Rolls

Ready in: 30 mins.

Serves: 12 to 14 egg role

Difficulty: medium

Ingredients:

- 2 tbsp. of vegetable oil (30 ml)

- 1 pound of ground pork (454 g)

- 3 cloves of garlic, crushed or minced

- 1 tbsp. of soy sauce (15 ml)

- 1 tsp. of ginger root, freshly grated (5 ml), optional

- 1/2 tsp. of kosher salt (2.5 ml), or to taste

- 1/2 tsp. of sesame seed oil (2.5 ml)

- Black pepper, freshly grated

- 1/2 cup of grated carrot (65 g), (about one medium carrot)

- 2 cups of cabbage (70 g), shredded thin

- 3 small green onions, chopped

- 14 egg roll wrappers (about 1 package)

- 1 egg, large

- oil spray or oil for coating the rolls

Peanut-Hoisin dip

- 1/4 cup of peanut butter (65 g)

- 1/2 cup of hoisin (140 g)

- Sriracha or hot chilli sauce (optional)

- 2 tsp. of vinegar (5 ml), or to taste

- 1/2 tsp. of sesame oil (2.5 ml), or to taste

- about half a cup of water

Directions:

- Fill each wrapper with 1-2 tbsp., of pork filling using egg roll wrappers (based on the size of the wrapper). Wrap the filling in the wrapper and tuck it inside.

- To effectively seal wrapper end, dab the top side of the wrapper with beaten egg or water. Then, continue wrapping the egg roll. Do this for each of the egg rolls. Rolls should be oiled using a brush or spray.

- Air fry for 12 to 16 minutes, turning halfway through at 195°C. Cook the wrapper until it becomes golden and crispy. In order to prevent the layers from becoming tough and chewy, if you use the bigger wrapper, cook the food for a bit longer.

- With warm peanut-hoisin dip, serve. These chicken and veggie egg rolls may also be eaten as lettuce-wrapped egg rolls!

Nutritional values per serving:

Total Calories: 152 kcal, Fats: 9g, Carbohydrates: 9g, Protein: 9g

5. Breaded Crispy Pork Chops

Ready in: 26 mins.

Serves: 3

Difficulty: medium

Ingredients:

- Some salt, to taste

- 3, 170g of pork chops (6oz.), rinsed and patted dry

- black pepper and smoked paprika, to taste

- Some garlic powder

- 1/2 cup of breadcrumbs (54 g), approximately

- Cooking spray to coat pork chops

- 1 egg, large

Directions:

- Season the pork chops on both sides with salt, smoked paprika, pepper, & garlic powder.

- Fill the medium bowl with the breadcrumbs. Beat the egg in a separate bowl.

- Coat each pork chop thoroughly with breadcrumbs after dipping it in the egg. Just before cooking, lightly mist the coated pork chops on both sides with cooking spray.

- For 4 minutes, preheat the air fryer up to 195°C. The pork chops will have a lovely, crispy crust as a result.

- Place in Air Fryer & cook for 8–12 minutes at 195°C. The pork chops should be cooked for a further 6 minutes after flipping them, or until browned and the internal temperature reaches 60–65°C.

- Serve hot.

Nutritional values per serving:

Total Calories: 361 kcal, Fats: 14g, Carbohydrates: 13g, Protein: 41g

6. Juicy Pork Chops

Ready in: 20 mins.

Serves: 3

Difficulty: medium

Ingredients:

- 2 tsp. of olive oil (10 ml) or any other preferred oil

- 3, six-ounce pork chops (170 g), rinsed and patted dry

- Some salt, to taste

- garlic powder and black pepper, to taste
- smoked paprika

Directions:

- Lightly spray or brush olive oil on the pork chops. Add smoked paprika, pepper, salt, and garlic powder for seasoning.
- Place pork chops into the Air Fryer & cook for 10–14 minutes at 194°C, turning the chops halfway through.
- Cook a bit longer if necessary to get the desired level of doneness. Serve hot.

Nutritional values per serving:

Total Calories: 287 kcal, **Fats:** 14g, Carbohydrates: 0g, **Protein:** 361g

7. Mushrooms Pork Bites

Ready in: 30 mins.

Serves: 4

Difficulty: medium

Ingredients:

- 8 oz. of mushrooms (227 g) (washed, cleaned and halved)
- 1 lb. of pork belly or pork chops (454 g), rinsed and patted dry
- 2 tbsp. of Butter or olive oil (30 ml), melted
- 1/2 tsp. of garlic powder (2.5 ml)
- 1 tsp. of soy sauce or Worcestershire sauce (5 ml)
- salt & black pepper, to taste

Directions:

- Heat Air Fryer for 4 minutes at 205°C. Pork will get a great sear from this.
- Combine the mushrooms and the pork chops after cutting them into 3/4" pieces (or your favourite veggie). Melt

the butter or use oil, & then sprinkle garlic powder, Worcestershire sauce, salt, and pepper over the pork and mushrooms. In the air fryer basket, distribute the pork & mushrooms in a uniform layer.

- Air-fried the pork belly for 10 to 18 minutes at 205°C, shaking and rotating it twice throughout the cooking duration.
- Inspect the bits of cooked pork chop to determine how done they are. Add an additional 2 to 5 mins of cooking time if you need it more done.
- If preferred, season with more salt and pepper. Serve warm and promptly. The pork bits will become tough if they become cold.

Nutritional values per serving:

Total Calories: 241 kcal, **Fats:** 14g, Carbohydrates: 2g, **Protein:** 26g

8. Frozen Pork Meatballs

Ready in: 10 mins.

Serves: 3

Difficulty: easy

Ingredients:

- oil spray for coating the meatballs
- 1 lb. of Frozen Meatballs (454 g), (454g / 16 oz.)
- Tomato or BBQ Sauce, optional

Directions:

- Spread out the frozen meatballs into an equal layer in an air fryer basket (cook in batches if needed). Spray oil evenly over the meatballs.
- Gently shake and flip the meatballs midway through air-frying at 195°C for 8–12 mins. (Based on size) or till well cooked.
- Before serving, if wanted, warm your preferred sauce (tomato, BBQ, etc.) and

combine it with the meatballs.

Nutritional values per serving:

Total Calories: 398 kcal, **Fats:** 32g, Carbohydrates: 0g, **Protein:** 26g

9. Corn Dogs

Ready in: 12 mins.

Serves: 4

Difficulty: easy

Ingredients:

- 4 Corn Dogs, Frozen (or about almost

12 oz. mini frozen corn dogs)

Directions:

- Spread out the corn dogs that are frozen into a single, uniform layer into the air fryer basket. (If your air fryer is smaller, you may have to shorten the stick a little bit to make the corn dog lie flat. The corn dogs shouldn't be tilted up near the cooking element. Oil spray is not required.

- Air fry regular-sized corn dogs for 8 minutes at 188°C. After turning the corn dogs over, cook them at 188°C for an additional 2-4 minutes, or until thoroughly cooked.

- Air fry mini-sized corn dogs for 6 minutes at 188°C. The small corn dogs should be given a little shake and turned over, then cooked at 188°C for an additional 2-4 minutes, or till heated through.

Nutritional values per serving:

Total Calories: 190 kcal, **Fats:** 9g, Carbohydrates: 18g, **Protein:** 7g

10. Pork Roast

Ready in: 1 hr. 5 mins.

Serves: 6

Difficulty: medium

Ingredients:

- 1 tbsp. of light olive oil

- 2 lb. of pork roast

- 2 tsp. of kosher salt

Directions:

- Blot the roast pork dry. If pork roast has a rind, slice the skin in a crisscross pattern with a sharp knife. Make sure to cut into the fat under the skin rather than the meat.

- Apply salt to the skin and massage it in. Allow the salt to extract the moisture out from the skin of the pork roast by leaving it on for 10 minutes.

- Once again, pat pork roast dry, then spray more oil over it and massage it in.

- Set the air fryer oven up to 180°C.

- Cook the pork roast for 50 minutes in the air fryer basket (25 mins. per lb. of meat).

- After the allotted time has passed, check the cookedness of the pork to make sure the thickest section has achieved a temperature of 63°C.

- Ten minutes before serving, remove the pork roast from the air fryer, cover it with aluminium foil, and let it rest.

- Cut into pieces before serving

Nutritional values per serving:

Total Calories: 241 kcal, **Fats:** 35g, Carbohydrates: 0g, **Protein:** 35g

11. Delicious Pork Belly Fry

Ready in: 30 mins.

Serves: 1

Difficulty: Medium

Ingredients:

- 1 clove of garlic, minced

- 1 1/2 pounds of pork belly

- 1 tbsp. of fresh ginger, minced

- 2 tbsp. of rice vinegar
- 1/3 cup of hoisin sauce
- 1 tsp. of sesame oil

Directions:

- Cut the pork belly into strips that are

about 3/4" and 1" broad. To fit inside the air fryer basket, cut items in half lengthwise as necessary (you'll probably need to cook in two batches).

- Put the pork belly into the air fryer and cook it there for 15 minutes at 205°C. Turn the strips to the other side and continue to air fry at 205°C for a further 7 minutes, or until golden and crisp.
- Combine the garlic, hoisin sauce, rice vinegar, ginger, and sesame oil into a small bowl and whisk to combine.
- Use a pastry brush to evenly coat the strips of pork belly in the basket of the air fryer with the sauce mixture.
- Continue to air fry for 3-4 more minutes at 205°C, or till the sauce bubbles & becomes golden.
- Take the crispy pig belly out of the basket, slice it, and serve.

Nutritional values per serving:

Total Calories: 371 kcal, Fats: 26g, Carbohydrates: 7g, Protein: 27g

12. Korean Pork Cheese Katsu

Ready in: 1 hr.

Serves: 8

Difficulty: medium

Ingredients:

For Pork:

- 1 lb. of pork loin (boneless), 2 oz., eight pieces
- 10 oz. of mozzarella cheese, cut into 8 or 2-inch long, 1-inch thick pieces
- salt & black pepper

For Panko:

- 3 cups of panko bread crumbs
- 3 tbsp. of avocado or any other cooking oil

Egg Mixture:

- 2 tbsp. of all-purpose flour
- 2 eggs
- 1/4 tsp. of black pepper
- 1/4 tsp. of salt

Directions:

- Sandwich a pork loin piece between two sheets of plastic or parchment paper. Pork should be flattened to a thickness of 1/8" using a heavy saucepan or meat tenderizer. Proceed with the remaining pork loin.
- Sprinkle a little salt and pepper over each pork loin piece, then top with a slice of cheese. Close the roll by rolling the side that is nearest to you, folding the right & left sides toward the centre, and rolling it shut. Pork will maintain its shape if plastic wrap is securely wrapped around it. Place for 15-30 minutes in the freezer.
- Heat a sizable skillet to a medium-high temperature. Add breadcrumbs and oil. Breadcrumbs should be toasted for 10 to 12 minutes until they are gorgeously golden brown. Frequently stir. Place aside.
- Set the air fryer to 185°C.
- Unwrap the cheese tonkatsu and dunk it in the egg mixture. Place it on the toasty breadcrumbs after evenly coating it. Spread out the bread crumbs evenly over the surface of the meat by softly pushing down. Place the cheese tonkatsu in a hot air fryer, and cook for 18-20 minutes.
- Cheese tonkatsu should be served with your preferred dipping sauce. Great sauces include steak sauce,

ketchup, BBQ sauce, and tonkatsu sauce.

Nutritional values per serving:

Total Calories: 280 kcal, **Fats:** 8.6g, Carbohydrates: 27.2g, **Protein:** 29.4g

13. Air-fried Brats

Ready in: 15min

Serves: 5

Difficulty: easy

Ingredients:

- 1 pack of brats (uncooked)

Directions:

- Arrange the raw brats in the basket of the air fryer.

- The brats should be air-fried at 170°C for 12 to 15 minutes, turning them over halfway through. Once they achieve an inside temperature of 74°C, they are finished.

- Use tongs to take the brats out from the air fryer basket, then let them sit for five minutes to rest, then delight in them!

Nutritional values per serving:

Total Calories: 57 kcal, **Fats:** 5g, **Carbohydrates:** 2g, **Protein:** 15g

14. Pork & bok-Choy

Ready in: 1 hr.

Serves: 6

Difficulty: medium

Ingredients:

- 4 cups of bok Choy, chopped (about 12 oz.)

- 1 tbsp. of fresh ginger, chopped

- 1 tsp. of canola oil

- 1 tbsp. of garlic, chopped (3 cloves of garlic)

- 1/4 tsp. of red pepper, crushed

- 4 ounces of ground pork

- 18 wonton wrappers (3, half-inch-square) or dumpling wrappers

- Cooking spray

- 2 tsp. of soy sauce, lower-sodium

- 2 tbsp. of rice vinegar

- 1 tsp. of sesame oil, toasted

- 1 tbsp. of scallions, finely chopped

- 1 1/2 tsp. of light brown sugar, packed

Directions:

- Place a large skillet over medium to high heat and add the canola oil. Bok Choy should be added and cooked for 6 to 8 minutes, frequently turning, until mostly dry. Ginger and garlic should be added. Stir continuously for 1 minute. Place bok Choy mixture on a platter and let it cool for five minutes. With a paper towel, dry the mixture.

- In a medium bowl, combine the ground pork, bok Choy combination, and crushed red pepper.

- Lay a dumpling wrapper out on the work surface and place about 1 spoonful of filling in the middle. The edges of wrapper should be gently wetted with water using your fingertips or a pastry brush. To create a half-moon shape, fold wrapper over and press the sides together to seal. Use the leftover wrappers and filling to complete the procedure.

- Lightly spray cooking spray on the air fryer basket. Leave space between each of the six dumplings as you place them in the basket and gently mist them with cooking spray. Cook for 12 minutes at 190°C until gently browned, flipping the dumplings over halfway through. Continue in the same manner, keeping the prepared dumplings warm.

- In the meanwhile, combine the scallions, soy sauce, rice

vinegar, sesame oil, and brown sugar in a small bowl and whisk until the sugar is dissolved. Put three dumplings and two tablespoons of sauce on each dish before serving.

Nutritional values per serving:

Total Calories: 140 kcal, Fats: 5g, Carbohydrates: 16g, Protein: 7g

15. Brussels Sprouts Pork Chops

Ready in: 25 mins.

Serves: 1

Difficulty: medium

Ingredients:

- Cooking spray
- 8 ounces of centre-cut, bone-in pork chop
- 1/8 tsp. of kosher salt
- 1 tsp. of olive oil
- 1/2 tsp. of black pepper, divided
- 1 tsp. of pure maple syrup
- 6 ounces of quartered Brussels sprouts
- 1 tsp. of Dijon mustard

Directions:

- Spray cooking spray lightly on the pork chop; season with salt & 1/4 tsp. of pepper. In a medium bowl, combine the remaining 1/4 teaspoon of pepper, syrup, oil, mustard, and mix in the Brussels sprouts.
- Arrange the marinated Brussels sprouts on one side of the air fryer basket and the pork chop on the other. Cook pork in air fryer at 205°C for 10–13 minutes, depending on how well-done you want your meat, or until it is golden brown and cooked through.

Nutritional values per serving:

Total Calories: 337 kcal, Fats: 11g, Carbohydrates: 21g, Protein: 40g

16. Pork Skewers with Sauce

Ready in: 35 min

Serves: 6

Difficulty: easy

Ingredients:

For skewers:

- 2 red bell peppers
- 1 lb. of pork tenderloin, fat trimmed
- ½ onion (medium)
- 2 cloves of garlic, minced or crushed
- 2 slices of bacon
- 1 tsp. of paprika
- ½ tsp. of black pepper
- ½ tsp. of salt
- 1 tbsp. of olive oil

For Creamy Maple Mustard Dipping Sauce:

- 1 tbsp. of Dijon mustard
- 2 tbsp. of mayo
- salt & pepper, to taste
- 2 tsp. of maple syrup

Directions:

- Put the diced pork into a medium bowl after cutting it into 1-inch pieces.
- Stir in the olive oil, salt, paprika, and pepper after adding the other ingredients. Place aside.
- Slice the bell peppers, onion, and bacon into 1-inch squares whilst the meat is marinating.
- Toss the chopped vegetables and bacon with the pork in the bowl to evenly distribute the marinade.
- Layer meat cubes, onions, bacon, and peppers onto metal or bamboo skewers to construct the kebabs. Use four pieces

of meat on each skewer and start and finish with peppers or onions.

- Air fry for 10 to 15 minutes at 185°C, or roast for 20 to 25 minutes at 230°C degrees, rotating once halfway through. The edges of the skewers should be thoroughly caramelized and appear golden.

- Combine the mustard, maple syrup, mayonnaise, salt, & pepper into a small bowl to create the maple mustard dipping sauce.

- If preferred, serve the pork skewers along with the dipping sauce.

Nutritional values per serving:

Total Calories: 160 kcal, Fats: 7.9g, Carbohydrates: 4g, Protein: 17.6g

17. Pork Loin Sandwich

Ready in: 20 min

Serves: 2

Difficulty: easy

Ingredients:

- 1/2 cup of flour

- 2 pork chops (boneless)

- 2 lightly beaten eggs

- Salt & black pepper

- 1 cup of Panko bread crumbs

- olive oil spray

Directions:

- Use the flat part of a meat tenderizer to pound 1 pork chop into a zip-top bag until it is just 1/4-inch thick.

- Gather a bowl and two plates. Fill a dish with flour. Whisk eggs, salt, and pepper in a bowl. Place bread crumbs on the final plate and season with salt and pepper.

- Take one chop that has been flattened and coat both sides with flour, then egg, and finally bread crumbs.

- Carefully put the meat in the air fryer. Spray some olive oil on.

- Air fry for five minutes at 205°C. Open the air fryer, turn, spray, & air fry for a further five minutes.

- Place on bun & top with pickles, mustard, mayo, and ketchup.

Nutritional values per serving:

Total Calories: 436 kcal, Fats: 15.1g, Carbohydrates: 39.1g, Protein: 35g

18. Veggie Stuffed Pork Chops

Ready in: 20 mins.

Serves: 4

Difficulty: medium

Ingredients:

- 1 chopped celery rib

- 1/2 tsp. of olive oil

- 1/4 cup of chopped onion

- 2 tbsp. of minced fresh parsley

- 4 slices of white bread, cubed

- 1/8 tsp. of salt

- 1/8 tsp. of white pepper

- 1/8 tsp. of rubbed sage

- 1/8 tsp. of dried marjoram

- 1/3 cup of chicken broth, reduced-sodium
- 1/8 tsp. of dried thyme

For chops:

- 1/4 tsp. of salt
- 4 (every 7 ounces) pork rib chops
- 1/4 tsp. of pepper

Directions:

- Heat the oil in a large skillet over medium-high heat. Cook and toss the celery and onion for 4-5 minutes, or until they are soft. Take it off the heat. Combine the bread and ingredients in a big bowl. A mixture of celery should be added together with broth.

- Slice each pork chop horizontally, nearly to the bone, to create a pocket. Add bread mixture to chops and, if necessary, secure with toothpicks.

- Set the air fryer up to 170°C. Chops should be salted and peppered. Arrange in a single layer in the air fryer basket on a greased tray. 10 minutes to cook. Turn the dish over and cook for an additional 6 to 8 minutes, or till a thermometer inserted in the stuffing's centre registers 74°C and one in the pork registers at least 74°C. After five minutes, remove toothpicks and serve.

Nutritional values per serving:

Total Calories: 10 kcal, **Fats:** 4g, **Carbohydrates:** 16g, **Protein:** 28g

Chapter 5: Air Fried Diabetic Diet - Poultry Recipes

1. Chicken Thighs

Ready in: 20 mins.

Serves: 4

Difficulty: easy

Ingredients:

- 1 tbsp. of olive oil
- 4 chicken thighs, bone-in (about 1 & 1/2 pounds)
- 3/4 tsp. of salt
- 1/4 tsp. of garlic powder
- 1/2 tsp. of paprika
- 1/4 tsp. of pepper

Directions:

- Set the air fryer up to 190°C. Apply oil to chicken and brush. Sprinkle the remaining ingredients over chicken after combining them. Put the chicken in the air fryer basket in one single layer on a tray with the skin-side up. Cook for 15–17 minutes, or until a thermometer placed into the chicken registers 70-75°C.

Nutritional values per serving:

Total Calories: 255kcal, **Fats:** 18g, **Carbohydrates:** 0g, **Protein:** 23g

2. Air fried Lemon Chicken

Ready in: 25 mins.

Serves: 4

Difficulty: medium

Ingredients:

- 3 cloves of garlic, minced
- 1/4 cup of butter, softened
- 2 tsp. of fresh rosemary, minced or 1/2 tsp. of rosemary (dried), crushed
- 1 tsp. of lemon zest, grated
- 1 tsp. of fresh thyme, minced or 1/4 tsp. of dried thyme
- 1 tbsp. of lemon juice
- 1/8 tsp. of salt
- 4 chicken thighs, bone-in (about 1 & 1/2 pounds)
- 1/8 tsp. of pepper

Directions:

- Set the air fryer up to 205°C. Combine the butter, rosemary, garlic, lemon juice, thyme, and zest in a small bowl. Each chicken thigh should have 1 tsp. of the butter mixture spread beneath the skin. Each thigh's skin should be covered with the remaining butter. Add salt and pepper to taste.

- Put the chicken in the air fryer basket with the skin-side up on a greased tray. 20 minutes of cooking, with one flip. Cook the chicken for a further 5 minutes, skin side up, or until a thermometer registers 75°–80°F.

Nutritional values per serving:

Total Calories: 329kcal, **Fats:** 26g, **Carbohydrates:** 111mg, **Protein:** 23g

3. Thai Air Fried Chicken Meatballs

Ready in: 10 mins.

Serves: 12

Difficulty: easy

Ingredients:

- 2 tbsp. of lime juice
- 1/2 cup of sweet chilli sauce
- 2 tbsp. of ketchup
- 1 egg (large), lightly beaten
- 1 tsp. of soy sauce
- 3/4 cup of panko bread crumbs
- 1 tbsp. of fresh cilantro, minced
- 1 finely chopped green onion
- 1/2 tsp. of salt
- 1 pound of lean ground chicken
- 1/2 tsp. of garlic powder

Directions:

- Set the air fryer up to 170°C. Combine the chilli sauce, lime juice, ketchup, and soy sauce in a small dish; save 1/2 cup for serving. Combine the egg, green onion, bread crumbs, cilantro, garlic powder, salt, and the final 4 tbsp. of the chilli sauce mixture in a sizable bowl. Add the chicken and stir just enough to combine. 12 balls should be formed.

- In the air-fryer basket, place the meatballs in batches in one single layer on a greased tray. Cook for 4-5 minutes, or until gently browned. For a further 4-5 minutes, turn the food over and cook it through until gently browned. Serve with the sauce you set out and top with more cilantro.

Nutritional values per serving:

Total Calories: 98kcal, **Fats:** 3g, **Carbohydrates:** 9g, **Protein:** 9g

4. Nashville Delicious Hot Chicken

Ready in: 10 mins.

Serves: 6

Difficulty: easy

Ingredients:

- 2 tbsp. of divided hot pepper sauce
- 2 tbsp. of divided dill pickle juice
- 1 tsp. of salt, divided
- 1 cup of all-purpose flour
- 2 pounds of chicken tenderloins
- 1/2 tsp. of pepper
- 1/2 cup of buttermilk
- 1 egg (large)
- Cooking spray
- 2 tbsp. of cayenne pepper
- 1/2 cup of olive oil
- 2 tbsp. of dark brown sugar
- 1 tsp. of chilli powder
- 1 tsp. of paprika
- Slices of Dill pickle
- 1/2 tsp. of garlic powder

Directions:

- Combine 1 tbsp. Pickle juice, 1 tbsp. hot sauce, and 1/2 tsp. Salt in a shallow dish or bowl. Add chicken & turn to coat. Refrigerate for at least an hour while covered. Drain the chicken, then throw away the marinade.

- Set the air fryer up to 190°C. Combine

the flour, pepper, and final 1/2 tsp. of salt in a small bowl. Whisk the buttermilk, and egg with, remaining 1 tbsp. Pickle juice and 1 tbsp. Spicy sauce in a separate shallow basin. Shake off extra flour after coating the chicken on both sides. Before dipping again, coat with the egg mixture.

- Place the chicken, in batches, in one single layer on a tray that has been well oiled and placed in the air fryer basket. Cook for 5 to 6 minutes or until golden brown. Toss with cooking spray and turn. Cook for another 5 to 6 minutes or until golden brown.

- The next six ingredients should be whisked together before being poured over cooked chicken and coated. Accompany with pickles.

Nutritional values per serving:

Total Calories: 413kcal, **Fats:** 21g, Carbohydrates: 20g, **Protein:** 39g

5. Piccata Chicken Pockets

Ready in: 20 mins.

Serves: 4

Difficulty: medium

Ingredients:

- 1-1/2 cups of rotisserie chicken, shredded

- 4 sweet orange or yellow peppers (medium)

- 1-1/2 cups of brown rice, cooked

- 1/2 cup of Havarti cheese, shredded

- 1 cup of prepared pesto

- Basil leaves (Fresh), optional

Directions:

- Set the air fryer up to 205°C. Remove the seeds and stems by halving the peppers lengthwise. Peppers should be put in one single layer in the air fryer basket on a tray in batches. Cook for 10-15 minutes, or until peppers are tender and skin begins to blister. 170°C is a good temperature for the air fryer.

- In the meanwhile, mix the chicken, rice, and pesto in a big bowl. Place chicken mixture into peppers after they are cold enough to handle. Cook in batches for 5 minutes or until well heated. Add

cheese and simmer for 3-5 minutes, or until it melts. Add some basil, if desired.

Nutritional values per serving:

Total Calories: 521kcal, **Fats:** 31g, Carbohydrates: 33g, **Protein:** 25g

6. Stuffed Fajita Chicken

Ready in: 15 mins.

Serves: 4

Difficulty: easy

Ingredients:

- 1 onion (small), halved & thinly sliced

- 4 skinless, boneless chicken breast, in halves (every 6 ounces)

- 1/2 green pepper (medium), thinly sliced

- 1 tbsp. of chilli powder

- 1 tbsp. of olive oil

- 1 tsp. of ground cumin

- 1/4 tsp. of garlic powder

- 1/2 tsp. of salt

- Optional: sour cream, Salsa, fresh cilantro (minced), jalapeno slices & guacamole

- 4 ounces of cheddar cheese in 4 slices

Directions:

- Set the air fryer up to 190°C. Each chicken breast's thickest region should have a pocket cut out of it horizontally. Add green pepper and onion to the space. Rub the chicken with a mixture of olive oil and spices from a small dish.

- Place the chicken in the air fryer basket in batches on a greased tray. 6 minutes to cook. Cheese pieces are added to the chicken and secured using toothpicks. Cook for another 6 to 8 minutes, or till a thermometer inserted into the chicken registers at least 74°C. Throw away toothpicks. Serve with your preferred toppings if you'd like.

Nutritional values per serving:

Total Calories: 347kcal, **Fats:** 17g, Carbohydrates: 5g, **Protein:** 42g

7. Almond Chicken

Ready in: 30 mins.

Serves: 2

Difficulty: medium

Ingredients:

- 1/4 cup of buttermilk

- 1 egg (large)

- 1 tsp. of garlic salt

- 1 cup of almonds (slivered), finely chopped

- 1/2 tsp. of pepper

- 2 skinless, boneless chicken breast, in halves (every 6 ounces)

- Optional: honey mustard or barbecue sauce, Ranch salad dressing,

Directions:

- Set the air fryer up to 170°C. Stir together the egg, buttermilk, garlic salt, and pepper in a small basin. Put almonds in a separate small dish. To help the coating stick, dip the chicken into the egg mixture and then into the almonds.

- Spread cooking spray on the greased tray where the chicken will be placed in the air fryer basket. Cook for 15–18 minutes, or until a thermometer is put into the chicken registers at least 74°C. Serve with some ranch dressing, barbeque sauce, or mustard, if preferred.

Nutritional values per serving:

Total Calories: 353kcal, **Fats:** 18g, Carbohydrates: 6g, **Protein:** 23g

8. Southern-Style Chicken

Ready in: 20 mins.

Serves: 6

Difficulty: medium

Ingredients:

- 1 tbsp. of fresh parsley, minced

- 2 cups of Ritz crackers, crushed (about 50)

- 1 tsp. of garlic salt

- 1/2 tsp. of pepper

- 1 tsp. of paprika

- 1/4 tsp. of ground cumin

- 1 egg (large), beaten

- 1/4 tsp. of rubbed sage

- Cooking spray

- 1 fryer/ broiler chicken (3-4 pounds) split up

Directions:

- Set the air fryer up to 190°C. Mix the first seven ingredients in a small dish. Put the egg in a different, small bowl. After dipping the chicken in the egg, coat it with the cracker mixture by patting it down. Chicken should be placed in single layers on a greased tray in the air fryer basket and sprayed with cooking spray in batches.

- Cook for ten minutes. Spray cooking spray after turning the chicken. Cook for 10–20 minutes more, or until the chicken is brownish and golden and the liquids are clear.

Nutritional values per serving:

Total Calories: 410kcal, **Fats:** 23g, Carbohydrates: 13g, **Protein:** 36g

9. Spicy Chicken Breasts

Ready in: 20 mins.

Serves: 8

Difficulty: medium

Ingredients:

- 2 tbsp. of Dijon mustard
- 1/2 tsp. of poultry seasoning
- 2 tsp. of salt
- 1-1/2 tsp. of garlic powder
- 2 tsp. of hot pepper sauce
- 8 (8 ounces each) chicken breast halves (bone-in), skin removed
- 1 cup of cornmeal
- 2 cups of soft bread crumbs
- 2 tbsp. of canola oil
- 1/2 tsp. of ground mustard
- 1/2 tsp. of poultry seasoning
- 1/2 tsp. of paprika
- 1/4 tsp. of dried oregano
- 1/2 tsp. of cayenne pepper
- 1/4 tsp. of parsley flakes, dried

Directions:

- Combine the first five ingredients in a big bowl. Chicken is added; turn to coat. Cover and refrigerate for an hour or overnight. The air fryer is up to 190°C.
- Drain the chicken and toss the marinade. In a small bowl, mix the remaining ingredients and whisk to blend. One piece of chicken at a time, add, & turn to coat. Place on an oiled tray in an air fryer basket in a single layer. Cook for approximately 20 minutes, rotating once halfway through or until a thermometer registers 60°C. Return all the chicken to the air fryer and heat through for an additional two to three minutes.

Nutritional values per serving:

Total Calories: 352kcal, Fats: 9g, Carbohydrates: 23g, Protein: 41g

10. Chicken Cordon Bleu

Ready in: 30 mins.

Serves: 4

Difficulty: medium

Ingredients:

- 1/4 tsp. of salt
- 4 skinless boneless (4 ounces each) chicken breast, in halves
- 1/4 tsp. of pepper
- 2 slices of halved Swiss cheese
- 4 slices of deli ham
- Cooking spray
- 1 cup of panko bread crumb

For sauce:

- 1/2 cup of 2% milk
- 1 tbsp. of all-purpose flour
- 1/4 cup of dry white wine
- 1/8 tsp. of salt
- 3 tbsp. of Swiss cheese, finely shredded
- Dash pepper

Directions:

- Set the air fryer up to 175°C. Chicken breasts should be salted and peppered. In the air-fryer basket, place it on a greased surface. Cook for ten minutes. Add one slice of ham and half a piece of cheese to the top of each chicken breast, covering the meat as much as you can with ham. Add some bread crumbs. Spray frying spray onto the crumbs with caution. Cook for a further 5-7 minutes or until a chicken thermometer registers 74°C.

- To make the sauce, stir together the milk and flour in a small pot. Stirring continuously, bring to a boil; simmer and stir for one to two minutes, or until thickened.

- Lower the heat to medium. Wine and cheese should be stirred in and cooked for two to three minutes, or till cheese is melted & the sauce is bubbling and thick. Add salt and pepper and stir. Keep heated till ready to serve over low heat. Serve alongside chicken.

Nutritional values per serving:

Total Calories: 272kcal, Fats: 8g, Carbohydrates: 14g, Protein: 32g

11. Feta Lemon Chicken

Ready in: 25 mins.

Serves: 2

Difficulty: medium

Ingredients:

- 1-2 tbsp. of lemon juice

- 2 skinless, boneless halves of chicken breast (2 ounces each)

- 2 tbsp. of feta cheese, crumbled

- 1/4 tsp. of pepper

- 1/2 tsp. of dried oregano

Directions:

- Set the air fryer up to 205°C. Put the chicken in an air fryer-compatible baking dish that has been gently oiled. Add oregano, feta cheese, and pepper after sprinkling the chicken with lemon juice.

- Cook for 20–25 minutes, or until a thermometer registers 74°C.

Nutritional values per serving:

Total Calories: 142kcal, Fats: 4g, Carbohydrates: 1g, Protein: 24g

12. Chicken Parmesan

Ready in: 45 mins.

Serves: 4

Difficulty: medium

Ingredients:

- ½ cup of panko bread crumbs, plain

- ½ cup of seasoned or plain bread crumbs

- 2¼ ounces of Parmesan (½ cup), grated

- 2 eggs, large

- 2 tbsp. of Italian seasoning

- 4-8 small skinless, boneless chicken breasts (each 4-5 ounces), pounded evenly

- ¼ cup of shredded mozzarella, or to taste

- 2 tbsp. of jarred or homemade marinara sauce, and some more for serving

- Some Pasta to serve

Directions:

- To generate 4 thin chicken pieces, carefully butterfly the chicken by slicing it in half lengthwise. Sprinkle salt & black pepper on both sides of the chicken.

- Put the flour in a small bowl and season with plenty of salt and black pepper. Eggs should be blended in another shallow basin. Combine Parmesan, panko, red pepper flakes, oregano, and garlic powder in a third shallow dish.

- Coat each chicken piece in flour, brushing off any excess as you go. Finally, dip in panko mixture, gently pushing to adhere and making sure both sides of the chicken are completely coated. Dip into the eggs, letting excess drop off.

- Place chicken in an air fryer basket in a single layer, working in batches as required. Cook for five minutes on each side at 205°C, rotating once. Add mozzarella and marinara to the chicken. About 3 minutes longer of cooking time at 205°C is required for the cheese to melt and get golden.

- Arrange the chicken on each platter. Add parsley as a garnish.

Nutritional values per serving:

Total Calories: 377kcal, **Fats:** 13g, **Carbohydrates:** 32g, **Protein:** 37g

13. Jamaican Chicken Curry

Ready in: 30 mins.

Serves: 4

Difficulty: medium

Ingredients:

- 2 tbsp. of Jamaican curry powder
- 1 pound of skinless, boneless chicken thighs
- 2 tsp. of paprika
- 1 tsp. of adobo seasoning
- ½-1 tsp. of cayenne pepper
- ½ tsp. of salt
- 3 cloves of garlic minced
- 1 diced yellow onion
- 1 tbsp. Of olive oil

Directions:

- To a large bowl, add chicken thighs and all of the seasonings (paprika, curry powder, adobo seasoning, cayenne pepper and salt). Olive oil, minced garlic cloves, and sliced yellow onion should all be added to the bowl.
- Combine the ingredients and massage the chicken with a spoon or your hands until it is evenly seasoned on both sides. Chicken should be marinated for 30 minutes at least, but preferably several hours. Cover the bowl.

- Set the air fryer's temperature to 190°C. After the basket has heated up, coat it with frying spray, then add chicken thighs and cook for 10-15 minutes.
- When the internal temperature of the chicken reaches 74°C, flip the chicken over and cook for an additional 8 to 10 minutes.
- Dish out and savour!

Nutritional values per serving:

Total Calories: 194kcal, **Fats:** 8.6g, **Carbohydrates:** 5.89g, **Protein:** 22.84g

14. Healthy Chicken & Veggies

Ready in: 20 mins.

Serves: 4

Difficulty: medium

Ingredients:

- 1 cup of broccoli florets (frozen or fresh)
- 1 pound of chopped chicken breast, in bite-sized pieces (2 to 3 chicken breasts, medium)
- 1 chopped zucchini
- 1/2 chopped onion
- 1 cup of chopped bell pepper (any colour)
- 2 cloves of garlic, crushed or minced
- 1/2 tsp. of each garlic powder, salt, chilli powder, pepper
- 2 tbsp. of olive oil
- 1 tbsp. of Italian seasoning

Directions:

- Turn the air fryer on at 205°C.
- Slice the vegetables and chicken into bite-sized pieces, then add them to a mixing bowl.
- Toss the spice and oil together in the bowl.

- Add vegetables and chicken to the already heated air fryer, and cook for 8-10 minutes, shaking the pan halfway through, or till the chicken is well cooked. You may need to fry them in two or three batches if the air fryer is tiny.

Nutritional values per serving:

Total Calories: 230kcal, Fats: 10g, Carbohydrates: 8g, Protein: 26g

15. Turkey Meatballs

Ready in: 15 mins.

Serves: 5

Difficulty: easy

Ingredients:

- 1 red bell pepper, medium
- 1 & ½ lbs. of ground turkey
- ½ cup of chopped Italian parsley
- 1 tbsp. of Italian seasoning
- 1 egg, large
- ½ tsp. of black pepper, ground
- ½ tsp. of salt

Directions:

- Turn the Air Fryer's temperature up to 205°C. Get a basket of air fryers ready.
- In a bowl, combine the ground turkey, parsley, bell pepper, egg, & spices. Mix thoroughly.
- Create 1 &1/4" meatballs out of each meatball using a tablespoon or a scooper.
- Arrange the meatballs in the air fryer basket in a single layer.
- Cook for 8 to 10 minutes at 205°C, or until well cooked.
- • After the cooked meatballs have been taken out of the air fryer, cook the rest of the meatballs.

Nutritional values per serving:

Total Calories: 149kcal, Fats: 3g, Carbohydrates: 2g, Protein: 28g

16. Stuffed Turkey Peppers

Ready in: 30 mins.

Serves: 3

Difficulty: medium

Ingredients:

- 1 tbsp. of olive oil
- 3 red bell peppers, medium
- 12 ounces of ground turkey
- ¼ cup of panko breadcrumbs
- ½ cup of brown rice, cooked
- ¾ cup of marinara sauce, low-sodium
- ¼ tsp. of ground pepper
- 3 tbsp. of flat-leaf finely chopped parsley
- ¼ cup of shredded mozzarella cheese, part-skim (1 oz.)
- ¼ cup of Parmesan cheese, grated (1 oz.)

Directions:

- Spray cooking spray on the air fryer's basket. Pepper tops should be cut off and saved. Set aside the pepper seeds.
- In a big skillet, heat the oil over medium-high heat. Add the turkey and heat for 4 minutes, stirring periodically, until browned. Add the rice and panko and toss. Cook for approximately a minute, stirring regularly until heated through. Stir in parsley, marinara, pepper, and Parmesan after taking the pan from the heat. Among the prepared peppers, distribute the mixture equally.
- Add the peppers to the air fryer basket that has been prepared. Place the tops of pepper in the basket's base. Cook the

peppers for approximately 8 minutes at 170°C or until they are soft. Add the mozzarella on top and heat for an additional 2 minutes or until the cheese is melted.

Nutritional values per serving:

Total Calories: 407kcal, **Fats:** 20.6g, **Carbohydrates:** 25.6g, **Protein:** 29.3g

17. Coconut Turkey Fingers

Ready in: 10 mins.

Serves: 6

Difficulty: easy

Ingredients:

- 2 tsp. of sesame oil

- 2 egg whites, large

- 1/2 cup of sweetened coconut (shredded), lightly toasted

- 2 tbsp. of sesame seeds, toasted

- 1/2 cup of bread crumbs, dry

- 1/2 tsp. of salt

- Cooking spray

- 1-1/2 pounds of turkey breast tenderloins in 1/2-inch strips

Dipping sauce:

- 1/3 cup of pineapple juice, unsweetened

- 1/2 cup of plum sauce

- 1-1/2 tsp. of prepared mustard

- Optional: lime wedges & Grated lime zest

- 1 tsp. of cornstarch

Directions:

- Set the air fryer up to 205°C. Whisk egg whites & oil together in a small bowl. Combine coconut, sesame seeds, bread crumbs, and salt in a separate shallow dish. To help the coating stick, pat the

turkey after dipping it in the egg mixture and the coconut mixture.

- Working in batches, arrange the turkey in the air-fryer basket on the oiled tray in a single layer. Mist with cooking spray. Cook for 3 to 4 minutes or until golden brown. Toss with cooking spray and turn. Cook for a further 3–4 minutes or until the turkey is golden brown and no longer pink.

- Meanwhile, combine the sauce's components in a small pot. Bring to boil; simmer and stir for 1-2 minutes or until thickened. Serve sauce with the turkey. Serve turkey strips with lime wedges and, at your discretion, lime zest on top.

Nutritional values per serving:

Total Calories: 292kcal, **Fats:** 9g, **Carbohydrates:** 24g, **Protein:** 31g

18. Turkey Burgers

Ready in: 30 mins.

Serves: 4

Difficulty: medium

Ingredients:

- 1 egg

- 1 pound of ground turkey

- 1 tbsp. of Worcestershire sauce

- ½ tsp. of garlic powder

- 1 tsp. of salt

- ¼ tsp. of black pepper

Directions:

- All ingredients should be combined in a big bowl, then divided and formed into four patties. For five to ten minutes, or until they are solid enough to handle, freeze the turkey burger patties.

- Add the patties into the air fryer & cook for 15 minutes at 178°C, turning once.

- Add the patties in burger buns and enjoy.

Nutritional values per serving:

Total Calories: 148kcal, Fats: 3g, Carbohydrates: 1g, Protein: 48g

19. Turkey Fajitas

Ready in: 30 mins.

Serves: 4

Difficulty: medium

Ingredients:

- 1 tbsp. of chilli powder
- 1 tbsp. of ground cumin
- ½ tbsp. of paprika
- ½ tbsp. of dried Mexican oregano
- 1 tsp. of black pepper, freshly ground
- 1 tsp. of garlic powder
- ½ tsp. of onion powder
- 2 divided limes
- 1 pound of boneless, skinless turkey breast, in ½" thick slices
- 1 & ½ tbsp. of vegetable oil, divided
- 1 red bell pepper (large), cut into strips
- 1 yellow bell pepper (medium), cut into strips
- 1 red onion (large), halved & sliced into strips
- 1 seeded jalapeno pepper, chopped, or some more to taste
- ¼ cup of fresh cilantro, chopped

Directions:

- In a small bowl, combine the chilli powder, paprika, cumin, oregano, garlic powder, pepper, and onion powder. Over the turkey breast, squeeze the 1 lime juice. Over the meat, sprinkle the spice mixture. Include 1 tablespoon of oil. Stir to coat, then put aside.

- Add the remaining oil to the bowl with the bell peppers, onion, and salt. Coat by tossing.

- As directed by the manufacturer, heat the air fryer up to 190°C.

- In preheated air fryer, cook bell peppers & onion for 8 minutes. 5 more minutes of cooking after a shake. Put jalapenos in. For five minutes, cook. Turkey strips are added to the veggies in a single layer after the basket is opened, shaken, and then opened again. Cook for 7-8 minutes after closing the basket. Open, shake the air fryer basket to spread the mixture, and cook for an additional 5 minutes or until the peppers are soft and the turkey strips are slightly crispy & not pink anymore in the middle.

- Take the basket out, then arrange the fajitas on a dish or in a bowl. Add cilantro on top and pour the remaining lime juice over it

Nutritional values per serving:

Total Calories: 247kcal, Fats: 7g, Carbohydrates: 15.3g, Protein: 32g

20. Mushroom Egg Turkey Burgers

Ready in: 50 mins.

Serves: 4

Difficulty: medium

Ingredients:

- 2 tbsp. of zucchini or mushrooms, finely grated
- 1 pound of turkey, ground (not extra lean)
- 1 egg yolk
- 1 tsp. of soy sauce
- 1 tbsp. of olive oil
- ¼ tsp. of garlic powder
- , salt & black pepper

Directions:

- In a large bowl, combine all the ingredients. Once combined, divide the mixture into four patties. For five to ten minutes, or until they are solid enough to handle, freeze the turkey burger patties.

- Place the patties into the air fryer & cook for 15 minutes at 178°C, turning once.

- Gently stir all the ingredients together in a bowl.

- Shape into 4 1/2-inch-thick patties. Make a tiny depression in the patties using your thumb. 30 minutes of refrigeration

- Set the air fryer up to 170°C.

- Arrange the patties into the air fryer basket in a single layer. 6 minutes to cook. Cook for a further 6 to 8 minutes on the other side or until well done (74°C).

- Top with chosen toppings and serve on buns.

Nutritional values per serving:

Total Calories: 17k6cal, Fats: 7g, Carbohydrates: 1g, Protein: 28g

21. Mustard Honey Turkey Breast

Ready in: 20 mins.

Serves: 5

Difficulty: medium

Ingredients:

- 2 tbsp. of olive oil

- 5 lb. of turkey (whole breast)

- 1 tsp. of salt

- 4-6 tbsp. of chopped herbs rosemary (fresh), sage, thyme

- 1 tsp. of black pepper

- 1 tbsp. of butter

- 2 tbsp. of Dijon mustard

- 3 tbsp. of honey

Directions:

- Cut the turkey along the middle to divide the 2 breasts, then preheat the air fryer up to 170°C. It should be noted that if you have a big air fryer, you might be able to cook the turkey breast in its whole.

- Rub the turkey breast with olive oil all over. Combine salt, pepper, and chopped herbs in a small bowl. Over the turkey breast, rub the herb mixture.

- Cook 1 of the halves for around 20 minutes in the air fryer. Cook the breast for 15 minutes more on the other side. Honey, Butter, and mustard are combined in a small pot over medium heat while the turkey cooks. After the butter has melted, incorporate by whisking. At this time, spread honey mustard glaze over the whole breast and put the air fryer back on for an additional 5 to 10 minutes, or until the outside is browned & crispy and the interior temperature reaches 74°C.

- Repetition is required with the other half of the turkey breast.

- Before slicing and serving, cover turkey breasts loosely with aluminium foil for 5 to 10 minutes.

Nutritional values per serving:

Total Calories: 110 kcal, Fats: 16g, Carbohydrates: 9g, Protein: 35g

22. Chicken Cutlets

Ready in: 20 mins.

Serves: 1

Difficulty: medium

Ingredients:

- ¼ cup of Parmesan cheese, grated

- 1 cup of gluten-free or whole-wheat panko breadcrumbs

- 1 tbsp. of olive oil

- ½ cup of whole buttermilk
- 1 tsp. of grated lemon zest
- 1 pound (4 cutlets) of chicken breast cutlets
- ½ tsp. of ground pepper
- ½ tsp. of salt

Directions:

- In a shallow dish, mix panko, Parmesan, oil, and lemon zest. Put the buttermilk in a different small dish.
- For five minutes, preheat the air fryer to 190°C. Spray cooking spray on the basket. Chicken should be salted and peppered. Dip in the buttermilk, allowing extra to drip off. Press the panko mixture into the surface as you dredge it. Place the basket, if required, in batches, and cook for 5 mins on each side, or till golden brown & a thermometer placed in the thickest section registers 74°C.

Nutritional values per serving:

Total Calories: 234kcal, Fats: 7g, Carbohydrates: 11g, Protein: 30g

23. Turkey Patty

Ready in: 30 mins.

Serves: 4

Difficulty: medium

Ingredients:

- 2 cloves of garlic, minced
- 1 lb. of ground turkey (454 g)
- 1 tbsp. of Worcestershire (15 ml), soy sauce or fish sauce
- 1/2 cup of minced onion (80 g)
- 1 tsp. of dried herbs (5 ml), oregano, dill, thyme, marjoram, basil
- 1/2 tsp. of salt (2.5 ml), or to taste
- Oil spray to coat
- Generous amount of Black pepper

Directions:

- For 5 minutes, preheat the air fryer to 193°C.
- Gently incorporate the turkey, dried herbs, salt, onion, pepper, Worcestershire sauce (or soy sauce or fish sauce), and garlic.
- Add ingredients for turkey patties in a bowl.
- Shape the turkey into four 4" broad patties. Apply oil evenly on both sides. You'll need to cook in 2 batches if your air fryer is smaller.
- Four patties made out of turkey flesh were coated with oil.
- Spray oil on the air fryer tray or basket or line it with a single layer of a perforated non-stick silicone liner. If necessary, cook in batches.
- Air fry for 10 to 12 minutes at 193 °C. Flip the patties after the first six minutes. Continue to Air Fry the food at 193°C for an additional 4-6 minutes, or until it reaches your ideal doneness or an internal temperature of 74°C. You may need to cook the patties for some more minutes if it is thicker. Cover the patties & let them rest for three minutes for the juiciest results.

Nutritional values per serving:

Total Calories: 144kcal, Fats: 1g, Carbohydrates: 3g, Protein: 27g

24. Rotisserie Chicken

Ready in: 1 hr. 20 mins.

Serves: 6

Difficulty: medium

Ingredients:

- 1 halved lemon

- 4 sprigs of thyme, fresh

- 1 whole chicken (3 & 1/2 - 4 pound), giblets removed

- ½ tsp. of ground pepper, divided

- ¾ tsp. of salt, divided

Directions:

- Insert lemon halves and thyme sprigs into chicken cavity. Utilize kitchen twine to truss the legs of chicken shut. 3/8 tsp. Salt and 1/4 tsp. Pepper should be distributed equally throughout the breasts and legs. Put the chicken in the air fryer basket with the breasts facing up.

- No need to preheat; set your air fryer up to 170°C and cook for 25-30 minutes. Cook the chicken for 15 minutes before carefully flipping it over. Once again, carefully flip the chicken over. Cook for 10 to 15 minutes, or until a thermometer placed in the thickest part of a thigh reads 74°C. After moving the chicken to the chopping board, let it for 10 minutes to rest.

- Carve the chicken; throw away the thyme, keeping the lemon halves for later. Sprinkle the remaining 3/8 tsp. Salt and 1/4 tsp. Pepper equally over the chicken before squeezing the juice from the saved lemon halves over it.

Nutritional values per serving:

Total Calories: 166kcal, **Fats:** 6.4g, Carbohydrates: 1g, **Protein:** 24.8g

Chapter 6: Air Fried Diabetic Diet - Lamb Recipes

1. Lamb Chops

Ready in: 45 mins.

Serves: 4

Difficulty: medium

Ingredients:

- 2 tbsp. of red-wine vinegar
- ¼ cup of olive oil
- 1 tbsp. of fresh rosemary, chopped
- 1 tsp. of grated lemon zest
- 1 ½ tsp. of fresh oregano, chopped
- 1 clove of garlic, grated
- 1 rack of lamb (1 & 1/4-lb.), trenched, removed silver skin, & cut into single chops (about 7-8 chops)
- ¾ tsp. of black pepper, cracked
- ½ tsp. of salt

Directions:

- In a zip-top large plastic bag, combine the oil, rosemary, vinegar, oregano, garlic, lemon zest, and pepper. Place the chops in the bag after salting them. The chops should be marinated, then let stand at normal temperature for 20 minutes while being turned regularly.
- For five minutes, preheat the air fryer to 193°C. Place the chops into the basket in one single layer, and cooking spray the basket lightly (based on size of the air fryer, this might require 2 batches).
- Cook the chops for approximately 4 minutes, or until they start to brown gently. Flip, then cook for 4 to 5 minutes, or until medium-rare (34°C). (If batch cooking, remove the chops to the platter, cover, and maintain warmth. With the remaining chops, repeat.)

Nutritional values per serving:

Total Calories: 133kcal, **Fats:** 7g, **Carbohydrates:** 0g, **Protein:** 16g

2. Air Fried Lamb Roast

Ready in: 20 mins.

Serves: 2

Difficulty: medium

Ingredients:

- 1 tbsp. of olive oil
- 10 oz. or 300 g of butterflied lamb roast
- 1 tsp. of rosemary, dried or fresh
- ½ tsp. of black pepper
- 1 tsp. of thyme, dried or fresh

Directions:

- Set the air fryer to 180°C.
- On a dish, combine olive oil, rosemary, and thyme.
- After patting the lamb roast dry, throw it in the mixture of herb oil and flip it to coat it completely.
- Put the lamb in the air fryer basket and cook it for 15 to 20 minutes at 180°C.
- You should get medium-sized lamb from this. To make sure it is cooked to your preference, use a thermometer to check the temperature. If you desire it more well-done, cook it for extra 3-minute intervals.

- Take the air-fried lamb out of the fryer, wrap it in aluminium foil, and let it rest for 5 mins before serving (this will allow the juices to reabsorb in the meat).
- To serve, cut the meat against the grain.

Nutritional values per serving:

Total Calories: 181cal, Fats: 11g, Carbohydrates: 1g, Protein: 18g

3. Lamb Spicy Curry Puffs

Ready in: 35 mins.

Serves: 4

Difficulty: medium

Ingredients:

- 1 Egg to brush the empanadas
- 1 thawed Biscuit Dough
- 3 tbsp. of Olive Oil
- 1 tsp. of Butter, for egg wash

For Filling:

- 1 Onion (Large), thinly chopped
- 1 Cup of Lamb Mince
- 1/2 Cup of Carrots-Peas, thawed

For Spices:

- 1/4 tsp. of Ginger Powder
- 1 tbsp. of Curry Powder
- 1/8 tsp. of Garlic Powder
- Salt
- 2 tbsp. of Hot Sauce
- Black pepper

Directions:

- Set the oven temperature to 190°C.
- Add chopped onions to a pan of hot oil. Golden brown onions should be sautéed.

- Add lamb mince now, and cook for two to three mins (over medium to low flames)
- Stir in the carrot-pea mixture and cook for a further 3 to 4 minutes over medium heat, sautéing every two minutes.
- Stirring every minute, add the "Spices" to the mixture and cook for an additional 4-5 minutes.
- Remove the mixture from the heat and allow it to cool.
- Combine butter and egg in a little bowl. Split a single ball of biscuit dough into two equal pieces.
- Roll one portion into a disc and hold it in your hand. Put 2 tablespoons of the lamb filling in the centre of the circle.
- To thoroughly seal the disc, fold and pinch its edges (to make a half-moon shape).
- In a similar manner, fill the remaining dough balls. Arrange all of the lamb hand pies or lamb curry puffs onto a baking sheet.
- Evenly brush them with the egg and butter mixture.
- Bake the tray in the oven for 15 to 18 minutes or until it becomes golden brown.
- Take the puffs out of the oven and set them on a serving platter. Accompany with preferred chutney.

Nutritional values per serving:

Total Calories: 215cal, Fats: 14g, Carbohydrates: 11g, Protein: 11g

4. Braised Delicious Lamb-shanks

Ready in: 40 mins.

Serves: 4

Difficulty: medium

Ingredients:

- 1 & ½ tsp. of kosher salt
- 4 lamb shanks
- ½ tsp. of black pepper, freshly ground
- 2 tbsp. of olive oil
- 4 cloves of garlic, crushed
- 3 cups of beef broth, divided
- 2 tbsp. of balsamic vinegar
- 4-6 sprigs of fresh rosemary

Directions:

- Season lamb shanks with salt & pepper before setting them on the baking or drip pan. Rub the lamb all over with the minced garlic. Apply olive oil to the seasoned lamb shanks and cover with rosemary before cooking.

- Position the lamb-filled prepared pan on the rack. Choose Dual Cook. Set the temperature first to Roast for 20 minutes at 230°C & then up to Low for 2 hours at 125°C.

- Roasting the lamb requires one rotation. When the oven is set to Low, add two cups of vinegar and broth. One hour of simmering time remains; add the remaining broth.

- Lamb is cooked when the meat readily separates from the bone.

Nutritional values per serving:

Total Calories: 447cal, Fats: 26g, Carbohydrates: 6g, Protein: 24g

5. Air Fried Lamb & Potatoes

Ready in: 1 hr. 15 mins.

Serves: 4

Difficulty: medium

Ingredients:

- 300 g of Potatoes
- 1.2 Kg of Lamb Roast

- 1 tbsp. of Olive Oil
- 1 tsp. of thyme
- 2 tsp. of Rosemary
- Salt & Black Pepper
- 1 tsp. of Bouquet Garni

Directions:

- Score the lamb, then season it with thyme, bouquet garni, salt, and pepper.

- Put the food into the air fryer basket & set the timer for 30 minutes at 160 C.

- Place sliced and peeled roast potatoes in a bowl. Use your hands to combine the extra virgin olive oil, rosemary, salt, and pepper.

- Rotate the lamb roast and add potatoes to the spaces when the air fryer beeps. Cook at the same time & temperature for an additional 25 minutes.

- Remove the potatoes when the beeper sounds, then let the lamb rest.

- If the centre is too pink, cut it in half and continue cooking for an additional 5 mins at the normal temperature.

- Cut your lamb into slices. Enjoy after serving.

Nutritional values per serving:

Total Calories: 464kcal, Fats: 21g, Carbohydrates: 1g, Protein: 63g

6. Leg of Lamb

Ready in: 1 hr. 5 min.

Serves: 4

Difficulty: medium

Ingredients:

- Roast Potatoes
- 1.4 kg of Leg Of Lamb
- Salt & Black Pepper

Directions:

- Salt and pepper your leg of lamb then set it on the top level of the air fryer oven.

- Do 20 minutes of cooking at 180 °C. Prepare the roast potatoes as it cooks.

- When it beeps, take a little amount of the lamb juices that have fallen to the bottom of the roast potatoes, stir them, and place them on the second level.

- Cook at the same temperature for 40 minutes further before serving.

Nutritional values per serving:

Total Calories: 639.84 kcal, **Fats:** 22.55g, **Carbohydrates:** 319g, **Protein:** 102.78g

7. Lamb Gyro

Ready in: 45 min

Serves: 4

Difficulty: medium

Ingredients:

- 2 tbsp. of oregano

- 1 pound of ground lamb

- One tbsp. of basil

- 1/2 tbsp. of garlic powder

- 1/2 tbsp. of onion flakes or onion powders

- 1/2 tbsp. of thyme

- 1/2 tbsp. of paprika

- 1/2 tbsp. of fennel

- 1 tbsp. of Harissa Seasoning

- 1/2 tbsp. of black pepper

For Toppings:

- Romaine Lettuce

- Pita Bread

- Tomatoes

- Kalamata Olives

- Tzatziki Sauce

- Feta Cheese

- Persian Cucumbers

Directions:

- Combine the ground lamb with the harissa spices, oregano, onion flakes, basil, garlic powder, fennel, thyme, and black pepper into a small bowl. Mix thoroughly.

- Make 2-inch-wide patties out of the meat. Place for 15 to 20 minutes in the refrigerator.

- Take them out of the fridge, place your silicone liner inside, and then spray cooking spray on the liner. Set 170°C on the setting of the air fryer for 8-10 minutes. Midway during the cooking period, flip.

- Use a meat thermometer to check the internal temperature of the meat; it should be 57°C.

- Put your gyro together and serve.

Nutritional values per serving:

Total Calories: 444cal, **Fats:** 26g, **Carbohydrates:** 20g, **Protein:** 33g

8. Spaghetti & Lamb meatball muffins

Ready in: 15 min

Serves: 24

Difficulty: medium

Ingredients:

- 2 cups of Pasta Sauce

- 8.8 oz. of Pasta

- 1 slightly beaten egg

- ½ cup of Parmesan cheese, grated

- 2 cups of mozzarella cheese, shredded

- 24 cooked Lamb meatballs

Directions:

- Prepare pasta as directed on the box.

- Add 1-12 cups of marinara to the spaghetti in a big bowl. Add the beaten egg.

- To the spaghetti mixture, add 1 cup of mozzarella and 1/2 cup Parmesan, and toss thoroughly.

- Use nonstick spray to coat silicone baking ware.

- Spoon the spaghetti mixture into each cup, pushing it down firmly to make it more compact.

- Your air fryer should now include the baking cups. Ensure there is adequate space around them so that air may circulate freely. Do not crowd. Until they are completely cooked, they may be prepared in stages.

- Cook at 198°C. for 4-5 minutes. Use big tongs to remove carefully from the air fryer.

- Fill the middle of muffin cup, each with a meatball. Add some more sauce and mozzarella on top.

- Go back to the air fryer & cook for 2 more mins at 198°C.

- Use tongs to remove and place aside to cool somewhat.

- Continue making more spaghetti & meatball muffins.

- After they have cooled, you may remove them from the silicone cups & set them on a serving tray. Extra spaghetti sauce should be served on the side.

- These muffins may be frozen for later use or individually packaged for lunchboxes and snacks.

- Place in the microwave for 1 minute to warm from frozen. If it's still chilly, extend the duration by 30 seconds.

Nutritional values per serving:

Total Calories: 120kcal, Fats: 6g, Carbohydrates: 9g, Protein: 7g

9. Meat Filled Air Fried Pita Pockets

Ready in: 20 min

Serves: 8

Difficulty: medium

Ingredients:

- 1 onion, small

- 1 lb. of ground lamb

- 1 tsp. of salt

- ½ tsp. of allspice, ⅛ tsp. of cinnamon, ⅛ tsp. of cloves)

- 1 tsp. of sumac powder

- 1 tsp. of red pepper, crushed

- ¼ cup of olive oil

- , ½ tsp. of black pepper

- 4 (cut in half) pita bread

Directions:

- Add ground lamb or beef to a big bowl. Utilizing a food processor, grind the onion. Add onion into the bowl after draining the liquid. Mix the spices into the meat mixture after adding them.

- To let the flavours meld for a few hours at least, cover the bowl and store it in the refrigerator.

- The meat should be divided into eight equal pieces. Each pita bread should be cut in half, and the meat mixture should be gently stuffed into every pita pocket to create a layer of meat.

- Set the oven to 190°C.

- Brush the filled pitas with some olive oil on both sides, then place them onto a baking sheet. Line your baking sheet with parchment paper or foil to make cleaning simpler. Bake the pita until crispy, and the meat is heated through, about 5 mins on each side.

Nutritional values per serving:

Total Calories: 289kcal, Fats: 18g, Carbohydrates: 18g, Protein: 16g

10. Lamb Meatball with Tahini Sauce

Ready in: 20 min

Serves: 4

Difficulty: medium

Ingredients:

Tahini Sauce:

- Juice of two lemons
- ¾ cup of tahini paste
- 1 & ½ tsp. of kosher salt, divided
- 2–3 cloves of garlic, coarsely chopped

Meatball:

- 1 lb. of ground lamb
- 2 tbsp. of bulgur wheat, finely ground
- ½ minced yellow onion
- 1 tsp. of cumin
- 1 tsp. of coriander
- ½ tsp. of black pepper
- Oil for spraying
- ¼ tsp. of ground cinnamon
- Pita bread to serve

Directions:

- To create the tahini sauce, blitz the lemon juice, tahini paste, garlic, and 1/2 tsp. of salt in a food processor or blender until a paste forms. Slowly add 1/2 cup of cold water while the motor is running; continue blending for 1 to 2 minutes, or till sauce is smooth & pourable. Depending on the thickness of tahini paste, if the mixture still is too dense to pour, add up to an extra 1/4 cup of cold water in the same way. The sauce should be kept cold until used.

- In a heat-resistant dish, combine the bulgur with 2 tbsp., of very hot water. Stir using a fork after letting stand for seven minutes to let all the water soak.

- In a medium bowl, add the softened bulgur, lamb, onion, 1 teaspoon of salt, and spices. Mix well with your hands to make the meatballs.

- Shape the mixture of lamb into 8 equal, closely packed oval patties using wet hands to avoid sticking. The patties should be placed on a platter, covered, and chilled for 30 minutes at least and maybe overnight.

- Set the air fryer up to 205°C for 3 minutes before beginning to cook the meatballs. Spray some oil on the basket to keep the patties from clinging.

- Thread half the patties onto the metal skewers & set them into the air fryer in one single layer, working in 2 batches to prevent overcrowding the basket.

- Cook the meatball for approximately 10 minutes, flipping once halfway through or until they are browned and register 70°C on an instant-read thermometer (like this one). Continue by making the 2nd batch of patties.

- To remove any extra oil, put the fried meatball on a platter lined with paper towels. Serve with warm tahini sauce to accompany.

Nutritional values per serving:

Total Calories: 621cal, Fats: 50.7g, Carbohydrates: 17.6g, Protein: 27.2g

11. Lamb kebab

Ready in: 20 min

Serves: 4

Difficulty: medium

Ingredients:

- 1 pound of ground lamb (480 g)
- 1 tbsp. of cooking oil

- 1/4 cup of fresh parsley, chopped
- 2 tbsp. of kebab spice mix
- 1 tbsp. of minced garlic
- 1 tsp. of kosher salt

Directions:

- All ingredients should be combined in a big mixing dish. Blend with an immersion blender until uniform. Refrigerate the lamb mixture for 30 minutes, at least with a cover on.
- For five minutes, preheat the air fryer up to 200 C.
- Take the chilled lamb mixture out of the fridge. The mixture should be shaped into four long sausages using your hands. Enter bamboo skewers that have been socked.
- Kebabs should be put in the basket of an air fryer. Fry for 8-10 minutes or till internal temperature reaches 70°C with tzatziki sauce, and serve.

Nutritional values per serving:

Total Calories: 140.9cal, Fats: 8.4g, Carbohydrates: 1.3g, Protein: 9.4g

12. Lamb & Cauliflower Rice

Ready in: 25 mins.

Serves: 2

Difficulty: medium

Ingredients:

- 1/3 cup of Frozen Corn (46g)
- 12 oz. bag of Cauliflower Rice, Frozen
- 1/3 cup of Peas & Carrots, Frozen (42g)
- 1 tbsp. of Soy Sauce (15g)
- 1 tbsp. of toasted Sesame Oil (16g)

Optional:

- 1/2 tsp. of Ginger, Ground
- 1/2 tsp. of Garlic Powder

Directions:

- Put the cauliflower rice into a dish that can be used in an air fryer or covers the bottom of basket with foil. 10 minutes of air frying at 205°C.
- Sesame oil & soy sauce should be added to the rice. Before adding the ginger & garlic powder and the other vegetables, give the rice a quick stir to coat it.
- Air-fried the rice for a further 10 to 15 minutes at 205°C while tossing regularly or until it reaches your desired crispiness. Add green onions as a garnish and season with some salt and pepper.

Nutritional values per serving:

Total Calories: 155cal, Fats: 7g, Carbohydrates: 15g, Protein: 7g

13. Butter Potato Lamb Chops

Ready in: 17 min

Serves: 1

Difficulty: easy

Ingredients:

- Salt & black pepper
- 350 g of lamb chops
- 1 tbsp. of butter
- 2 potatoes (large)
- 3-4 stalks of rosemary herbs

Directions:

- Rub salt, pepper, & rosemary herbs all over lamb chops to make a marinade.
- Peel and chop the potatoes into tiny pieces. Combine the butter, salt, and pepper with the rosemary sprigs that have been crushed.
- Heat up the air fryer.
- Put the ingredients in the air fryer and cook for 10 minutes at 200°C. To make sure food is cooked evenly when air

frying, shake and turn the contents halfway through.

- Enjoy!

Nutritional values per serving:

Total Calories: 380kcal, **Fats:** 20g, **Carbohydrates:** 34g, **Protein:** 28g

14. Stuffed Lamb Feta Burgers

Ready in: 50 mins.

Serves: 5

Difficulty: medium

Ingredients:

For burger patties:

- 1 lb. of ground lamb
- 8 oz. of mushrooms
- ¼ tsp. of salt
- 4 oz. of crumbled feta
- ¼ tsp. of pepper

For pickled red onions:

- ½ cup of water
- 1 sliced thinly red onion
- ½ cup of distilled white vinegar
- 1 tsp. of salt
- 2 tbsp. of honey

For yoghurt sauce:

- 1 tbsp. of lemon juice
- ½ cup of plain Greek yoghurt, nonfat

- ½ tbsp. of olive oil
- ¼ tsp. of garlic powder
- ¼ tsp. of salt
- 1 tbsp. of fresh parsley
- 1 tbsp. of fresh dill

For assembling burger:

- ¾ cup of baby arugula
- 5 hamburger buns

Directions:

- Make the hamburger patties first. The mushrooms should first be roughly chopped and added to the food processor. Several pulses are needed to achieve extremely fine chopping.

- Combine the minced mushrooms, salt, ground lamb, and pepper in a big bowl. Mix well using your hands. Divide into ten equal pieces.

- Make a patty by taking one piece of lamb mixture. In the middle, sprinkle some feta. Place another patty made from leftover lamb mixture on top, sealing the sides by squeezing them together. To create 5 filled burger patties, repeat the process with the leftover lamb mixture and feta.

- The patties should be placed on a platter and chilled in the refrigerator for 20 minutes at least.

- If you want to make pickled red onions from scratch, get started on them in the meanwhile. In a mason jar, put your finely sliced onion. Combine the vinegar, water, honey, & salt in a small saucepan. After bringing it to a boil, turn off the heat. After covering the onions with the vinegar mixture, wait 10 minutes.

- Additionally, make the yoghurt sauce. Greek yoghurt, olive oil, lemon juice, salt, dill, garlic powder, and parsley should all be mixed together in a bowl. Combine and put away for the time being.

- When the patties are cool enough to handle, take them from the burgers and put them in the air fryer's basket. Work in batches if necessary.

- Air-fried the lamb patties at 190°C for 15 to 18 minutes, or until they reach an inside temperature of 70°C.

- The Greek yoghurt sauce, arugula, a dollop of the pickled red onions, & the lamb patties should be placed on a bun. Enjoy!

Nutritional values per serving:

Total Calories: 480kcal, **Fats:** 11.5g, **Carbohydrates:** 1.5g, **Protein:** 32g

Chapter 7: Air Fried Diabetic Diet ~ Fish & other Seafood Recipes

1. Breaded Sea Scallops

Ready in: 15 mins.

Serves: 4

Difficulty: easy

Ingredients:

- ½ tsp. of garlic powder
- ½ cup of buttery crackers, finely crushed
- ½ tsp. of seafood seasoning
- 1 pound of sea scallops (dry)
- 2 tbsp. of butter, melted
- 1 cooking spray

Directions:

- Set the air fryer's temperature to 198°C.
- In a small bowl, combine the garlic powder, cracker crumbs, and seafood seasoning. Put butter in a 2nd shallow dish after it has melted.
- Roll each scallop in breading till thoroughly covered, then dip in the melted butter. Repeat with remaining scallops, then place on a dish.
- Lightly spritz cooking spray in the air fryer basket. You may have to work in batches. Arrange the scallops into the prepped basket so that they're not overlapping.
- Do 2 minutes of cooking in the already heated air fryer. With a tiny spatula, carefully flip the scallops over and cook for an additional 2 minutes or until opaque.

Nutritional values per serving:

Total Calories: 282kcal, **Fats:** 17.6g, **Carbohydrates:** 13.7g, **Protein:** 16.6g

2. Crumbed Fish

Ready in: 25 mins.

Serves: 4

Difficulty: medium

Ingredients:

- 4 flounder fillets
- ¼ cup of vegetable oil
- 1 sliced lemon
- 1 beaten egg

Directions:

- Set an air fryer up to 180°C.
- Combine oil and bread crumbs in a small bowl; whisk until the mixture is loose and crumbly.
- Shake off any extra egg after dipping fish fillets in it. Dip the fillets into the bread crumbs mixture and completely coat them.
- Gently place the coated fillets into the air fryer basket and heat for 12 minutes, or until the fish with a fork easily flakes. Serve with lemon slices as a garnish.**Nutritional values per serving:**

Total Calories: 353kcal, **Fats:** 17.7g, **Carbohydrates:** 22.5g, **Protein:** 26.9g

3. Salmon Cakes & Sriracha Mayo

Ready in: 40 mins.

Serves: 4

Difficulty: medium

Ingredients:

Sriracha Mayo:

- 1 tbsp. of Sriracha
- ¼ cup of mayonnaise

Salmon Cakes:

- ⅓ cup of almond flour
- 1 pound of salmon fillets (skinless), cut into 1-inch pieces
- 1 lightly beaten egg
- 1 coarsely chopped green onion
- 1 ½ tsp. of seafood seasoning
- 1 pinch of seafood seasoning
- cooking spray

Directions:

- In a small bowl, combine Sriracha and mayonnaise. Put 1 tablespoon of the Sriracha mayo into the food processor's bowl, then chill the remaining mixture until needed.
- To the Sriracha mayo, add the salmon, egg, almond flour, 1 1/2 tsp. of seafood spice, and green onion. Pulse briskly for 4-5 seconds, just until the ingredients are incorporated, but there are still tiny pieces of salmon visible. (Avoid over-processing as it will make the mixture mushy.)
- Spread cooking spray on hands and cover a dish with waxed paper. Make 8 little patties out of the salmon mixture, then place them on a platter. Place in the fridge for 15 minutes or until cooled and stiff.
- Set the air fryer's temperature to 200°C. Spray cooking oil on the air fryer basket.
- Take the salmon cakes out of the fridge. Working in the batches, if required to prevent crowding, lightly coat both sides with the cooking spray before placing it into the air fryer basket.
- Cook for 6-8 minutes in the already heated air fryer. Place on a serving tray and serve with any leftover Sriracha mayo and, if preferred, a small dusting of Old Bay seasoning.

Nutritional values per serving:

Total Calories: 340kcal, **Fats:** 24.7g, Carbohydrates: 3.6g, **Protein:** 25.5g

4. Lemon Pepper Shrimp

Ready in: 15 mins.

Serves: 2

Difficulty: medium

Ingredients:

- 1 juiced lemon
- 1 tbsp. of olive oil
- 1 tsp. of lemon pepper
- ¼ tsp. of garlic powder
- ¼ tsp. of paprika
- 1 sliced lemon
- 12 ounces of medium shrimp (uncooked), peeled & deveined

Directions:

- Set an air fryer to the manufacturer's recommended temperature of 200°C.
- Oil, lemon pepper, lemon juice, paprika, & garlic powder should all be combined in a bowl. Add the shrimp and coat well.
- Cook shrimp into the preheated air fryer for 6 to 8 minutes, or until the outsides are brilliant pink and the interiors are opaque. Add lemon wedges to the dish.

Nutritional values per serving:

Total Calories: 215kcal, **Fats:** 8.6 g, Carbohydrates: 12.6g, Protein: 28.9g

---

5. Lobster Tails with Garlic-Lemon Butter

Ready in: 20 mins.

Serves: 2

Difficulty: medium

Ingredients:

- 4 tbsp. of butter
- 2 lobster tails (4 ounces)
- 1 tsp. of lemon zest
- salt & black pepper (ground), to taste
- 1 clove of garlic, grated
- 2 lemon wedges
- 1 tsp. of fresh parsley, chopped

Directions:

- Set an air fryer up to 195°C.
- Use kitchen shears to cut longitudinally through the centres of the flesh and hard top shells of lobster tails. Cut up to the bases of the shells but not beyond them. Disperse the tail parts. Place the lobster meat-facing-up on the tails in air fryer basket.
- In a saucepan set over medium heat, melt the butter. Add garlic and lemon zest; cook for 30 seconds or until garlic is aromatic.
- Spoon 2 tablespoons of the butter mixture into a small dish, then brush it over the lobster tails. Discard any excess butter to prevent cross-contamination with the raw lobster. Use salt and pepper to season lobster.
- Cook in the already heated air fryer for 5 to 7 minutes, or until the lobster flesh is opaque.
- Pour the saucepan's saved butter over the lobster flesh. Serve with lemon wedges and parsley on top.

Nutritional values per serving:

Total Calories: 313kcal, **Fats:** 25.8g, Carbohydrates: 3.3g, Protein: 18.1g

---

6. Salmon Nuggets

Ready in: 35 min

Serves: 4

Difficulty: hard

Ingredients:

- ¼ tsp. of dried chipotle pepper, ground
- ⅓ cup of maple syrup
- 1 pinch of sea salt
- 1 egg (large)
- 1 ½ cups of garlic-flavoured croutons & butter
- cooking spray
- 1 centre-cut, skinless salmon fillet (1 pound), cut in 1 & 1/2-inch of chunks

Directions:

- In a saucepan, combine salt, maple syrup, and chipotle powder. Heat to a simmer. To stay warm, turn the heat down to low.
- In the bowl of the small food processor, add the croutons and pulse several times to create fine crumbs. Place in a small bowl.
- Set the air fryer up to 198°C and whisk the egg in a different bowl.
- Lightly season salmon with sea salt. Salmon should be lightly dipped into the egg mixture, allowing excess drop-off. Shake off any excess crouton breading after coating the fish. Put onto a plate and give a gentle cooking spray mist.
- Cooking spray should be used on the air fryer's basket. If necessary, add salmon nuggets within, working in the batches to prevent crowding.

- Do 3 minutes of cooking in a preheated air fryer. Turn the salmon pieces gently, spritz with a little oil, and cook for an additional 3 to 4 minutes, or until the fish is well cooked. Drizzle heated chipotle maple syrup over the dish before serving. Serve right away.

Nutritional values per serving:

Total Calories: 364cal, Fats: 16.4g, Carbohydrates: 27.2g, Protein: 25.8g

7. Fish Sticks

Ready in: 20 mins.

Serves: 4

Difficulty: easy

Ingredients:

- ¼ cup of all-purpose flour
- 1 pound of cod fillets
- 1 egg
- ¼ cup of grated Parmesan cheese
- ½ cup of panko bread crumbs
- 1 tbsp. of parsley flakes
- ½ tsp. of black pepper
- 1 tsp. of paprika
- cooking spray

Directions:

- Set an air fryer up to 200°C.
- Cut fish into 1x3-inch sticks after patting it dry with paper towels.
- Fill a shallow plate with flour. In a separate, shallow dish, beat the egg. In a 3rd shallow dish, mix panko, parsley, Parmesan cheese, paprika, & pepper.
- Use flour to cover each fish stick before dipping it in a beaten egg and then coating it with a seasoned panko mixture.
- Coat the air fryer's basket with nonstick frying spray. Make sure none of the sticks contacts you when you arrange half of them in the basket. Each stick's top should be sprayed with cooking spray.
- Five minutes of cooking in the already heated air fryer. Cook the fish sticks on the other side for five more minutes. With the remaining fish sticks, repeat.

Nutritional values per serving:

Total Calories: 200kcal, Fats: 4.1g, Carbohydrates: 16.5g, Protein: 26.3g

8. Panko-Crusted Mahi Mahi

Ready in: 20 mins.

Serves: 4

Difficulty: medium

Ingredients:

- 2 tbsp. of Grapeseed oil
- 4 Mahi Mahi fillets (4 ounces)
- 2 cups of panko bread crumbs
- ½ tsp. of garlic salt
- 1 tsp. of everything bagel seasoning
- ½ tsp. of ground turmeric
- Cooking spray
- ½ tsp. of ground black pepper
- 1 lemon (medium), cut in 4 wedges
- 1 tsp. of fresh parsley, chopped

Directions:

- For five minutes, preheat the air fryer up to 200°C.
- Mahi Mahi fillets should be placed on a tray and covered with Grapeseed oil in the meanwhile.
- In a shallow dish, combine panko, garlic salt, bagel seasoning, turmeric, & pepper. Place the fillets in the basket of the air fryer in one single layer after coating each with the panko mixture. Use nonstick spray to coat.
- Cook in the already heated air fryer for 12 15 minutes, turning halfway through, or till fish easily flakes with a fork.
- Take out of the air fryer. Lemon wedges and parsley are used as a garnish. Serve right away.

Nutritional values per serving:

Total Calories: 304kcal, **Fats:** 9.4g, **Carbohydrates:** 40.6g, **Protein:** 26.7g

9. Spicy Bay Scallops

Ready in: 15 mins.

Serves: 4

Difficulty: easy

Ingredients:

- 2 tsp. of smoked paprika
- 1 pound of bay scallops, rinsed & patted dry
- 2 tsp. of chilli powder
- 1 tsp. of garlic powder
- 2 tsp. of olive oil
- ⅛ tsp. of red cayenne pepper
- ¼ tsp. of ground black pepper

Directions:

- Set an air fryer up to 200°C.
- Stir the following ingredients in a bowl: bay scallops, chilli powder, smoked paprika, garlic powder, olive oil, pepper, & cayenne pepper. Transfer to the basket of an air fryer.
- Shake the basket halfway through air-frying the scallops for 8 minutes, or until they are well done.

Nutritional values per serving:

Total Calories: 179kcal, **Fats:** 3.8g, **Carbohydrates:** 7.2g, **Protein:** 28.9g

10. Crunchy Seasoned Cod Fillets

Ready in: 22 mins.

Serves: 3

Difficulty: medium

Ingredients:

- ⅓ cup of panko bread crumbs, unseasoned
- Cooking spray (avocado oil)
- ⅓ cup of yellow cornmeal, stone-ground

- 1 tsp. of paprika
- 2 tsp. of seasoning mix
- ½ tsp. of salt
- 3 cod fillets (5 ounces)
- ½ cup of buttermilk
- 1 tbsp. of all-purpose flour

Directions:

- In the base of the basket of the air fryer, make a 3-inch wide foil sling that extends across the bottom & up the sides. Make some holes in the foil sling's bottom that correspond to the holes in the basket. Use avocado oil to spritz on the sling.

- Set the air fryer's temperature to 200°C.

- In a separate bowl, mix the panko crumbs, seasoning mix, yellow cornmeal, paprika, and salt. Add buttermilk to a different bowl.

- After gently dusting both sides of the cod fillets with flour, pat them dry with paper towels. Each flour-coated fillet should be dipped into buttermilk before being coated with the crumb mixture. Place each fillet on a foil sling, if you're using it, or onto the rack of the shelf-style air fryer, and pat all sides with the crumb mixture. Spray avocado oil on each fish fillet.

- Cook in the air fryer for 10 to 12 minutes, or till the fish flakes easily. Cod fillets should be taken out of the air fryer using the sling and served right away.

Nutritional values per serving:

Total Calories: 224kcal, Fats: 2.3g, Carbohydrates: 23.1g, Protein: 29.5g

11. Salmon Patties

Ready in: 25 mins.

Serves: 6

Difficulty: easy

Ingredients:

- 1 tbsp. of brown sugar
- 2 tbsp. of grill seasoning
- ¾ tsp. of ground cumin
- ¼ tsp. of cayenne pepper
- ½ tsp. of ground coriander
- 2 pounds of skin on salmon fillets

Directions:

- For 2 minutes, preheat the air fryer to the 165°C setting for fish.

- In a small bowl, mix the cayenne pepper, cumin, brown sugar, coriander, & steak seasoning. Each salmon fillet should receive around 2 tsp. (or more, as preferred) of the seasoning mixture. Salmon should be layered into the air fryer basket.

- Cook salmon into the air fryer for approximately 18 minutes, or until it easily flakes with a fork, working in batches if required. Place cooked salmon on a platter and rewarm on the lowest setting of the oven. The remaining salmon fillets, and repeat. Serve right away.

Nutritional values per serving:

Total Calories: 230kcal, Fats: 9.8g, Carbohydrates: 3.5g, Protein: 30.2g

12. Lemon-Garlic Salmon

Ready in: 25 mins.

Serves: 2

Difficulty: medium

Ingredients:

- ½ tsp. of minced garlic
- 1 tbsp. of melted butter
- 2 fillets of salmon fillets, centre-cut (6 ounces), with skin
- ⅛ tsp. of dried parsley

- ¼ tsp. of lemon-pepper seasoning
- 3 thin slices of lemon in half
- cooking spray

Directions:

- Set the air fryer's temperature to 200°C.
- Melted butter & minced garlic are combined in a small bowl.
- Salmon fillets should be rinsed and dried with paper towels. Brush with the butter mixture and garnish with parsley and lemon-pepper seasoning.
- Cooking spray should be used on the air fryer's basket. Put three lemon halves on top of each salmon fillet into the basket, skin side down.
- Cook for 8-10 minutes in the already heated air fryer. Take out of the air fryer, then wait two minutes before serving.

Nutritional values per serving:

Total Calories: 293kcal, Fats: 16.4g, Carbohydrates: 1.4g, Protein: 33.6g

13. Crispy Parmesan Cod

Ready in: 25 mins.

Serves: 4

Difficulty: medium

Ingredients:

- salt and black pepper
- 1 pound of cod filets
- 1/2 cup of flour
- 1/2 tsp. of salt
- 2 eggs (large)
- 1 cup of Panko
- 2 tsp. of old bay seasoning
- 1/2 cup of grated parmesan
- olive oil spray

- 1/2 tsp. of garlic powder

Directions:

- Cod fillets should be salted and peppered.
- Establish a station for breading fish. Add the flour to a bowl. The eggs and salt should be combined in the second bowl. Add the Panko, old bay seasoning, parmesan cheese, and garlic powder to the final bowl.
- Cod should first be floured.
- Next, add the egg concoction.
- In the Panko, finally.
- Apply olive oil with a spray bottle to the basket's bottom. Put the fish into the air fryer's basket. Cook for 10 minutes at 205°C. Flip the fish gently. Cook the meat for a further 3–5 minutes, or until it reaches a temperature of 57°C, inside.

Nutritional values per serving:

Total Calories: 303 kcal, Fats: 3 g, Carbohydrates: 24g, Protein: 32g

14. Chili Lime Tilapia

Ready in: 10 mins.

Serves: 2

Difficulty: easy

Ingredients:

- 2 tsp. of chilli powder
- 12 oz. of tilapia fillets, 6 to 8 oz. each
- 1 tsp. of cumin
- 1/2 tsp. of oregano
- 1 tsp. of garlic powder
- 1/2 tsp. of sea salt
- 1 Lime zest
- 1/4 tsp. of ground black pepper
- Juice of half lime

Directions:

- If the air fryer has to be heated up, do it at 205°C. Use your preferred cooking oil to coat the air fryer tray or basket.

- Use a paper towel to pat the tilapia fillets dry.

- Place all the spices in a small bowl, except the lime juice, and mix to blend.

- Apply the spice mixture evenly over the fish.

- Cook fish into the air fryer, apart from one another, for 8 to 10 minutes, or until opaque and flaky.

- Serve right after adding lime juice.

Nutritional values per serving:

Total Calories: 178kcal, Fats: 3g, Carbohydrates: 3g, Protein: 35g

15. White Fish with Lemon Pepper and Garlic

Ready in: 16 mins.

Serves: 2

Difficulty: easy

Ingredients:

- 2 tbsp. of olive oil

- 4 white fish filets (6 oz.)

- 2 tsp. of garlic powder

- 1 tsp. of freshly cracked pepper

- 1 tsp. of Celtic sea salt

- 1 sliced lemon, in thin rounds

- 2 tsp. of Italian herbs

- 1 tsp. of lemon juice

Directions:

- Place the fish fillets in a big bowl, add the lemon juice and olive oil, and toss to coat the fish evenly.

- Season liberally with Italian herbs, salt, and pepper.

- Arrange the fish fillets in the air fryer basket so that they don't contact one another excessively.

- Fish should be placed in an air fryer basket with lemon slices all around it.

- For fish with a slight bit of red in the centre, preheat the air fryer up to 205°C & cook for 10 minutes.

- For fish without any red in the centre, cook for 12 minutes; for well-done or fatter fish fillets, cook for 14.

- Dish out and savour!

Nutritional values per serving:

Total Calories: 462kcal, Fats: 28g, Carbohydrates: 13g, Protein: 39g

16. Crispy Fish Tacos & Pineapple Slaw

Ready in: 35 mins.

Serves: 4

Difficulty: easy

Ingredients:

- 1 & 1/4 tsp. of garlic powder

- 1 cup of panko bread crumbs

- 1 & 1/2 tsp. of chilli powder

- 1 tsp. of ground cumin

- 1/2 tsp. of onion powder

- 3/4 tsp. of kosher salt

- 24 oz. of barramundi (4 filets)

- 1/4 tsp. of black pepper

- 1 egg, large, plus 2 tbsp. of water

- sour cream & lime juice, to serve

- 16 flour tortillas

Salsa:

- 2 tsp. of honey

- 2 tbsp. of lime juice

- 1 clove of garlic (small), grated

- 1/2 tsp. of ground cumin
- 1/2 tsp. of kosher salt
- 1/2 tsp. of chilli powder
- 5 cups of shredded cabbage
- 2 tbsp. of olive oil
- 1 jalapeno, diced
- 1/4 cup of chopped cilantro
- 1 cup of chopped pineapple
- 1/4 cup of red onion, diced

Directions:

- Set the fryer's temperature to 195°C for five minutes.

- Combine the panko, salt, cumin, black pepper, chilli powder, garlic powder, onion powder, and chilli powder in a shallow plate or bowl. To blend, stir.

- In a bowl or shallow dish, combine the egg and water. Combine by whisking.

- Use paper towels to pat dry the fish. Cut fish into 4, 1x4 pieces using a sharp knife. Add salt and pepper to taste.

- Submerge every piece of the fish in the egg. Allow the extra to trickle off. Add the bread crumbs to coat. Ensure the breadcrumbs are pushed into the fish using your fingers. Continue with the remaining fish.

- Fill the air fryer with half the fish. Use a lot of olive oil spritz on the top. For 4 minutes, cook. Flip over the fish by removing the tray. Use olive oil spray to spritz. Cook for a further 2 minutes or until crispy and golden. After every batch, clean the air fryer's bottom. It is really fast and simple & prevents fish from burning later. Repeat with the second fish, half of it.

- While the fish is cooking, in a medium bowl, combine the honey, lime juice, garlic, cumin, salt, chilli powder,

and olive oil. Combine by whisking. Add the cilantro, red onion, pineapple, cabbage, and jalapenos. Toss to evenly distribute the dressing. Use salt and pepper to taste to season.

- Microwave tortillas to a warm state. Over an open heat, you may burn the tortillas if you want.

- Fill each tortilla with a little amount of slaw. Add a slice of fish on top. Add additional coleslaw on top. Serve with some lime juice & sour cream.

Nutritional values per serving:

Total Calories: 82kcal, **Fats:** 3g, **Carbohydrates:** 5g, **Protein:** 9g

17. Swordfish Steak & Mango Citrus Salsa

Ready in: 15 mins.

Serves: 1

Difficulty: easy

Ingredients:

- 1/2 mango
- 1 swordfish steak
- half jalapeno
- 1 tbsp. of orange juice
- 1/4 onion
- juice of half lime
- salt and black pepper, to taste
- Some cilantro

Directions:

- Swordfish should be salted and peppered. Cook for 8 to 10 mins at 205°C in the air fryer. No flipping is required.

- Make a medium bowl of chopped mango, onion, jalapeño, and cilantro for the citrus salsa. Juices from the orange and lime may be added; mix.

- Remove the fish from the air fryer with care, place it on a dish, and cover it with salsa. Enjoy!

Nutritional values per serving:

Total Calories: 442kcal, Fats: 9g, Carbohydrates: 65g, Protein: 27g

18. Crab Cakes

Ready in: 40 mins.

Serves: 6

Difficulty: medium

Ingredients:

- 2 tbsp. of butter (unsalted), melted
- 2 eggs (large)
- 1 tbsp. of fresh basil, chopped
- 2 tsp. of Worcestershire sauce, lower-sodium
- 2 tsp. of fresh tarragon, chopped
- 1 tsp. of lemon zest (grated), plus some lemon wedges, to serve
- ½ tsp. of garlic powder
- 1 tsp. of Old Bay seasoning, reduced-sodium
- ½ tsp. of onion powder
- 2 tbsp. of fresh chives (thinly sliced), divided
- ½ cup of sour cream (light), divided
- 1 pound of lump crabmeat (fresh) or 3 cans of lump crab meat (6 ounces), drained & picked over
- Cooking spray
- ½ cup of panko breadcrumbs, whole-wheat
- 6 butter lettuce leaves (large)

Directions:

- Set a 6 & 1/2-quart air fryer up to 195°C before using. In a large bowl, combine eggs, butter, chives, tarragon, basil, Worcestershire, lemon zest, garlic powder, Old Bay, onion powder, and 1/3 cup sour cream. Gently toss in the panko and crab meat.

- Using clean hands, form the mixture into six crab cakes, each measuring 1/3 cup. Spray frying oil on the fry basket liberally. 3 crab cakes should be added, each of which should be covered with frying spray. Cook for 15 to 18 minutes, rotating once and spraying halfway with extra frying spray, until well browned & crispy on both sides. Place on a platter and cover to maintain warmth. Continue by making the rest of 3 crab cakes.

- Arrange one lettuce leaf and one crab cake on each of the six dishes. 1 & 1/2 tsp. of sour cream & 1/2 tsp. of chives should be placed on top of each crab cake. If desired, garnish with lemon slices. Remove the fish from the air fryer with care, place it on a platter, and cover it with salsa. Enjoy!

Nutritional values per serving:

Total Calories: 209kcal, Fats: 4g, Carbohydrates: 7g, Protein: 22g

19. Bacon Wrapped Shrimp

Ready in: 30 mins.

Serves: 8

Difficulty: medium

Ingredients:

- 8 slices of bacon in thirds
- 24 tail on jumbo shrimps (raw), deveined, thawed from frozen or fresh
- 1 tbsp. of olive oil
- 1 ~2 cloves of garlic, minced
- 1 tsp. of paprika
- 1 tbsp. of fresh parsley, finely chopped

Directions:

- Combine olive oil, garlic, paprika, and parsley in a small bowl.

- If necessary, peel the tails off of the raw shrimp and set them in a medium dish.

- Drizzle the shrimp with the olive oil mixture and gently swirl to coat.

- Place each shrimp on a small baking sheet and wrap a bacon strip around the centre, seam side down.

- Chill for 30 minutes. (Bacon is kept in place during cooking, thanks to this.)

- Set the air fryer at 205°C.

- Place the shrimp seam-side down, snugging the bacon again if required. Take care to avoid having the shrimp overlapping or touching. (Depending on the size of the air fryer, cooking may need to be done in batches.)

- Cook the bacon for 8-10 minutes or until it is completely done. If required, repeat with the remaining shrimp. Serve right away.

Nutritional values per serving:

Total Calories: 111kcal, **Fats:** 11g, **Carbohydrates:** 1g, **Protein:** 3g

20. Shrimp Scampi

Ready in: 15 mins.

Serves: 4

Difficulty: medium

Ingredients:

- 1 tbsp. of Lemon Juice

- 4 tbsp. of Butter

- 1 tbsp. of Garlic, Minced

- 1 tbsp. of chives (chopped), or 1 tsp. of dried chives

- 2 tsp. of Red Pepper Flakes

- 1 tbsp. of fresh basil (chopped), or 1 tsp. of dried basil

- 1 lb. of Raw Shrimp (453.59 g), (21 to 25 count)

- 2 tbsp. of Chicken Stock

Directions:

- Your air fryer should be set at 165°C. While you collect your ingredients, set a metal pan (6 x 3) inside of it to begin heating.

- Add the garlic, butter, & red pepper flakes to a heated 6-inch pan.

- Cook for two minutes while stirring only once, or till the butter has melted. Don't miss this procedure. Everything tastes so nice because the butter has been infused with garlic as a result.

- Turn on the air fryer, then add the ingredients listed in the order given— butter, lemon juice, minced garlic, chives, red pepper flakes, chicken stock, basil, and shrimp—gently stirring between each addition.

- Cook the shrimp for five minutes, stirring once. The butter should now be completely melted and liquid, coating the shrimp with delicious flavour.

- Combine well, remove the six-inch pan with silicone gloves, and let it sit on the counter for a minute. By doing this, you prevent the shrimp from unintentionally overcooking and becoming rubbery by letting it cook in the residual heat.

- Stir for 1 minute. At this stage, the shrimp must be well cooked.

- Add more fresh basil leaves; enjoy

Nutritional values per serving:

Total Calories: 221kcal, **Fats:** 13g, **Carbohydrates:** 1g, **Protein:** 23g

21. Lime Garlic Shrimp Skewers

Ready in: 13 mins.

Serves: 2

Difficulty: easy

Ingredients:

- 1 clove of garlic
- 1 cup of raw shrimp
- 1 lime
- freshly ground black pepper
- 1/8 tsp. of salt
- 5 wooden skewers (6-inch)

Directions:

- Soak wooden skewers for 20 minutes in water.
- Thaw frozen shrimp. Turn the Air Fryer on at 175°C.
- Combine shrimp with minced garlic & lime juice. Including salt and pepper.
- Thread shrimp onto each skewer. Place 8 minutes in the air fryer, flipping halfway through.
- Top with chopped cilantro and your preferred dip before serving.

Nutritional values per serving:

Total Calories: 76kcal, **Fats:** 0g, **Carbohydrates:** 4g, **Protein:** 13g

22. French Classic Mussels

Ready in: 12 mins.

Serves: 4

Difficulty: easy

Ingredients:

- 2 tbsp. of garlic minced
- 1 pound of mussels
- 4 tbsp. of butter melted & unsalted
- 2 tbsp. of heavy cream

- 2 tbsp. of dry white wine

Directions:

- Place the mussels in a large bowl and stir in the butter, garlic, white wine, & heavy cream.
- Place the mussels in the basket or on the rack.
- Set the oven to 205°C for 5 minutes, then shake or toss the basket with them. Set for a further two to five minutes.

Nutritional values per serving:

Total Calories: 97kcal, **Fats:** 5g, **Carbohydrates:** 5g, **Protein:** 8g

23. Garlic Butter Lobster Tails

Ready in: 10 mins.

Serves: 4

Difficulty: easy

Ingredients:

- 6 tbsp. of butter melted
- 4 lobster tails, take the meat out from shell, keep it adhered at the base & place it on the top of shelf.
- 1 tbsp. of packed cilantro, some more to garnish (or you can use any of the other greens as chives or parsley)
- 1 tsp. of Dijon mustard
- 2 cloves of garlic
- 2 tbsp. of lemon juice
- Some salt & black pepper
- 1/8 tsp. of creole seasoning

Directions:

- With the exception of the lobster tails, mix all the ingredients in a blender. Divide sauce into 2 bowls.
- Turn the air fryer on at 195°C. Place the lobster tails in the air fryer, coat them with half of garlic butter sauce, cover

the lid, and cook for 5 to 7 minutes, or till the lobster is well cooked.

- Drizzle the heated lobsters with the remaining garlic butter, then top with fresh cilantro. Serve with mashed potatoes & a cucumber salad.

Nutritional values per serving:

Total Calories: 204kcal, **Fats:** 18g, **Carbohydrates:** 1g, **Protein:** 11g

24. Chili & Garlic Baby Octopus

Ready in: 40 mins.

Serves: 6

Difficulty: medium

Ingredients:

- 12 prawns (large), deveined and peeled (fresh or frozen)
- 8 baby octopus, whole (fresh or frozen)
- 4 garlic cloves, minced
- 1 tbsp. of olive oil
- 1 tsp. of chilli flakes
- Salt to taste

For salad:

- 125g of halved grape tomatoes
- 60g of lettuce leaves, mixed
- 2 Spring onions sprigs, chopped
- Half Spanish onion, sliced and quartered

For dressing:

- Olive oil
- 1 cup of chimichurri sauce

Directions:

- Toss the frozen prawns, baby octopus, chopped garlic, chilli flakes, olive oil, and salt in a big dish. Preheat the air fryer to 180°C. Thoroughly blend

- Put prawns and seasoned baby octopus in the air fryer. Cook for 12 minutes at 180 °C.
- When finished, remove.

For salad:

- Toss the ingredients for the salad in a big bowl.
- To the salad, add half a cup of chimichurri sauce.
- Depending on how much olive oil is already in your chimichurri sauce, you may need to add a little additional. If there is enough to incorporate into the salad, you won't need any.
- Combine salad and sauce.

To serve:

- Add prawns and tiny octopus to the salad as garnish.
- Spoon the leftover chimichurri sauce over the prawns and baby octopus.
- Dish out and savour!

Nutritional values per serving:

Total Calories: 60kcal, **Fats:** 1g, **Carbohydrates:** 7g, **Protein:** 5g

25. Charred Baby Octopus

Ready in: 30 mins.

Serves: 6

Difficulty: medium

Ingredients:

- 1 big Onion piece, diced

- 6 Baby Octopus pieces

- 1 diced carrot, small

- 1 slice of Lemon

- 2 tbsp. of Teriyaki Sauce

- 1 tsp. of sesame oil

- 6 pieces of wooden skewers

- Dash of black pepper

Directions:

- Bring some water to boil in a saucepan. Baby octopus should be added, parboiled for 3 minutes, and then the heat should be turned off. Drain thoroughly after removing the baby octopus.

- Olive oil, salt, and pepper are used to season sliced onion and carrots.

- The six wooden skewers should be soaked in warm water.

- Marinate the octopus for three to four hours in the refrigerator with sesame oil, teriyaki sauce, and a sprinkle of pepper.

- Take out of the fridge, skewer marinated baby octopus in between pieces of carrot and onion.

- Air-fry lemons and octopus skewers for approximately five minutes at 190°C on a well-oiled grill or skillet.

- Enjoy right now with your preferred dipping sauce or chilli.

Nutritional values per serving:

Total Calories: 45kcal, Fats: 1.5g, Carbohydrates: 1g, Protein: 7g

Chapter 8: Air Fried Diabetic Diet - Vegetarian Recipes

1. Honey Brussels Sprouts

Ready in: 23 mins.

Serves: 6

Difficulty: easy

Ingredients:

- 1 tbsp. of olive oil
- 1 pound of halved Brussels sprouts
- 1 tsp. of kosher salt
- 1/4 cup of garlic chilli paste
- 1 tsp. of white pepper
- 1 tbsp. of honey
- Sesame seeds, to garnish
- 2 tbsp. of water

Directions:

- In a big bowl, combine the salt, olive oil, and pepper, and toss Brussels sprouts to coat them evenly.
- Put Brussels sprouts in the air fryer's basket; they don't have to be arranged in a single layer, but doing so will make them extra crispy. Cook the sprouts in batches. For nine minutes, set your air fryer up to 195°C. Shake the basket &

cook for an extra nine minutes after the allotted time has passed.

- In a small bowl, combine the honey, garlic chilli paste, and two tbsp. of water. For one mins or till the sauce is hot, place the bowl into the microwave and cook while covered.
- When Brussels sprouts are finished cooking, transfer them to a large bowl and immediately combine them with the sauce.
- Sprinkle sesame seeds on top. To get the crispiest results, serve right away.

Nutritional values per serving:

Total Calories: 77kcal, **Fats:** 3g, **Carbohydrates:** 13g, **Protein:** 2g

2. Air Fried Tofu

Ready in: 1 hr. 20 mins.

Serves: 4

Difficulty: medium

Ingredients:

- 1/3 cup of soy sauce, low sodium
- 16 ounces of extra-firm tofu
- 1/4 cup of rice vinegar
- 1 tbsp. of grated ginger
- 1 1/2 tbsp. of canola oil (or any other oil, neutral flavour)
- 1 tbsp. of brown sugar
- 1 1/2 tsp. of minced garlic
- 2 tsp. of sesame oil, toasted
- 1 tbsp. of green onions (sliced) to garnish (optional)

Directions:

- Place the tofu on a baking sheet with a rim and cover it with a fresh kitchen towel. Alternatively, spread some paper towels over the tofu and cover it. Put some heavy objects on the top of the tofu, such as a pan, a big book, or a chopping board, to weigh it all down. This will assist in pressing the tofu's extra moisture out. Give the tofu roughly 30 minutes to stand.

- In a separate bowl, combine the vinegar, soy sauce, canola oil, brown sugar, ginger, sesame oil, & garlic while the tofu is still standing.

- Tofu marinade into a bowl with a whisk

- Cubes of pressed tofu should be cut into 1-inch pieces and put in a baking dish (shallow) or another nonreactive container.

- Place diced extra-firm pressed tofu into a dish

- Over the tofu, pour the marinade mixture. Refrigerate the dish with a cover for 30 mins–1 hour.

- Turn the air fryer on at 195°C. The tofu cubes should be arranged in the basket of the air fryer & cooked until crisp for 12-15 minutes, flipping them over every 3-4 minutes.

- Put tofu from an air fryer in a little serving dish.

- The tofu cubes may be served hot or cold.

Nutritional values per serving:

Total Calories: 125kcal, Fats: 3g, Carbohydrates: 2g, Protein: 3g

3. Roasted Bell Peppers

Ready in: 12 mins.

Serves: 2

Difficulty: easy

Ingredients:

- 2 tsp. of oil, avocado or coconut

- 3 Bell peppers (any colour)

- ¼ tsp. of salt

- 1 heaped tsp. of taco seasoning

- ¼ tsp. of white or black pepper

Directions:

- After washing the bell peppers, you can dry them using a paper towel or a clean kitchen towel. Now split them in half, remove the seeds, and cut them into cubes or long or short strips, as you choose. Keep in mind that depending on size you cut them, the time of your air frying may vary significantly.

- Place the diced bell peppers in a bowl and season with taco spice, salt, and pepper.

- Fill your air fryer with the seasoned bell peppers, being careful not to overcrowd them. For the feature of air frying to function properly, it is crucial to provide room between the pieces.

- Now, air-fry them for 10-12 minutes at 195°C. If you first place the pieces correctly with sufficient space between them, there is no need to toss the basket halfway through. If you prefer the chargrilled appearance, you may even roast a bit longer.

Nutritional values per serving:

Total Calories: 74kcal, Fats: 4.3g, Carbohydrates: 9.2g, Protein: 1.3g

4. Air fried Pickles

Ready in: 20 mins.

Serves: 6

Difficulty: medium

Ingredients:

- 1 cup of flour

- 2 cups of hamburger pickles (sliced)

- 1 tbsp. of garlic powder

- ½ tbsp. of Cayenne pepper

- 1 tbsp. of Cajun seasoning

- Olive oil

Directions:

- Before starting, place the pickles on a piece of paper towel to assist to drain any extra pickle juice. This will help the flour mixture adhere to the pickles more effectively.

- Combine the flour, Cajun spice, garlic powder, and cayenne pepper in a medium bowl.

- Coat all sides of the pickles by dipping them into the flour mixture.

- Rub both sides with olive oil.

- Arrange the pickles into the air fryer in a single layer, being careful to keep them from touching.

- Cook for 10 minutes at 205°C. Cook for five more minutes after flipping.

Nutritional values per serving:

Total Calories: 55kcal, **Fats:** 1.3g, **Carbohydrates:** 8.7g, **Protein:** 2.4g

5. Zucchini Pizza

Ready in: 20 mins.

Serves: 4

Difficulty: medium

Ingredients:

- salt and black pepper

- 1 zucchini (medium), sliced into ¼" rounds

- ½ cup of pizza sauce

- pepperoni, in small pieces (optional)

- ½ cup of mozzarella cheese, shredded

- Black olives (sliced), cut into small pieces (optional)

Directions:

- Cut the zucchini lengthwise into 1/4" rounds, then season with salt & pepper. For two minutes, preheat your air fryer at 175°C.

- Put seasoned zucchini slices on top

- Use nonstick spray to coat the air fryer basket, then gently add as many slices of zucchini as will fit within. Cook for 4 minutes at 175°C.

- Take each zucchini slice out of the air fryer using tongs. Pizza sauce, pepperoni, cheese, and olives are placed on top of each slice.

- Reposition the slices into the air fryer & cook for an additional 4-5 minutes at 175°C. Use the tongs to remove the pizza bits from the air fryer, then let them cool before eating.

Nutritional values per serving:

Total Calories: 59kcal, **Fats:** 0g, **Carbohydrates:** 0g, **Protein:** 0g

6. Shishito Peppers

Ready in: 15 mins.

Serves: 4

Difficulty: easy

Ingredients:

- avocado oil cooking spray

- 8 ounces of shishito peppers

- salt, to taste

Directions:

- Wash and well dry the peppers before cooking. Don't take the stems off. Leave the shishito peppers' stems on.

- Spray them with avocado oil after they have been cleaned and dried. They are now prepared for the air fryer.

- Shishito peppers should be arranged in one single layer into the air fryer's basket or tray.

- Heat the air fryer up to 205°C for cooking. A timer for 7-8 minutes has been set.

- There isn't any need to wait for it to heat up before adding the peppers. The ideal amount of time for air frying is 8 minutes, plus roughly 2-3 minutes for preheating.

- They could hiss and pop as they cooked. That's okay; they should just expand while they cook rather than explode.

- They are prepared when the timer sounds. They need to have black burned spots and blisters.

- Use tongs to carefully transfer them to a dish or bowl.

- Add salt to them as required. Immediately serve as it is or with the preferred dipping sauces.

Nutritional values per serving:

Total Calories: 45kcal, **Fats:** 3.5g, **Carbohydrates:** 3g, **Protein:** 1g

7. Onion Bites

Ready in: 25 mins.

Serves: 2

Difficulty: medium

Ingredients:

- 1 4th cup of gram flour, plus add some more if required

- 1 red onion (large), sliced lengthwise

- 1 tbsp. of rice flour

- 1-2 finely chopped green chillies

- 1 tsp. ginger grated

- 1 stalk of finely chopped curry leaves

- ¼ tsp. of carrom seeds

- 1 4th cup of finely chopped coriander leaves

- ¼ tsp. of turmeric

- ½ tsp. garam masala

- ½ tsp. of chilli powder (red)

- ½ tbsp. of hot oil

- oil to air fry

- half tsp. of salt

Directions:

- Thinly slice one big red onion (approximately 250 grams). They should not be very thick or thin.

- Place the thinly sliced onions in a big bowl. To a mixing bowl, add all the things except the gram flour, rice flour, and oil. With your fingers, rub the onions gently.

- Let the bowl rest for 10 minutes with a plate on top to assist the onions release moisture.

- Add rice flour and gram flour after 10 minutes. Mix well to get a firm, non-soggy mixture. The moisture from the onions must be enough to create the dough; do not add any more water. Add 1/2 tbsp. of heated oil next. Onion bites remain soft on the inside as a result of this. Don't skip it.

- Set air fryer at 205°C. Add onion mixture in batches into the air fryer and let it cook for 10 minutes.

Nutritional values per serving:

Total Calories: 140kcal, **Fats:** 5g, **Carbohydrates:** 20g, **Protein:** 5g

8. Paneer Tikka Fry

Ready in: 50 mins.

Serves: 4

Difficulty: medium

Ingredients:

Tikka Marinade Masala:

- 1 tbsp. of chickpea flour (or gram flour)

- ½ cup of Greek yogurt

- 1 tbsp. of garlic ginger paste

- 1 tsp. red chilli powder

- ¼ tsp. of turmeric powder

- ½ tsp. cumin powder

- ½ tsp. garam masala
- 1 tsp. of chaat masala powder
- 1 tsp. of dried fenugreek leaves
- one tbsp. of oil
- 1 tsp. of lemon juice
- Some salt

Other things:

- 1~2 bell peppers, medium (mix of red, green, and yellow) in 1-inch cubes
- 300 grams of Paneer (about two cups) cut in 1-inch cubes
- 1 red onion (medium) cut in 1-inch cubes

Garnish:

- slices of onion
- lemon wedges
- mint sauce
- chaat masala

Directions:

- Combine the Greek yoghurt, gram flour, garlic-ginger paste, cumin powder, turmeric powder, red chilli powder, fenugreek seeds, chaat masala, salt, lemon juice, & oil in a large bowl.
- Include the bell peppers, onion, and Paneer. To coat, well, toss. Cover the bowl & place in the refrigerator for 30 minutes at least or up to 1 day. To avoid burning, whether using an air fryer, oven, or grill, soak the wooden skewers into cold water for 10 minutes at least.
- Using a skewer, carefully thread Paneer, bell peppers, and onions in alternation. Assemble the remaining skewers in a similar manner.
- Set the air fryer's temperature to 180°C. Place each prepared skewer in the basket, spacing them out 1/2 inch apart. Oil should be brushed or sprayed on top to prevent the Paneer and vegetables from drying out.
- Do 5 minutes of cooking at 180°C. The skewers should be turned after 5 minutes, brushed or gently sprayed with oil, and cooked for a further 2~3 minutes.
- Remove to a serving dish, pour some lime juice over it, top with chaat masala, and serve right away with mint chutney.

Nutritional values per serving:

Total Calories: 293kcal, **Fats:** 23g, **Carbohydrates:** 8g, **Protein:** 14g

9. Cauliflower Manchurian

Ready in: 30 mins.

Serves: 2

Difficulty: medium

Ingredients:

For Batter:

- ¼ cup of corn flour/corn starch
- 2 ~ 2.5 cups of cauliflower, cut in florets (almost about 20 to 22 florets)
- ¼ cup Of all-purpose flour
- 2 tsp. of ginger-garlic paste
- one tsp. of red chilli powder
- 2 tsp. of tomato ketchup
- Some water
- salt & pepper to taste

For Sauce:

- 1 tsp. of ginger minced
- 1 tbsp. of oil
- 1 tsp. of garlic minced
- ¼ cup of bell pepper
- ½ cup of finely chopped onion
- 1 tbsp. of soy sauce

- ¼ cup of tomato Sauce
- 2 tsp. of red chilli sauce
- 1 tbsp. of white distilled vinegar
- 2 tbsp. of finely chopped spring/green onion
- 2 tbsp. of finely chopped cilantro
- salt to taste

Directions:

For Batter:

- Combine all the ingredients listed under "batter" and add some water at a time to the mixture to get a pancake consistency.
- Ensure that the batter is smooth and free of lumps.

Frying Cauliflower Florets:

- Include cauliflower florets in the batter, and deep-fry until golden and crisp.
- Only add 7 to 8 florets at one time; do not overcrowd.
- Once all of the florets are mature. On paper towels, set them aside.

Manchurian Sauce:

- Add the ginger and garlic to the hot, Smokey oil and cook for 20 seconds.
- Include onion and pepper as well. Cook for 30 to 90 seconds.
- After adding the vinegar, continue tossing the mixture while adding each sauce one at a time.
- After adding the vinegar, continue tossing the mixture while adding each sauce one at a time.
- Add fried cauliflower florets last, season with salt (if necessary), and combine for two minutes. Add spring onions & coriander/cilantro. After one last toss, serve it right away with tomato ketchup.

- To prepare Gobi Manchurian into an air fryer, dunk the florets into the batter and arrange them in a single layer on the air fryer's tray.
- Apply some oil to the basket of the air fryer using a brush or spray. For 12 to 15 minutes, or till they are browned & crispy, air fried them in an air fryer that has been set to 200°C. Shake them once you've finished.

Nutritional values per serving:

Total Calories: 236kcal, **Fats:** 16g, **Carbohydrates:** 22g, **Protein:** 3.1g

10. Tandoori Potatoes

Ready in: 1 hr.

Serves: 4

Difficulty: medium

Ingredients:

Tikka Marinade:

- 1 tbsp. of chickpea flour (or gram flour)
- ½ cup of Greek yogurt
- 1 tbsp. of garlic ginger paste
- 1 tsp. red chilli powder
- ¼ tsp. turmeric powder
- ½ tsp. cumin powder
- ½ tsp. garam masala
- one tsp. chaat masala powder
- 1 tsp. dried fenugreek leaves
- one tbsp. of oil
- 1 tsp. of lemon juice
- salt to taste

Other Ingredients:

- 1 bell pepper, medium (yellow or red), cut in 1-inch cubes
- 1 pound of baby potatoes (around 16)

- 1 red onion (medium), cut in 1-inch cubes

Garnish:

- onion slices
- lemon wedges
- mint sauce
- chaat masala

Directions:

- The baby potatoes must first be parboiled. The baby potatoes may be parboiled in an Instant Pot at High Pressure for ~12 minutes, followed by a Natural Pressure Release, or they can be pressure cooked in a stovetop pressure cooker for 1 whistle.

- After that, thoroughly drain the potatoes, wipe them dry using a kitchen towel, and remove the skin.

Making a Marinade:

- Hung curd, gram flour, ginger-garlic paste, red chile, turmeric, cumin, chaat masala, garam masala, fenugreek seeds, salt, lemon juice, and oil should all be combined in a big bowl.

- Add the onion, bell peppers, and baby potatoes that have been parboiled. To coat, well, toss. Refrigerate for about 1 day or 30 minutes at least with the bowl covered in the fridge.

- In the meanwhile, immerse wooden skewers in the cold water for 10 minutes at least to avoid scorching if using an oven, grill, or air fryer.

- Using a skewer, carefully thread potatoes, onions and bell peppers in alternation. Prepare the rest of the skewers in a similar manner.

- Set the air fryer's temperature to 180°C. Place each prepared skewer in the basket, spacing them out 12 inches apart. Oil may be brushed or sprayed on top to prevent the potato and vegetables from drying out.

- Do 15 minutes of cooking at 180°C. Turn the skewers after 10 minutes, roast for a further 5 minutes, then gently spritz or brush with oil.

Nutritional values per serving:

Total Calories: 164kcal, Fats: 4g, Carbohydrates: 26g, Protein: 6g

11. Stuffed Okra

Ready in: 22 mins.

Serves: 4

Difficulty: medium

Ingredients:

- 2 tbsp. of oil (1 to 2 tsp. to air fry)
- 230 grams of okra (about 20 to 22)

Stuffing Masala:

- 1 tbsp. of coriander powder
- three tbsp. of roasted peanut powder
- 1 tsp. of cumin powder
- 1 tsp. of red chilli powder
- ¼ tsp. of turmeric powder
- half tsp. of garam masala
- ½ tsp. of fennel powder, optional
- ½ tsp. of lime juice
- 2 tsp. of oil
- salt to taste

Directions:

- Okra should first be rinsed and dried with a fresh towel. Trim the okra's top and bottom portions. Slit in the middle.

- For preparing the stuffing masala, take a small bowl and add salt, lime juice, coriander powder, roasted peanut powder, red chilli powder, cumin powder, turmeric powder, & garam masala. Mix thoroughly.

- After that, add a spoonful of oil and thoroughly mix. When stuffing the okra, oil is applied to assist the spices in adhering.

- Fill the okra with the prepared masala and set it aside. If necessary, remove the big seeds from the okra before filling.

- Set the air fryer's temperature to 180°C. Spread the filled okra in a single layer in the basket of air fryer (cook in batches if required). Spray or gently brush some oil on the surface.

- Air fry them for 10 to 12 minutes at 180°C. Flip the okra after around 8 minutes and remove the basket. If the stuffed okra seems to be dry, brush some oil over it.

- Take out stuffed okra from the air fryer, and serve with a slice of lime on the side.

Nutritional values per serving:

Total Calories: 166kcal, **Fats:** 15g, **Carbohydrates:** 7g, **Protein:** 3g

12. Roasted Cauliflower Potatoes

Ready in: 30 mins.

Serves: 4

Difficulty: medium

Ingredients:

- 2 Potatoes (small), cut in ¾" pieces (almost about 1 cup)

- 1 Cauliflower head (medium) cut in florets (almost about 3 cups)

- 2-3 tbsp. of Olive Oil

- 1 Green Chili, cut lengthwise

- 1 tbsp. of minced Ginger-Garlic

- 1 Onion sliced (medium), about ¾ to 1 cup

- 1 tbsp. of Lime juice

- 1 diced Tomato, medium (about half cup)

- 2 tbsp. of Coriander leaves to garnish

Spices:

- ½ tsp. of Turmeric powder

- ½ tsp. of Red chilli powder

- ½ tsp. of Cumin powder

- ½ tsp. of Garam masala

- 1 tsp. of Coriander powder

- Salt to taste

Directions:

- Combine the cauliflower, potato, onions, tomatoes, green chillies, minced ginger, garlic, and oil in a large mixing basin.

- For three to four minutes, preheat your air fryer to 195°C.

- Next, if desired, lightly oil the air fryer plate, and then lay the potato-cauliflower mixture out in one single layer (do not cram it on there).

- Place for 12–15 minutes at 195°C in an air fryer. At the midway point, shake the basket.

- Add some cilantro and lime juice as a garnish. Serve warm.

Nutritional values per serving:

Total Calories: 191kcal, **Fats:** 8g, **Carbohydrates:** 28g, **Protein:** 5g

13. Tandoori Cauliflower

Ready in: 35 mins.

Serves: 4

Difficulty: medium

Ingredients:

For Marinade:

- 1 tbsp. of chickpea flour (or gram flour)

- ½ cup of Greek yogurt

- 1 tbsp. of garlic ginger paste

- 1 tsp. of red chilli powder

- ¼ tsp. of turmeric powder
- ½ tsp. of cumin powder
- ½ tsp. of garam masala
- 1 tsp. of chaat masala powder
- 1 tsp. of dried fenugreek leaves
- 1 tbsp. of oil
- 1 tsp. of lemon juice
- salt to taste

Vegetables:

- 1 cauliflower (medium), about 18-20 florets

Garnish:

- onion slices
- lemon wedges
- mint sauce
- chaat masala

Directions:

- Clean, then slice the whole head of cauliflower into about equal-sized bite-sized florets for uniform cooking.

- Combine hanging curd, gram flour, turmeric powder, ginger-garlic paste, cumin powder, red chilli powder, fenugreek seeds, chaat masala, salt, lemon juice, and oil in a big bowl.

- After that, stir in the cauliflower florets to thoroughly coat each one in the marinade. For 15 to 20 minutes, cover the bowl & place it in the fridge.

- Set the air fryer's temperature to 180°C. Spread out the marinated florets of cauliflower in a single layer in the basket of the air fryer (cook in batches if required). Oil may be brushed or sprayed on top.

- Air fry them for 14–18 minutes, or until the edges begin to crisp and brown, at 180°C. At the midway point, shake the basket.

- Remove to a serving dish, pour some lime juice over it, top with chaat masala, and serve right away with mint sauce.

Nutritional values per serving:

Total Calories: 96kcal, **Fats:** 4g, **Carbohydrates:** 10g, **Protein:** 6g

14. Tofu Tikka

Ready in: 55 mins.

Serves: 6

Difficulty: medium

Ingredients:

For Marinade:

- 1 tbsp. of chickpea flour (or gram flour)
- ½ cup of Greek yogurt
- 1 tbsp. of garlic ginger paste
- 1 tsp. of red chilli powder
- ¼ tsp. of turmeric powder
- ½ tsp. of cumin powder
- ½ tsp. of garam masala
- 1 tsp. of chaat masala powder
- 1 tsp. of dried fenugreek leaves
- 1 tbsp. of oil
- 1 tsp. of lemon juice
- salt to taste

Other Ingredients:

- 1-2 medium bell peppers (mix of green, red, and yellow) cut into 1-inch cubes
- 16 oz. extra-firm tofu pressed for 30 minutes, cut into 1" cubes
- 1 small red onion cut into 1-inch cubes

Garnish:

- onion slices
- lemon wedges
- mint sauce

- chaat masala

Directions:

- For 30 minutes at least, press the tofu with any heavy objects. It will remove the extra moisture.

- The tofu should then be diced.

- Mix together in a sizable bowl the hanging curd, gram flour, turmeric powder, ginger-garlic paste, red chilli powder, chaat masala, roasted cumin powder, garam masala, lemon juice, fenugreek seeds, salt, and oil. Mix everything well.

- After that, include bell peppers, tofu cubes, and onions. Gently toss the tofu and vegetables to cover them evenly.

- Place the bowl in the refrigerator for 30 minutes at least and up to 1 day with the lid on.

- In the meanwhile, soak bamboo skewers or toothpicks in water for 15 minutes least to prevent scorching.

- On a toothpick, delicately thread the tofu, onion and bell peppers.

- Set the air fryer's temperature to 200°C. Make cautious not to crowd the prepped toothpicks or skewers as you arrange them. To prevent the tofu and vegetables from drying out, spray or brush some oil on top.

- Do 5 minutes of cooking at 200°C. Turn the toothpicks/skewers after 5 minutes, cook for a further 3 to 4 minutes, and then gently brush or spritz with oil.

- Transfer to a serving platter, squeeze lime juice over it, top with chaat masala, and serve the air-fried tofu tikka right away with the mint sauce.

Nutritional values per serving:

Total Calories: 11kcal, Fats: 0.1g, Carbohydrates: 3g, Protein: 0.4g

15. Air Fried Samosa

Ready in: 10 mins.

Serves: 4

Difficulty: easy

Ingredients:

- 1 tbsp. of oil

- 4 frozen samosas (large)

Directions:

- Set the air fryer's temperature to 193°C. In the air fryer basket, add the frozen samosas, allowing space between each one. The samosas' tops should be oiled with a spray or brush.

- Air fry them for 8 to 12 minutes, or until they are crisp and golden brown, at 193 °C. Using kitchen tongs, carefully turn the samosas halfway through.

- The size, brand of used frozen samosas, and air fryer will all affect how long they take to cook.

- Take the samosa out of the air fryer & serve it hot with your preferred chutney or dipping sauce. Such a treat!

Nutritional values per serving:

Total Calories: 155kcal, Fats: 8g, Carbohydrates: 15g, Protein: 5g

16. Beetroot Cutlet

Ready in: 30 mins.

Serves: 3

Difficulty: medium

Ingredients:

- 2 boiled & grated potatoes, medium (about 1 cup)

- 1 grated beetroot, large (about almost 1.25 cup)

- ¼ cup of roasted peanuts, crushed

- 1 tsp. of ginger grated

- 3 tbsp. of corn flour or bread crumbs or rice flour
- 2 finely chopped green chillies
- ½ tsp. of garam masala
- 2 tbsp. of finely chopped cilantro
- 1 tsp. of chat masala powder
- salt to taste
- ½ tsp. of lime juice

Directions:

- Boil the potatoes for 3–4 whistles on medium heat in a pan or pressure cooker with some salt and water.
- Mash or Grate the potatoes after finishing.
- Beets should be peeled, grated, and their surplus juice squeezed out.
- The beets in this recipe have not been cooked.
- Take a bowl for mixing. Mix all the ingredients together well. As a binding agent, you may instead use rice flour or corn flour in place of the breadcrumbs. If the mixture is too wet, add additional bread crumbs.
- Use a tsp. of oil to grease your hand to prevent the mixture from sticking.
- Create a ball about the size of a lemon, flatten it between the palms, and then shape it into a cutlet. Repeat the procedure with the leftover mixture to create additional cutlets.
- Put some parchment paper or aluminium foil that has been gently greased in the basket or tray.
- Place cutlets in a single layer at this point.
- Set the temperature up to 190°C in an air fryer, choose the duration to be 12 minutes.

- Place the tray in the air fryer. Carefully turn the cutlets after an interval
- Beetroot cutlets should be served hot with mint sauce or ketchup after they are crispy & golden brown.

Nutritional values per serving:

Total Calories: 271kcal, **Fats:** 7g, **Carbohydrates:** 46g, **Protein:** 9g

17. Crispy Corn Fritters

Ready in: 20 mins.

Serves: 2

Difficulty: medium

Ingredients:

- ½ finely chopped onion
- 1 cup of corn kernels (sweet), boiled & crushed coarsely
- ¼ cup of gram flour or chickpea flour
- 2-3 finely chopped green chillies
- 1 tbsp. of rice flour
- ¼ tsp. of turmeric
- 1 tsp. of garam masala powder
- 1 tsp. of garlic ginger paste
- ¼ cup of finely chopped cilantro
- ½ tsp. of cumin
- few chopped curry leaves
- Some oil
- salt to taste

Directions:

- The boiling sweet corn kernels should be ground coarsely. Use a mixer or blender to pulse a few times.
- Combine the roughly crushed sweet corn with the onions, ginger-garlic paste, green chillies, turmeric, coriander leaves, chat masala powder, gram flour, cumin, rice flour, & salt in a large bowl.

- Combine and thoroughly blend without adding water. If needed, add extra gram of flour.

- Set the air fryer to 200°C for 3–4 minutes.

- Fill the basket with a layer of aluminium foil or parchment paper, gently oil it, and add the corn fritter mixture. Fry the fritters for 10 to 12 minutes, rotating them halfway through.

Nutritional values per serving:

Total Calories: 104kcal, **Fats:** 1g, **Carbohydrates:** 21g, **Protein:** 3g

18. Tandoori Broccoli

Ready in: 40 mins.

Serves: 4

Difficulty: medium

Ingredients:

For Marinade:

- 1 tbsp. of chickpea flour (or gram flour)
- ½ cup of Greek yogurt
- 1 tbsp. of garlic ginger paste
- 1 tsp. of red chilli powder
- 1 4th tsp. of turmeric powder
- ½ tsp. of cumin powder
- ½ tsp. of garam masala
- 1 tsp. of chaat masala powder
- 1 tsp. of dried fenugreek leaves
- one tbsp. of oil
- 1 tsp. of lemon juice
- salt to taste

Other Ingredients:

- 1 head of broccoli, large (about 20 to 22 florets, medium-sized)

Garnish:

- onion slices

- lemon wedges
- mint sauce
- chaat masala

Directions:

- To ensure consistent cooking, clean and slice the head of broccoli in bite-sized florets.

- The broccoli must be blanched in the next step. Using high heat, bring a pot (medium-sized) of salted water to boil. Broccoli should be cooked for one minute in boiling water before being transferred to a bowl of ice cubes and water. Cubes.

- After they have cooled, remove the water from them and use a paper or kitchen towel to pat them dry. Or you may use your Instant Pot to steam the broccoli.

- Combine hanging curd, grammes flour, ginger-garlic paste, cumin powder, red chilli powder, turmeric powder, fenugreek seeds, chaat masala, salt, lemon juice, and oil in a large bowl.

- After that, stir in the broccoli florets that have been blanched or steam-cooked until each one is well covered in the marinade. For 15 to 20 minutes, cover the bowl & place it in the fridge.

- Set the air fryer's temperature to 180°C. Spread the marinated florets of broccoli in a single layer in the basket of the air fryer (cook in batches if required). The broccoli won't dry out if some oil is brushed or sprayed on the top.

- Air fry for 8–10 minutes at 180°C or until the edges begin to brown and become crispy. At the midway point, shake the basket.

- Take it out onto a serving platter, sprinkle with chaat masala, squeeze lime juice over it, and serve it right away with mint sauce.

Nutritional values per serving:

Total Calories: 108kcal, Fats: 4g, Carbohydrates: 12g, Protein: 7g

19. Cottage Cheese Popcorn

Ready in: 25 mins.

Serves: 3

Difficulty: medium

Ingredients:

- 1 tsp. of ginger garlic paste
- 1 cup of cottage cheese (1-inch cubes)
- ½ tsp. of chilli powder (red)
- ½ tsp. of mixed dried herbs
- ½ tsp. of garam masala powder
- 1 4th tsp. of pepper powder
- 2 tsp. of oil for spraying
- ¼ cup of refined flour or corn flour
- salt to taste

For Crust:

- ¼ tsp. of red chilli powder
- ½ cup of bread crumbs
- ⅛ tsp. of salt

Directions:

- Ginger garlic paste, garam masala, red chilli powder, pepper powder, mixed herbs, and salt should be added to a bowl. Then mix thoroughly before adding the cottage cheese.
- To produce a paste, use 1/4 cup of maize flour and add as much water as is necessary.
- Combine salt, red chilli powder, and breadcrumbs; set aside.
- Next, dip the cheese cubes in the paste, shake off any excess batter, and fully cover each cheese cube with the bread crumbs mixture. For 15 minutes at least, refrigerate.

- Coat the fryer basket and the cheese cubes with the cooking spray, and then put the bread-coated cheese cubes in the fryer basket in a single layer.
- Popcorn should be cooked for 6 minutes at 190°C. It should take another 5 minutes to brown and crisp after flipping. If you believe the food is not fully done, stir it and cook it for two more minutes. With the remaining cheese popcorn, repeat.
- Remove the popcorn from the fryer and place it on a serving platter. Serve right away with your preferred dipping sauce.

Nutritional values per serving:

Total Calories: 290kcal, Fats: 18g, Carbohydrates: 17g, Protein: 12g

20. Cajun Potatoes

Ready in: 25 mins.

Serves: 2

Difficulty: medium

Ingredients:

Cajun Mayonnaise:

- 1 tsp. garlic powder
- 4 tbsp. of mayonnaise
- 1 tsp. onion powder
- ½ tsp. of thyme (dried)
- ½ tsp. of dried oregano
- ½ tsp. ground black pepper
- 2 tbsp. of milk (optional)
- 1 tsp. of red chilli powder
- 1 tsp. of tomato ketchup
- salt to taste

Crispy Potatoes:

- 2 tbsp. of corn flour
- 10 to 12 baby potatoes

- oil
- salt to taste
- 1 tbsp. of finely chopped coriander leaves
- 2 tbsp. of finely chopped onions

Directions:

Preparing Mayonnaise Dressing:

- In a bowl, combine the tomato ketchup, mayonnaise, and all of the spices listed under "Cajun Mayonnaise Ingredients."
- Place aside. 1-2 tbsp. of milk may be added if the dressing is very thick.
- Getting the Potatoes Ready:
- Cleanse the potatoes to remove any debris.
- Boil the potatoes until they are just soft (90 percent cooked).
- Next, set the potatoes onto a cutting board and pound each tiny potato with a hefty spoon until the skin slightly breaks (do not break).
- Sprinkle some cornflour over the potatoes, then toss them to evenly cover all sides.
- Fill the air fryer basket with the floured baby potatoes in a single layer at this point. Apply some oil to the potatoes' surface.
- Place the potatoes on the platter after they are crispy & golden brown.
- Lastly, arrange the fried potatoes on a platter for serving. On each potato, sprinkle coriander, finely chopped onions, and Cajun Mayonnaise.

Nutritional values per serving:

Total Calories: 253kcal, Fats: 8g, Carbohydrates: 43g, Protein: 5g

21. Vegetable Chilli Cheese Toast

Ready in: 15 mins.

Serves: 4

Difficulty: easy

Ingredients:

- 1 cup of mozzarella cheese, shredded
- 4 bread (white or brown)
- ¼ cup of coloured (any) bell peppers
- 1-2 finely chopped jalapeno or green chillies
- 2 tbsp. of tomato, finely chopped (deseeded)
- 1 tsp. of garlic, minced
- ½ tsp. of oregano (or any other mixed herbs)
- 1 tbsp. of finely chopped coriander leaves, optional
- salt & pepper, to taste

Directions:

- Dice or chop the veggies finely.
- In a mixing dish, combine the cheese, veggies, and seasonings. Set apart.
- Toast the bread on one side just with butter.
- On the toasted side of the bread, spread the chilli cheese mixture.
- Set the air fryer's temperature to 165°C. The bread slice should be cooked in the basket of air fryer at 165°C for 5 to 6 minutes, or until the cheese is melted and the top is beginning to brown. Continue by adding more slices.

Nutritional values per serving:

Total Calories: 169kcal, Fats: 8g, Carbohydrates: 16g, Protein: 9g

22. Bread Pizza

Ready in: 20 mins.

Serves: 2

Difficulty: medium

Ingredients:

- ½ cup of Pizza sauce
- 4 Slices of Bread
- 1 cup of Processed/Mozzarella Cheese, shredded
- ¼ cup of finely chopped onion
- ¼ cup of green bell peppers
- ¼ cup of tomato, finely chopped (deseeded)
- 2 tsp. of red chilli flakes
- 2 tsp. of pizza seasoning or any other mixed herbs
- Salt, to taste
- 2 tbsp. of butter

Directions:

- Spread some butter onto the pan and toast the bread until it is crisp and brown on one side.
- Spread your pizza sauce on the toasted bread, and toast the side up.
- Sprinkle some pizza seasoning, mozzarella cheese, onion, bell pepper, tomato, and chilli flakes.
- Set the air fryer's temperature to 165°C. Slices of bread pizza should be placed on the basket of air fryer and cooked for 7-8 minutes at 330°F, or till the cheese melts & the top is lightly browned. Continue by adding more slices.

Nutritional values per serving:

Total Calories: 130kcal, **Fats:** 4.1g, **Carbohydrates:** 18.2g, **Protein:** 5.5g

23. Veggie Bread Roll

Ready in: 45 mins.

Serves: 4

Difficulty: easy

Ingredients:

- ½ tsp. of salt
- 4 potatoes (medium-sized), peeled & chopped
- water as required

Spices:

- 1 tsp. of cumin seeds
- 1 tbsp. of olive oil
- 1-2 green chillies, chopped
- 1 tsp. of cumin powder
- 1 tsp. of coriander powder
- ½ tsp. of turmeric powder
- 1 tsp. of garam masala
- salt as needed
- 1 tbsp. of lime juice
- 12 slices of white bread
- ¼ cup of chopped cilantro

Directions:

- Potatoes should be boiled.
- In a sauté pan, heat the oil over medium heat. Fill the pan with oil.
- Add the cumin seeds to the heated oil. Green chillies should be added when they begin to sizzle. They need around 10 seconds of sautéing.
- Add salt, turmeric powder, garam masala, cumin powder, and coriander powder. After thoroughly combining, add the potatoes, lime juice, and cilantro right away.

- Mash the ingredients with a potato masher or the back of a spatula until there are no more lumps.

- Using a rolling pin, flatten the bread pieces one at a time.

- Place a flattened piece of bread on top of around 1.5 teaspoons of the potato filling.

- Form a long cylinder out of the firmly rolled bread pieces. To seal the bread's edges, dab them with water.

- Carry out the same procedure with the remaining bread pieces.

- Turn the air fryer on at 205°C. Allow it to warm up for approximately five minutes.

- Put the rolls into the basket and bake it at 205°C for about 10 minutes.

- Serve hot with ketchup or mint sauce.

Nutritional values per serving:

Total Calories: 244kcal, Fats: 4g, Carbohydrates: 44g, Protein: 8g

24. Eggplant Parmesan Pasta

Ready in: 45 mins.

Serves: 8

Difficulty: medium

Ingredients:

- 2 tbsp. of nutritional yeast, plus 1 tsp.

- 4 crispy bread crackers

- 1 tsp. of garlic powder

- ¼ cups of unflavored, unsweetened . plant milk, like almond, cashew, soy, or rice

- 1 tsp. of Italian seasoning (dried), crushed

- 1 eggplant, medium (1 lb.), peeled & sliced in half-inch rounds

- 1 chopped onion (1 cup)

- 10 oz. of dry linguine (whole grain)

- 1 chopped green bell pepper (1 cup)

- 1 jar of marinara sauce, oil-free (22- to 23-oz.)

- 1 package of fresh button mushrooms, sliced (8-oz.)

- ¼ cup of fresh basil, chopped

- 1 can of no-salt-added tomatoes, diced (14.5-oz), undrained

Directions:

- Set air fryer to a 187°C temperature. Place crackers, 2 tablespoons of nutritional yeast, garlic powder, & Italian seasoning in a food processor. Place in a narrow bowl after processing until finely chopped undercover. Milk should be poured into another small dish. Each eggplant slice should be dipped into the milk, followed by the crumbs, to gently cover both sides. Set in a baking pan.

- If required, add the eggplant slices to the air fryer in stages so that they don't contact. Slices of eggplant should be air-fried for 12 to 15 minutes, or until they are soft and the breading is crunchy.

- Prepare the linguine in the meanwhile according to the instructions on the box. Drain and put the pot back. Cook bell pepper, onion, and mushrooms in a large pan over medium-high heat for 5-7 minutes or till soft stirring regularly & adding water, 1-2 Tbsp. At a time, as required to avoid sticking. Transfer to pasta-filled pot. Tomatoes and marinara sauce are added; combine thoroughly. Cook for 5 minutes, or until well heated.

- Add eggplant to the linguine mixture on top. Add the basil and the last teaspoon of nutritional yeast.

Nutritional values per serving:

Total Calories: 810 kcal, Fats: 29g, Carbohydrates: 110g, Protein: 31g

25. Kale & Sweet Potato Calzones

Ready in: 1hr. 30 mins.

Serves: 6

Difficulty: medium

Ingredients:

- 2¼ cups of potato flakes (or 3 tbsp. + ½ cup of potato flour)
- ⅓ cup of raw cashews
- 1 cup of whole wheat flour
- 2½ cups of white sweet potato (peeled), finely chopped
- ½ tsp. of sea salt
- 1 cup of onion, finely chopped
- 3 cloves of garlic, minced
- 1 cup of red bell pepper, coarsely chopped
- 1 tbsp. of fresh thyme, chopped (or 1 & ½ tsp. of dried crushed thyme)
- 2 cups of steamed kale, chopped
- 1 tbsp. of fresh oregano, chopped (or 1 & ½ tsp. of crushed dried oregano)
- 1 & ¼ cups of unflavored, unsweetened plant-based milk
- 1 tbsp. of white wine vinegar
- 6 tbsp. of nutritional yeast
- 1½ cups of marinara sauce (oil-free), warmed
- Red pepper (crushed), to taste

Directions:

- Soak the cashews in 1 & 1/2 cups of hot water for 20 minutes to make dough. Blend the cashews & soaking liquid until smooth in a blender. Combine 1 & 3/4 cups of potato flakes or 1/2 cup of the potato flour with the wheat and 1/4 tsp. of salt in a bowl. Stir in the cashew paste until dough forms.

- To make the filling, mix the next 6 ingredients with 1/4 cup of water in a saucepan. Bring to a boil, then moderately lower heat. Stirring periodically, heat the sweet potato for approximately 5 minutes until it is halfway done. Add the kale after stirring. When the sweet potato is ready, uncover and simmer for a further 5 minutes, adding water and 1-2 tbsp. At a time, as necessary, to avoid sticking.

- Add the remaining 1/2 cup of potato flakes or 3 tablespoons of potato flour, nutritional yeast, milk, and vinegar to a blender; until smooth, blend. Add the remaining 1/4 tsp. Salt, the milk mixture, and the crushed red pepper to the veggies. To taste and season as necessary.

- For 15 minutes, preheat the air fryer to 175°C. Four 8 by 11-inch pieces of parchment paper should be cut out. Add whole wheat flour and sift it onto a clean board. Four parts of dough should be formed into balls. Roll 1 ball into a circle (8-inch) on a floured surface. Leave a 1-inch margin after spooning 1/2 cup of filling into the circle's bottom half. To create a half-moon, fold the empty half over the filled half. With a fork, seal the edge, then brush more milk on top.

- Dust one piece of parchment with flour. On parchment, place the calzone. Place paper in air fryer by lifting by the edges for 8 minutes or till the top is browned in the air fryer.

- Repeat the process with the rest of the dough balls & filling. Serve marinara sauce with the calzones.

Nutritional values per serving:

Total Calories: 400kcal, **Fats:** 12g, **Carbohydrates:** 60g, **Protein:** 6g

26. Air Fried Mixed Veggies

Ready in: 45 mins.

Serves: 4

Difficulty: easy

Ingredients:

- 6-8 cauliflower florets (medium)
- 1 tbsp. of oil
- ½ green bell pepper (medium), cubed
- 1 carrot (medium), chopped
- ½ red bell pepper (medium) cubed
- ¼ cup of peas
- 1 potato (medium), chopped

Spices:

- 3 tbsp. of curry paste
- 1 tbsp. of oil
- 1 tbsp. of coriander powder
- 1 tsp. of red chilli powder or paprika, or to taste
- ¼ tsp. of turmeric powder
- 1 tbsp. of garam masala powder
- salt to taste

Directions:

- Combine chopped carrots, cauliflower florets, and potatoes in a mixing basin with the oil.
- For 10 minutes, preheat your air fryer at 180°C.
- With 1 tablespoon oil, toss the vegetables (chopped carrots, cauliflower, and potatoes) and air fry for 7 minutes.
- Combine the curry paste, oil, and all the spices—turmeric, paprika or red chilli powder, garam masala powder, and coriander powder—in a separate bowl.
- Blend them well.
- Place the peas, along with the green and red peppers, in a bowl.
- Pour the spice blend into a mixing dish.
- The semi-fried veggies (potato, cauliflower, and carrots) should now be added to the mixing bowl.
- With a spoon, combine everything to evenly distribute the spice mixture over each veggie.
- Reload the basket of air fryer with the hot veggies.
- At 180°C, air fried all the veggies for 10 minutes.
- Provide hot with bread or rice.

Nutritional values per serving:

Total Calories: 110kcal, **Fats:** 4g, **Carbohydrates:** 38g, **Protein:** 14g

27. Stuffed Eggplant

Ready in: 20 mins.

Serves: 4

Difficulty: medium

Ingredients:

- 2 tsp. of Oil divided
- 8 Baby Eggplants, rinse & pat dry
- 1 tbsp. of Cilantro leaves for garnishing

Spice Stuffing:

- 1 tsp. of Ground Cumin
- ¾ tbsp. of Coriander powder
- ½ tsp. of Red Chili powder
- ½ tsp. of Garlic powder
- ½ tsp. of Ground Turmeric
- 1 tsp. of Salt
- ¾ tbsp. of Dry Mango powder

Directions:

- Combine the stuffing spices in a bowl.

- Take the eggplants & keep the stems whole. Slit the middle of each eggplant, starting at the bottom and continuing up to just above stem. It should not break into two parts when you cut it. The eggplant should now be turned 90 degrees, and a new incision should be cut from the middle. Cut the eggplant in half lengthwise while retaining the stem.

- You may also add a tsp. of oil to the spice mixture. Fill each of the eggplants' slits with spices using a small spoon or knife.

- Arrange the eggplants in the Air Fryer in a single layer. Oil each eggplant by brushing it. Brush oil on opposite side as you turn around.

- Turn on the air fryer and wait 8 to 12 minutes at 180°C. When they are cooked, their colour will change. At 8 minutes, check, and cook for longer if necessary. At roughly six minutes, you may flip them around, although it is not required.

- Enjoy with cilantro as a garnish!

Nutritional values per serving:

Total Calories: 106 kcal, Fats: 3g, Carbohydrates: 20g, Protein: 3g

28. Stuffed Bitter Gourd

Ready in: 50 mins.

Serves: 6

Difficulty: medium

Ingredients:

- 3 sliced onions

- 12 bitter gourds, small

- 1 tbsp. of ginger garlic paste

- 1 tbsp. of coriander powder

- 1 tsp. of cumin powder

- 1 tsp. of aniseed powder

- 1 tsp. of cayenne

- ½ tsp. of garam masala

- 1 tsp. of tamarind paste

- 1/2 tsp. of fenugreek seeds

- salt to taste

- Mustard oil for frying

Directions:

- Use a knife to delicately scrape the bitter gourd.

- Cut a vertical split through the bitter gourd from top to bottom, and then scoop out the meat and seeds.

- Throw away the seeds. Apply some salt to the interior and exterior of the bitter gourd to lessen its bitterness, and then set it aside for 30 minutes.

- After 30 minutes, rinse the bitter gourd to remove all of the salt, dry it, and set it away. To mildly cook the bitter gourd, either microwave it for two minutes or parboil it for two to three minutes with a little tamarind paste (approximately one-fourth teaspoon).

Prepare the stuffing:

- In a pan, add 1 teaspoon of mustard oil. Add the minced ginger and garlic and cook till golden brown. When it has cooled, mix into a thick paste. Cook for a further period of time after adding salt and all the spice powders. Make the stuffing substantial. Examine the flavour and adjust the spice. Allow the filling to cool totally.

Get the bitter gourd ready:

- Take the bitter gourd that has been split open now, and liberally pour the filling inside. To keep them intact, wrap the regular sewing thread around them.

- Preheat the air fryer for five minutes at 200°C. On the basket of the air fryer, spray or brush oil.

- Place the basket with the stuffed bitter gourd in it and air fried for 6 to 8 minutes, or until the bitter gourd is golden brown and just beginning to crisp up. Continue to check every 3 to 4 minutes. Remove them, then serve them hot with bread.

Nutritional values per serving:

Total Calories: 73 kcal, **Fats:** 1g, **Carbohydrates:** 15g, **Protein:** 3g

29. Pumpkin Pie

Ready in: 30 mins.

Serves: 5

Difficulty: medium

Ingredients:

- ½ cup of granulated sugar
- 1 can (15 ounces) of pure pumpkin
- ½ cup of brown sugar
- ½ tsp. of ground ginger
- 1 tsp. of ground cinnamon
- ½ tsp. of ground nutmeg
- ½ cup of heavy cream or milk
- 2 eggs (large)
- ½ cup of evaporated milk (not condensed sweetened milk)
- 1 pie crust

Directions:

- Roll the pie dough into the pie pan to prepare it for baking. Place the pie's shell in the basket of the air fryer and cook for approximately 5 minutes at 175°C. In contrast, making the filling, set it aside.

- To make the filling, combine the sugar, pumpkin puree, brown sugar, ginger, cinnamon, and nutmeg in a mixing bowl. Continue blending while remaining together.

- Add the eggs and combine everything with a whisk. Milk and evaporated milk should be added gradually. Once the filling is combined, smooth, and creamy, continue stirring.

- Gently pour the prepped pie crust with the filling of pumpkin pie within. Place the pie into the air fryer for a further 25 to 30 minutes, or until the middle is no longer wobbly. You may have to add an extra two to three minutes.

Nutritional values per serving:

Total Calories: 353 kcal, **Fats:** 12g, **Carbohydrates:** 58g, **Protein:** 7g

Chapter 9: Air Fried Diabetic Diet ~ Snack Recipes

1. Coconut Crusted Air Fried Turkey Fingers

Ready in: 30 mins.

Serves: 6

Difficulty: easy

Ingredients:

- 2 tsp. of sesame oil
- 2 egg whites (large)
- 1/2 cup of shredded coconut (sweetened), lightly toasted
- 2 tbsp. of sesame seeds, toasted
- 1/2 cup of dry bread crumbs
- 1/2 tsp. of salt
- Cooking spray
- 1~1/2 pounds of turkey breast tenderloins in half-inch strips

Dipping sauce:

- 1/3 cup of pineapple juice, unsweetened
- 1/2 cup of plum sauce
- 1 tsp. of cornstarch
- 1~1/2 tsp. of prepared mustard
- Optional: lime wedges and Grated lime zest

Directions:

- Set the air fryer up to 205°C. Whisk the egg whites & oil together in a small bowl. Combine coconut, sesame seeds, bread crumbs, and salt in a separate shallow dish. To help the coating stick, pat the turkey after dipping it in the egg mixture and the coconut mixture.

- Working in batches, arrange the turkey in the air-fryer basket on the oiled tray in a single layer. Mist with cooking spray. Cook for 3 to 4 minutes or until golden brown. Toss with cooking spray and turn. Cook for a further 3–4 minutes or until the turkey is golden brown and no longer pink.

- Meanwhile, combine the sauce's components in a small pot. Bring to boil; simmer and stir for 1-2 minutes or until thickened. Serve sauce with the turkey. Serve turkey strips with lime wedges and, at your discretion, lime zest on top.

Nutritional values per serving:

Total Calories: 292 kcal, **Fats:** 9 g, **Carbohydrates:** 24 g, **Protein:** 31 g

2. Turkey Croquettes

Ready in: 30 mins.

Serves: 6

Difficulty: easy

Ingredients:

- 1/2 cup of grated Parmesan cheese
- 2 cups of mashed potatoes (with added butter and milk)
- 1/2 cup of Swiss cheese, shredded
- 2 tsp. of fresh rosemary (minced), or 1/2 tsp. of rosemary (dried), crushed
- 1 finely chopped shallot
- 1 tsp. of fresh sage, minced or 1/4 tsp. of sage leaves, dried
- 1/4 tsp. of pepper

- 1/2 tsp. of salt
- 3 cups of cooked turkey, finely chopped
- 2 tbsp. of water
- 1 egg (large)
- 1-1/4 cups of panko bread crumbs
- Sour cream (optional)
- Cooking spray, Butter-flavored

Directions:

- Set air fryer up to 175°C. Mash potatoes with cheeses, rosemary, shallot, sage, salt, & pepper in a large bowl; mix in turkey. Lightly but thoroughly combine. Form into twelve patties that are 1 inch thick.

- Eggs and water should be whisked in a small bowl. Another small bowl should be filled with bread crumbs. Croquettes should be dipped in a mixture of egg, then coated with bread crumbs by patting them down.

- Working in batches, arrange the croquettes in one single layer on the prepared baking sheet within the air-fryer basket. Cook for 4-5 minutes, or until golden brown. Toss with cooking spray and turn. Cook for 4-5 minutes, or until golden brown. Serve with sour cream, if preferred.

Nutritional values per serving:

Total Calories: 322 kcal, Fats: 12 g, Carbohydrates: 22g, Protein: 29 g

3. Fish & Chips

Ready in: 35 mins.

Serves: 2

Difficulty: medium

Ingredients:

- 1 tbsp. of olive oil
- 1 potato (medium)
- 1/8 tsp. of salt

- 1/8 tsp. of pepper

For Fish:

- 1/8 tsp. of pepper
- 3 tbsp. of all-purpose flour
- 1 egg (large)
- 1/3 cup of crushed cornflakes
- 2 tbsp. of water
- 1-1/2 tsp. of grated Parmesan cheese
- 1/8 tsp. of salt
- Dash of cayenne pepper
- 1/2 pound of cod or haddock fillets
- Tartar sauce (optional)

Directions:

- Set the air fryer up to 205°C. Potatoes should be peeled and cut into 1/2-in. Slices should be thick and sliced into 1/2-in. -heavy sticks.

- Toss the potato with the oil, pepper, and salt in a large bowl. Place the potato pieces in the air fryer basket in a single layer, and cook for 5 to 10 minutes, or until just soft. Re-distribute the potatoes in the basket and cook for a further 5–10 minutes, or until they are crisp and lightly browned.

- Meanwhile, combine the flour and pepper in a small bowl. Whisk egg and water in a separate shallow bowl. Mix cornflakes, cheese, and cayenne in a third bowl. After salting the fish, cover both sides with the flour mixture, and brush off the excess. After dipping in the egg mixture, massage the coated object to help the coating stick.

- Take out the fries and keep them heated. Put the fish in the air fryer basket in a single layer. Cook for 8 to 10 minutes, flipping once until the fish is gently browned and just starting to easily flakes with a fork. Avoid overcooking. Heat up the fries in the basket once more. Serve right away. Serve with tartar sauce, if preferred.

Nutritional values per serving:

Total Calories: 304 kcal, **Fats:** 9 g, Carbohydrates: 33 g, **Protein:** 23 g

4. Crusted Sweet Potato Chicken Nuggets

Ready in: 25 mins.

Serves: 4

Difficulty: easy

Ingredients:

- 1/4 cup of all-purpose flour
- 1 cup of sweet potato chips
- 1 tsp. of salt, divided
- 1/4 tsp. of baking powder
- 1/2 tsp. of pepper, coarsely ground
- 1 tbsp. of cornstarch
- Cooking spray
- 1 pound of chicken tenderloins, in 1-1/2" pieces

Directions:

- Set air fryer up to 205°C. Grind the chips, flour, pepper, baking powder, and 1/2 tsp. Salt in a food processor. Place on a small plate.
- Toss the chicken with the cornstarch mixture and the rest of 1/2 tsp. Salt. Combine potato chip mixture with chicken and toss to coat.
- Place the chicken, in batches, in one single layer on the oiled pan within the air fryer basket. Spray with cooking spray. Cook for 3 to 4 minutes or until golden brown. Toss with cooking spray and turn. Cook for a further 3–4 minutes or until the chicken is golden brown and no longer pink.

Nutritional values per serving:

Total Calories: 190 kcal, **Fats:** 4 g, Carbohydrates: 13g, **Protein:** 28 g

5. Potato Chips

Ready in: 35 mins.

Serves: 6

Difficulty: easy

Ingredients:

- Olive oil cooking spray
- 2 potatoes (large)
- Fresh parsley (Minced), optional
- 1/2 tsp. of sea salt

Directions:

- Set the air fryer up to 175°C. Slice potatoes into extremely tiny pieces using a vegetable peeler or mandoline. Transfer to a big basin and cover with cold water. Drain after a 15-minute soak. 15 additional minutes of soaking after adding more cold water.
- Potatoes should be drained, placed on towels, and dried. Potatoes should be sprayed with cooking spray and salt. Put potato slices in one single layer on the oiled tray in the air fryer basket in batches. Cook for 15–17 minutes, tossing and rotating every 5-7 minutes, until crisp & golden brown. Add some parsley, if desired.

Nutritional values per serving:

Total Calories: 148 kcal, **Fats:** 1 g, Carbohydrates: 32g, **Protein:** 4 g

6. Cauliflower Gnocchi & Marinara Sauce

Ready in: 20 mins.

Serves: 8

Difficulty: medium

Ingredients:

- 3 tbsp. of extra-virgin olive oil, divided
- 2 packages of cauliflower gnocchi, frozen (10 ounces), thawed & divided

- ½ cup of Parmesan cheese (grated), divided

- 1 cup of marinara sauce (reduced-sodium), warmed

- 2 tbsp. of chopped flat-leaf parsley, fresh

Directions:

- Set the air fryer up to 190°C. In a big bowl, combine 1 package of gnocchi, 1 1/2 teaspoons of oil, and 2 tablespoons of Parmesan.

- Spray cooking spray on the air fryer's basket. Once in the basket, add the gnocchi mixture and cook for 5 minutes, flipping once. Transfer to a big bowl. The remaining gnocchi, oil, and tbsp. Parmesan should be used in a similar manner. The rest of 1/4 cup of Parmesan and the parsley should be added to the cooked gnocchi. Serve alongside marinara.

Nutritional values per serving:

Total Calories: 160 kcal, **Fats:** 9 g, Carbohydrates: 14 g, Protein: 3g

7. Bacon Wrapped Scallops

Ready in: 20 mins.

Serves: 6

Difficulty: medium

Ingredients:

- 3 thin bacon slices, center-cut

- 12 sea scallops, medium (about almost 9 ounces total)

- ¼ tsp. of ground pepper

- 1 tsp. of olive oil

- ¼ tsp. of paprika

Directions:

- Set the air fryer up to 190°C. Pat the scallops dry. Each scallop's side muscle should be removed and discarded. To create 12 strips of bacon, cut each piece in half lengthwise and then across. Wrap 1 strip of bacon around each scallop, gently overlapping the ends. To hold the bacon in place, put one wooden pick through the other side of the scallop and through both of the bacon ends. Along with a little oil brush, evenly distribute the pepper and paprika over the scallops.

- Place the scallops into the fryer basket in an equal layer. Cook for 10 to 12 minutes, or till the bacon is starting to crisp & the scallops get firm yet soft.

Nutritional values per serving:

Total Calories: 43 kcal, **Fats:** 2 g, Carbohydrates: 1 g, Protein: 5 g

8. Feta Beets

Ready in: 30 mins.

Serves: 4

Difficulty: easy

Ingredients:

- 1 tbsp. of olive oil

- 1 pound of beets (3 small or 2 large), trimmed & peeled, cut in one-inch pieces

- ¼ tsp. of salt

- ¼ cup of feta cheese, crumbled

- ¼ tsp. of ground pepper

- 1 tbsp. of chopped fresh oregano

Directions:

- Set the air fryer up to 205°C and wait five minutes. Beets should be placed in a large bowl with oil, salt, and pepper. Toss to coat.

- Place the beets into the fryer basket in a single layer, and cook for 8-10 minutes. Be careful while flipping the beets, and cook for 6 to 8 minutes, or until the edges are caramelized and crispy. Add feta and oregano to the serving plate after transfer.

Nutritional values per serving:

Total Calories: 106 kcal, **Fats:** 6 g, Carbohydrates: 12g, **Protein:** 3 g

9. Cinnamon Apples

Ready in: 10 mins.

Serves: 2

Difficulty: easy

Ingredients:

- 1 tsp. of Ground Cinnamon
- 2 Apples (Large)
- 1/8 tsp. of Salt

Directions:

- Set air fryer up to 198°C.
- In a mixing dish, combine sugar and cinnamon.
- Each apple should be cut into eighths.
- Combine the sugar and cinnamon with the apples.
- Arrange the apple wedges into the air fryer in a single layer.
- Do 4 minutes of cooking at 198°C.
- After flipping, sauté the apple wedges for a further 4 minutes, or until they are crisp.
- The apple wedges should be placed on a wire rack to cool fully.
- Continue frying apple wedges in single layers until they are all done and cooled.
- Consume immediately or keep in an airtight container.

Nutritional values per serving:

Total Calories: 50 kcal, **Fats:** 2 g, Carbohydrates: 15 g, **Protein:** 4 g

10. Zucchini Fries

Ready in: 30 mins.

Serves: 6

Difficulty: medium

Ingredients:

For Zucchini Fries:

- ½ cup of almond flour
- 2 Zucchinis, cut in fries (medium)
- ¼ cup of pork rinds (ground), plain
- 1 tsp. of garlic sea salt
- ¼ cup of parmesan cheese, grated
- 1 tsp. of dried parsley
- ½ tsp. of oregano
- 1 tsp. of dried basil
- 2 beaten eggs

For sauce:

- 2 tsp. of prepared horseradish
- ½ cup of mayonnaise
- 2 tbsp. of ketchup (without sugar)
- 1 tsp. of garlic salt
- 1 tsp. of smoked paprika
- ½ tsp. of fresh lemon juice

Directions:

- Set a regular oven to 205°C if you're baking them in an air fryer.
- Establish the breading station. In a bowl, combine the almond flour, pork rinds, cheese, basil, parsley, oregano, and garlic salt. Eggs should be combined in a separate bowl.
- After dipping the zucchini in the egg, coat it with the breading (lightly, don't press in the mixture). Shake off any extra breading before placing the food onto a baking rack coated with

parchment or Silpat) that has been sprayed with olive oil.

- After all of the breaded zucchini are placed on the baking trays, coat the tops with the olive oil spray & bake at 205°C for 15 to 20 minutes, or till golden brown. About halfway through cooking, rotate or switch the pans.

- Make the dipping sauce while zucchini fries are baking. In a bowl, mix and whisk all the sauce components until well incorporated.

- Before serving, give the zucchini fries a little time to cool.

Nutritional values per serving:

Total Calories: 257 kcal, **Fats:** 22 g, Carbohydrates: 5 g, **Protein:** 8 g

11. Chicken Wings

Ready in: 55 mins.

Serves: 10

Difficulty: medium

Ingredients:

- 1 pound of Chicken Wings
- 2 tbsp. of Berbere
- 2 tbsp. of Olive Oil
- 1 tsp. of garlic powder
- Salt & pepper to taste

Directions:

- Combine the olive oil, chicken wings, salt, garlic powder, and Berbere in a zip lock bag.

- Overnight marinating gives them more taste, but 30 minutes will suffice if you want them right away.

- Spray some olive oil on the air fryer tray (or pam). As a result, the wings won't adhere to the tray.

- In accordance with the manufacturer's instructions, air fry them.

- Serve and savour!

Nutritional values per serving:

Total Calories: 420 kcal, **Fats:** 20 g, Carbohydrates: 0 g, **Protein:** 60 g

12. Bolognese Zucchini Boats

Ready in: 27 mins.

Serves: 4

Difficulty: medium

Ingredients:

- 2 Zucchinis (Medium)
- 300 g of Pork Mince
- ½ Diced Onion (Large)
- 400 g of Tinned Tomatoes
- 1 Tbsp. of Garlic Puree
- 2 Tsp. of Oregano
- 50 g of Hard Cheese, optional
- Salt & black Pepper

Directions:

- Fill the cake pan of air fryer with your garlic, minced pork, sliced onion, salt, and pepper. In the air fryer, cook for 8 mins at 180°C.

- Add the oregano and canned tomatoes, and simmer for 2 minutes further at 200°C.

- Cut the zucchini lengthwise in half, then use a spoon to scoop out the centre.

- When air fryer beeps, fill the zucchini boats with the cooked Bolognese and set them on the grill pan in the air fryer. Cook at 180°C for 10 minutes further.

- After the beep, top with cheese and cook for an additional 2 minutes at 200°C.

Nutritional values per serving:

Total Calories: 309 kcal, **Fats:** 21 g, Carbohydrates: 13 g, **Protein:** 19 g

13. Onion Rings

Ready in: 25 mins.

Serves: 5

Difficulty: medium

Ingredients:

- 1 & ¼ cup of Flour
- 1 Onion, Sliced
- 1 tsp. of Baking Powder
- 1 cup + 1 tsp. of Milk
- 1 Beaten Egg
- ¾ cup of Bread Crumbs Seasonings

Directions:

- Set your air fryer up to 185°C and prepare a nonstick basket.
- Combine the flour, baking powder, and spices in a mixing dish.
- Add the egg and milk after combining (or beer). Move into a small dish.
- Your bread crumbs should be placed in a small basin. Take the 1st slice of onion and, using a fork, thoroughly dredge it in the ingredients from the first bowl.
- Next, coat this piece with bread crumbs. After that, put it in the basket. Repeat this with the remaining slices, being careful not to overlap them too much.
- After 8 minutes, turn the onion rings over in the air fryer. Continue air frying for a further 8 minutes.

Nutritional values per serving:

Total Calories: 172 kcal, **Fats:** 4 g, Carbohydrates: 15 g, **Protein:** 11 g

14. Crab Rangoon

Ready in: 30 mins.

Serves: 8

Difficulty: medium

Ingredients:

- 2 ounces of cream cheese at room temp
- 2 ounces of imitation crab meat
- 1½ tbsp. of chopped green onions, small
- 16 wonton wrappers
- ½ tbsp. of Worcestershire sauce
- oil for spritzing

Directions:

- In a small bowl, combine the cream cheese, green onions, crab meat, and Worcestershire sauce.
- For 10 minutes, preheat the air fryer on broil while the basket of air frying is inside.
- Begin folding your crab Rangoon while the air fryer is heating up. On a cooling rack, arrange eight wonton wrappers. They won't get too wet because of this. Each wonton should have 1 1/2 tbsp. of filling in the middle. Apply a little amount of water just outside the corner filings. Fold into the shape.
- Spray some oil on the basket. 8 crab Rangoon should be placed in the basket. Set the temperature to 149°C. Air fry for 4-5 minutes. Each one should be turned over and given another oil spritz. 3-5 more minutes, or till golden brown.
- Take out and let cool until you're ready to serve on the cooling rack. Continue with the second batch. Enjoy! Serve with your preferred dipping sauce!

Nutritional values per serving:

Total Calories: 76 kcal, **Fats:** 3 g, Carbohydrates: 11g, **Protein:** 2 g

15. Air Fried Churros

Ready in: 20 mins.

Serves: 4

Difficulty: medium

Ingredients:

- 1/3 cup of butter (unsalted), cut into cubes
- 1 cup of water
- 2 Tbsp. of granulated sugar
- 1 cup of all-purpose flour
- 1/4 tsp. of salt
- 2 eggs (large)
- oil spray
- 1 tsp. of vanilla extract

Sugar cinnamon coating:

- 3/4 tsp. of ground cinnamon
- 1/2 cup of granulated sugar

Directions:

- Place an oil spray-coated baking sheet on top of a silicone baking mat.
- Combine water, sugar, butter, and salt in a medium pot. Heat to a rolling boil over medium-high.
- Flour is added to the pot when the heat is reduced to medium-low. Cook while regularly mixing the dough using a rubber spatula until it comes together & is smooth.

- Remove the dough from the heat and place it in a mixing bowl. Allow cooling for four minutes.
- Use a stand mixer or electric hand mixer to combine the dough by adding the eggs & vanilla extract into the mixing bowl. It will resemble sticky mashed potatoes. Put lumps in a ball with your hands & transfer them to a big piping bag with a huge star-shaped tip.
- Use a pastry bag to pipe churros into 4-inch lengths, then trim the ends with scissors.
- On the baking sheet, chill the piped churros for an hour.
- Carefully transfer the churros to the basket of Air Fryer using a cookie spatula, allowing a gap of approximately 1/2 inch between each one. Churros should be sprayed with oil. The size of the air fryer will determine how many batches you need to cook them.
- Air fry until golden brown for 10 to 12 minutes at 190°C.
- Combine cinnamon and granulated sugar in a small basin.
- As soon as the churros are done baking, put them in to bowl with the mixture of sugar & toss to coat. Doing so in groups. Serve hot with chocolate or Nutella dipping sauce

Nutritional values per serving:

Total Calories: 204 kcal, **Fats:** 9 g, **Carbohydrates:** 27 g, **Protein:** 3 g

16. Egg Rolls

Ready in: 46 mins.

Serves: 12

Difficulty: medium

Ingredients:

- 1/2 onion

- 1/2 pound of ground pork
- 1/2 bag of coleslaw mix
- 1 stalk of celery
- 4 ounces of mushrooms
- 12 wrappers of egg roll
- 1/2 tsp. of salt

Directions:

- A skillet should be heated to medium.

- Cook the onion and ground pork together until the meat loses its pink colour.

- Season the pan with salt and add the celery, mushrooms, and coleslaw mixture. The veggies should cook for 5 mins to soften.

- Place the package on the cutting board. To the upper corner of the egg roll wrapper, add 1/3 cup of the filling ingredients. Over the filling, fold the top down. After that, roll up the wrapper while tucking the edges in. When you reach the bottom, wet the wrapper's edges with your fingertips to secure it in place.

- Keep rolling the egg rolls till all of the fillings have been used.

- If desired, gently mist the egg rolls with cooking spray. The egg rolls will be evenly browned as a result.

- Cook egg rolls for 6 to 8 minutes at 205°C, turning them over with tongs once halfway through.

Nutritional values per serving:

Total Calories: 76 kcal, Fats: 5g, Carbohydrates: 3g, Protein: 5 g

17. Stuffed Mushrooms

Ready in: 18 mins.

Serves: 12

Difficulty: easy

Ingredients:

- 6 oz. of softened Cream Cheese
- 16 oz. of White Button Mushrooms (Whole)
- 3 tbsp. of Sour Cream
- ½ tsp. of Garlic Powder
- ¼ cup of Cheddar Cheese, Shredded
- ½ tsp. of Salt
- Chives (Chopped) for topping
- Dash of black Pepper
- Oil Spray

Directions:

- Clean off any dirt or debris from the mushrooms using a moist paper towel (they can get slimy if rinsed underwater.) Trim or remove the mushroom stems.

- Cream cheese, garlic powder, sour cream, salt, & pepper should all be combined in a bowl. The mixture should be placed into each mushroom cap's "well." Add chives and cheddar cheese shavings to the top of each.

- Oil spray the air fryer basket to stop it from sticking. In the basket, arrange the mushrooms in a single layer. Cook for 8–10 minutes at a temperature of 185°C. Prior to serving, let it cool somewhat.

Nutritional values per serving:

Total Calories: 86 kcal, Fats: 2g, Carbohydrates: 3g, Protein: 2 g

18. Pretzel Bites

Ready in: 21 mins.

Serves: 30

Difficulty: medium

Ingredients:

- 2 & 1/4 tsp. of quick rise yeast

- 1 1/2 cups of water
- 4 cups of all-purpose flour
- 1 tbsp. of sugar/honey
- 1 tsp. of sea salt
- 4 cups of water
- 1/3 cup of baking soda
- 1 beaten egg
- 1 tbsp. of water
- 3 tbsp. of melted butter

Optional:

- Baking Soda Bath
- Pretzel salt
- Egg Wash
- Butter topping

Directions:

Prepare the Dough:

- Water and yeast should be combined in a mixing bowl. Stir.
- Stir in the sea salt, sugar, & flour until largely incorporated.
- Lightly dust your hands and use your hands to knead the dough for 1 minute, forming a ball. The dough should be divided into eighths.
- Form dough ropes on a surface that has been gently dusted with flour.
- Cut the dough into pieces that are 1 inch long using a floured knife.
- Lightly olive oil brush the air fryer's basket. Give the pretzel bits space to expand as you add them to the basket.
- Cook for 5-6 minutes at 198°C, or until the top is just beginning to brown. Brush heated pretzel bits with melted butter and pretzel salt if you're using the butter technique.

Nutritional values per serving:

Total Calories: 37 kcal, Fats: 1g, Carbohydrates: 8g, Protein: 1g

19. Pretzel Dogs

Ready in: 27 mins.

Serves: 8

Difficulty: medium

Ingredients:

- 1/2 cup of warm water
- 8 hot dogs
- 3/4 tsp. of quick rise yeast
- 1/4 tsp. of sea salt
- 1 1/3 cup of all-purpose flour, and some more for dusting}
- 1/4 tsp. of sugar
- pretzel salt, optional
- 2 tbsp. of melted butter
- olive oil
- sesame seeds, optional

Directions:

- Water and yeast should be combined in a mixing bowl. Stir in the sugar, flour, and sea salt until mostly incorporated.
- Using a little flour, knead the dough using your hand for a minute, forming a ball as you go. The dough should be divided into eighths.
- Based on the size of the hot dog, shape the dough into ropes that are 14 to 20 inches long on a lightly dusted surface.
- Roll the dough as you wrap it around the hot dog, starting at 1 of the ends. To keep the dough pieces together, gently squeeze each end.
- Olive oil should be brushed over the air fryer's basket. Put the pretzel dogs in the

basket, allowing them to expand slightly.

- Cook for 7 mins at 198°C, or until the top is just beginning to brown. Pretzel salt or sesame seeds may be added after brushing heated pretzel bits with melted butter.

Nutritional values per serving:

Total Calories: 213 kcal, **Fats:** 10g, Carbohydrates: 24 g, **Protein:** 7g

20. Air-Fried Ravioli

Ready in: 30 mins.

Serves: 6

Difficulty: easy

Ingredients:

- 1/4 cup of Parmesan cheese, shredded
- 1 cup of bread crumbs, seasoned
- 2 tsp. of dried basil
- 2 eggs (large), lightly beaten
- 1/2 cup of all-purpose flour
- 1 package of frozen beef ravioli (9 ounces), thawed
- Fresh basil (minced), optional
- Cooking spray
- 1 cup of marinara sauce, warmed

Directions:

- Set the air fryer up to 170°C. Combine basil, Parmesan cheese, and bread crumbs in a small bowl. Put the flour and the eggs in separate, small dishes. Shake off excess flour after coating the ravioli on both sides. In order to make the coating adhere, dip in the eggs, then into the crumb mixture.

- Ravioli should be arranged in one single layer on a greased tray in the air fryer basket and sprayed with cooking spray in batches. Cook for 3 to 4 minutes or until golden brown. Toss with cooking

spray and turn. Cook for 3–4 more minutes, or until golden brown. Sprinkle basil and extra Parmesan cheese right away, if preferred. With marinara sauce, serve warm.

Nutritional values per serving:

Total Calories: 40kcal, **Fats:** 1g, **Carbohydrates:** 6g, **Proteins:** 2g

21. Cheeseburger Onion Rings

Ready in: 40 mins.

Serves: 8

Difficulty: medium

Ingredients:

- 1/3 cup of ketchup
- 1 pound of ground beef, lean (90% lean)
- 2 tbsp. of prepared mustard
- 1 onion (large)
- 1/2 tsp. of salt
- 4 ounces of cheddar cheese in 8 squares
- 2 tsp. of garlic powder
- 3/4 cup of all-purpose flour
- 2 eggs (large), lightly beaten
- Cooking spray
- 1-1/2 cups of panko bread crumbs
- Ketchup, optional

Directions:

- Set the air fryer at 160°C. Beef, ketchup, mustard, and salt are combined in a small bowl while being softly but completely mixed. Slice onion into 1/2-inch rings after cutting it. Place half of the meat mixture into 8 slices (save other onion rings for one other use).

Add the square of cheese & the leftover meat mixture to each.

- Mix flour & garlic powder in a small bowl. Put eggs in one shallow dish, followed by bread crumbs. Shake off excess flour after dipping stuffed onion rings in it to cover both sides. To help the coating stick, dip in the egg, then coat in the bread crumbs

- On a greased tray in the air fryer basket, arrange onion rings in one single layer in batches and spritz with the cooking spray. Cook for 12 to 15 minutes, or until the beef thermometer reaches 80°C and the surface is golden brown. Serve with spicy ketchup, if preferred.

Nutritional values per serving:

Total Calories: 258kcal, **Fats:** 11g, Carbohydrates: 19g, **Proteins:** 19g

22. Sriracha Crispy Spring Rolls

Ready in: 1 hr.

Serves: 24

Difficulty: medium

Ingredients:

- 3 chopped green onions

- 3 cups of coleslaw mix (almost about 7 ounces)

- 1 tbsp. of soy sauce

- 1 pound of skinless, boneless chicken breasts

- 1 tsp. of sesame oil

- 1 tsp. of seasoned salt

- 2 tbsp. of Sriracha chilli sauce

- 2 packages of cream cheese (8 ounces each), softened

- 24 wrappers of spring roll

- Optional: more green onions and Sweet chilli sauce

- Cooking spray

Directions:

- Set the air fryer up to 178°C. As the chicken cooks, combine the coleslaw mix, soy sauce, green onions, and sesame oil. Put the chicken in the air fryer basket in one single layer on an oiled tray. Cook for 18–20 minutes, or until a thermometer placed in the chicken registers 80°C. Remove chicken, and let it cool. Chicken should be chopped finely and then salted.

- Heat the air fryer to 205°C. Cream cheese & Sriracha chilli sauce should be combined in a big bowl before adding the chicken and coleslaw combination. Put roughly 2 teaspoons of filling directly below the wrapper's centre, with one corner facing you. (Until ready to use, cover the leftover wrappers with a wet paper towel.) Fold the bottom corner over the filling and wet the other corners. Over the filling, fold the side corners toward the centre. Roll firmly, pushing the tip to seal. Repeat.

- Spring rolls should be arranged in one single layer on a greased tray in the air fryer basket and sprayed with cooking spray in batches. Cook for 5 to 6 minutes, until gently browned. Toss with cooking spray and turn. Cook for a further 5 to 6 minutes, or until crisp and golden. Serve with green onions and sweet chilli sauce, if preferred.

Nutritional values per serving:

Total Calories: 127kcal, **Fats:** 7g, Carbohydrates: 10g, **Proteins:** 6g

23. Air-Fried Calamari

Ready in: 30 mins.

Serves: 5

Difficulty: medium

Ingredients:

- 1/2 tsp. of salt

- 1/2 cup of all-purpose flour

- 1 egg (large), lightly beaten
- 1 cup of panko bread crumbs
- 1/2 cup of 2% milk
- 1/2 tsp. of seasoned salt
- 8 ounces of cleaned, frozen or fresh calamari, thawed & cut into half-inch rings
- 1/4 tsp. of pepper
- Cooking spray

Directions:

- Set the air fryer up to 205°C. Flour and salt should be combined in a small bowl. Whisk the egg and milk in a separate shallow dish. Combine bread crumbs, seasoning salt, and pepper in a third small bowl. Calamari should be covered in a flour mixture, then dipped in egg mixture and bread crumbs combination.

- Calamari should be placed in single layers on a greased tray in the air fryer basket and sprayed with cooking spray in batches. 4 minutes to cook. Toss with cooking spray and turn. Cook for 3-5 more minutes, or until golden brown.

Nutritional values per serving:

Total Calories: 11kcal, Fats: 0g, Carbohydrates: 1g, Proteins: 1g

24. Mushroom Roll-Ups

Ready in: 40 mins.

Serves: 10

Difficulty: easy

Ingredients:

- 8 ounces of Portobello mushrooms (large), finely chopped & gills discarded
- 2 tbsp. of olive oil
- 1 tsp. of dried oregano
- 1/2 tsp. of crushed red pepper flakes
- 1 tsp. of dried thyme

- 1/4 tsp. of salt
- 4 ounces of ricotta cheese, whole-milk
- 1 package of cream cheese (8 ounces), softened
- 10 (8 inches) flour tortillas
- Mint sauce
- Cooking spray

Directions:

- Heat oil in a skillet over medium heat. Add the mushrooms and cook for 4 minutes. Add salt, pepper flakes, oregano, and thyme. Sauté for 4-6 minutes, or until mushrooms are browned. Cool.

- Combine the cheeses, then thoroughly fold in the mushrooms. Place 3 tablespoons of the mushroom mixture in the middle of each tortilla's bottom. Roll firmly, then use toothpicks to fasten.

- Set the air fryer up to 205°C. Place roll-ups in the air fryer basket in batches on a greased tray and spritz with the cooking spray. Cook for 9 to 11 minutes or until golden brown. Discard toothpicks after roll-ups have cooled enough to handle. Eat with mint sauce.

Nutritional values per serving:

Total Calories: 291kcal, Fats: 16g, Carbohydrates: 31g, Proteins: 8g

25. Garlic Bread

Ready in: 20 mins.

Serves: 8

Difficulty: easy

Ingredients:

- 3 tbsp. of Parmesan cheese, grated
- 1/4 cup of butter, softened
- 2 cloves of garlic, minced
- 8 slices of ciabatta/French bread
- 2 tsp. of minced parsley (fresh) or 1/2 tsp. of parsley flakes (dried)

Directions:

- Set the air fryer up to 170°C. Spread over bread after combining the first 4 ingredients in a small dish.
- Place the bread on the tray in the air fryer basket in batches. Cook for 2 to 3 minutes or until golden brown. Serve hot.

Nutritional values per serving:

Total Calories: 122kcal, **Fats:** 7g, **Carbohydrates:** 14g, **Proteins:** 3g

Chapter 10: Air Fried Diabetic Diet - Dessert Recipes

1. Chocolate Donuts

Ready in: 18 mins.

Serves: 12

Difficulty: medium

Ingredients:

Donuts:

- ¼ cup of erythritol
- 1 cup of almond flour
- 2 tsp. of baking powder
- ½ tsp. of espresso powder
- 2 tbsp. of Cocoa Powder
- ½ tsp. of xanthan gum
- ¼ cup of melted butter
- 4 eggs (large)
- 2 tbsp. of whipping cream (heavy), 35% Cream
- ½ tsp. of vanilla extract

Chocolate Glaze:

- ½ tbsp. of butter
- ½ cup of chocolate chips, sugar-free

Directions:

- Set the air fryer to 170°C and combine dry ingredients into a large mixing bowl. Add wet ingredients and stir to thoroughly combine.
- Fill the little silicone donut moulds with the mixture after transferring them to a piping bag.
- Put the food in the air fryer basket & cook it there for 8 minutes at 170°C.
- Let the donuts cool fully before removing them from the moulds.
- Combine the butter and chocolate chips in a small bowl.
- Melt in the microwave on high for 30-second intervals. Blending between each increment.
- After the donuts have cooled, dip them in the chocolate glaze & let them dry on a rack.

Nutritional values per serving:

Total Calories: 158kcal, **Fats:** 13g, **Carbohydrates:** 3g, **Protein:** 3g

2. Peanut Butter Cookies

Ready in: 9 mins.

Serves: 8

Difficulty: easy

Ingredients:

- 1 cup of sugar substitute
- 1 beaten egg
- 1 tsp. of liquid stevia drops
- 1 cup of peanut butter, all-natural

Directions:

- Mix ingredients to make a dough.
- Create 24 balls out of the dough.
- Use a fork to push balls onto a baking sheet or cutting board to make a traditional crisscross pattern.

- Place 6-7 cookies spread out into the basket air fryer.

- Air Fry for 10 minutes at 150°C.

- After a minute or two, remove the cookies with a spatula & transfer them to a dish to complete cooling.

- Finish making the remainder of the cookies into batches.

Nutritional values per serving:

Total Calories: 198kcal, **Fats:** 17g, Carbohydrates: 7g, **Protein:** 9g

3. Cheesecake Bites

Ready in: 30 mins.

Serves: 5

Difficulty: medium

Ingredients:

- 1/2 cup of erythritol, plus 2 tbsp.

- 8 ounces of cream cheese

- 4 Tbsp. of heavy cream, divided

- 1/2 cup of almond flour

- 1/2 tsp. of vanilla extract

Directions:

- Give the cream cheese 20 mins to soften on the counter.

- Attach a paddle to a stand mixer.

- Blend the vanilla, softened cream cheese, heavy cream, and 1/2 cup erythritol until smooth.

- Scoop onto a baking sheet lined with parchment paper.

- Freeze until firm for about 30 minutes.

- In a small bowl, combine the 2 Tablespoons of erythritol with the almond flour.

- Roll the cheesecake bites in the mixture of almond flour after dipping them in two tablespoons of cream.

- Cook for two minutes at 145°C in an air fryer.

Nutritional values per serving:

Total Calories: 80kcal, **Fats:** 7g, **Carbohydrates:** 2g, **Protein:** 2g

4. Chocolate Cake

Ready in: 20 mins.

Serves: 6

Difficulty: medium

Ingredients:

- 1/3 cup of Truvia (0.33 g)

- 3 Eggs

- 4 tbsp. of Butter

- 1 tsp. of Vanilla extract

- 1/2 cup of Heavy Whipping Cream (119 g)

- 1/4 cup of Coconut Flour (30 g)

- 2 tbsp. of Cocoa Powder, Unsweetened

- 1 tsp. of Baking Powder

- 1/4 tsp. of Kosher Salt

For Chocolate Ganache:

- 1 tbsp. of Butter

- 3/4 cup of Heavy Whipping Cream

- 1 cup of Chocolate Chips, Sugar-Free

Directions:

- Preheat the air fryer to 170°C.

- Grease the air fryer tray and set it aside.

- Microwave the butter in a sizable mixing bowl for 30 to 60 seconds.

- Take out and add Truvia to the butter.

- Use a mixer to combine the heavy whipping cream, eggs, and vanilla extract.

- Put an end to the mixer and fill the bowl with all the dry ingredients.

- Mix again till the batter is thoroughly mixed and somewhat smooth.

- Coconut flour's absorbency varies. Mix in a bit of extra heavy whipping cream if the mixture is thicker than the typical cake batter.

- Fill the oiled tray with the batter. A toothpick inserted should come out clean after 20 minutes of air frying, and the tops should faintly bounce back when pressed.

- Let it cool.

Ganache made with chocolate:

- The chocolate chips should be put in a bowl and left alone.

- Microwave-safe bowl with heavy cream & butter heated for one minute.

- After adding the warm cream to the chocolate chips, wait a few minutes. Once the chocolate gets melted, and the mixture is smooth, stir it occasionally.

- Use the hot glaze right away, or let it cool for a bit.

- To prepare to frost, let the Ganache chill for 20 to 30 minutes before whipping the frosting with a stand mixer until it is frothy and light. This may be used as icing on top or as a filling in between layers of cake.

Nutritional values per serving:

Total Calories: 194 kcal, Fats: 18g, Carbohydrates: 5g, Protein: 4g

5. Cheese Biscuits

Ready in: 25 mins.

Serves: 8

Difficulty: medium

Ingredients:

- 2 tbsp. of agave nectar

- 4 tbsp. of softened butter (or some coconut oil)

- 2 tbsp. of Water

- 1 Egg

- 1/3 cup of Truvia or a half cup of sugar

- 2.5 cups of Almond Flour

- 2 tsp. of ground ginger

- ½ tsp. of Ground Nutmeg

- 1 tsp. of Ground Cinnamon

- ¼ tsp. of Kosher Salt

- 1 tsp. of Baking Soda

Directions:

- Set the Air fryer up to 170°C.

- Use parchment paper to line the cookie sheet and have it handy.

- Combine the butter, egg, agave nectar, and water in a hand blender.

- Add all of the dry ingredients to this mixture and combine thoroughly on low speed.

- Scoop out two teaspoon-sized balls, and place them on a parchment-lined baking sheet. They don't actually spread out too much, but they do leave some space between each other.

- Air fry for 12 to 15 minutes, or until the tops are just beginning to brown.

- After cooling, place the item in an airtight container. Before you consume every cookie, for instance, for the hour, they will be available.

Nutritional values per serving:

Total Calories: 122kcal, Fats: 10g, Carbohydrates: 5g, Protein: 3g

6. Air Fried Smores

Ready in: 7 mins.

Serves: 4

Difficulty: easy

Ingredients:

- 2 bars of chocolate
- 4 graham crackers
- 4 marshmallows

Directions:

- Use parchment paper to line the basket of the air fryer or a nonstick frying spray.
- Put graham cracker square pieces in the basket of an air fryer.
- Place a marshmallow on top of the Graham Cracker.
- Air fry the marshmallow for 7 minutes at 190°C, or until it has melted and become golden.
- Add some chocolate bar on top of the heated marshmallow and graham cracker.
- On top of a chocolate bar, place a second graham cracker.

Nutritional values per serving:

Total Calories: 165kcal, Fats: 7g, Carbohydrates: 23g, Protein: 2g

7. Carrot Cake

Ready in: 55 mins.

Serves: 8

Difficulty: medium

Ingredients:

- 1 tsp. of Baking Powder
- 1 ¼ cup of All Purpose Flour
- ½ tsp. of Baking Soda
- ¾ cup of Splenda
- 1 tsp. of Pumpkin Pie Spice
- 2 Eggs
- ¾ cup of Canola Oil
- 2 cups of grated Carrots, about 5 carrots (regular sized), grated

Directions:

- Set your air fryer up to 170°C and thoroughly prepare your nonstick cake pan. Mix the baking powder, flour, baking soda, and pumpkin pie spice in a mixing bowl using a fork or whisk. Next, whisk or combine the sugar substitute, eggs, and oil in a big mixing dish.
- The dry ingredients in the first bowl will be added to the big mixing bowl in the next step. Stirring in between additions, add half of the dry ingredients at a time. Next, include the carrots. After gently transferring the cake pan to a basket of air fryers, add the batter cake to the prepped cake pan.
- Check the cake's top after 30 minutes of air-frying to make sure it is not turning too black. If so, you may air fry the cake until a wooden skewer or toothpick inserted into the centre of the cake comes out clean (40 minutes total). Before removing the cake from the pan, let it cool completely on a rack.

Nutritional values per serving:

Total Calories: 287kcal, Fats: 22g, Carbohydrates: 19g, Protein: 4g

8. Vegan Beignets

Ready in: 5 mins.

Serves: 24

Difficulty: easy

Ingredients:

For powdered baking:

- 1 tsp. of corn starch (organic)
- 1 cup of Sweetener Baking Blend

For proofing:

- 3 tbsp. of powdered baking blend
- 1 cup of coconut milk (full-fat) from a can

- 1 1/2 tsp. of active baking yeast

For dough:

- 2 tbsp. of aquafaba, can of chickpeas, drained

- 2 tbsp. of coconut oil, melted

- 3 cups of white flour (unbleached), with some extra for sprinkling on the cutting board

- 2 tsp. of vanilla

Directions:

- Fill your blender with the Baking Mix and corn starch, and blend until completely smooth.

- Heat coconut milk till it is warm yet cold enough to touch without being burned. The yeast will be killed by excessive heat. Combine it with the yeast and sugar in the bowl of a stand mixer. 10 minutes should pass for the yeast to start to froth.

- Combine the aquafaba, coconut oil, and vanilla with the yeast mixture using the paddle attachment. After that, gradually add flour to the mixture, one cup at a time.

- If you have a dough hook, switch to it after the flour has been incorporated and the dough has begun to pull away from the mixer's sides. If not, you should continue using the paddle.

- In your mixer, knead yeast dough for around 3 minutes. Even though the dough would be wetter compared to if you were baking a bread loaf, you should still be able to scoop it out and roll it into a ball without sticking it to your hands.

- Put the dough in a big bowl, cover it with a fresh dish towel, and let it rise for an hour.

- On a floured surface, roll the dough out into a rectangle which is approximately 1/3 inch thick. Before cooking, divide into 24 squares & let proof for 25-30 minutes.

- Set your air fryer's thermostat to 198°C. In your warmed air fryer basket, place paper on the bottom. You may either poke holes in the parchment or use the perforated parchment that has been trimmed to fit your basket.

- You can fit 3-6 beignets in the air fryer basket at once, based on the size of the air fryer. Just be sure to arrange them in one single layer.

- Three minutes on each side of the food. Cook for a further two minutes after flipping. You may have to cook them for an additional minute or two in your air fryer to get a golden brown colour.

- Generously top with the powdered baking mixture you created earlier and savour!

- Cook them in batches till they are all finished.

Nutritional values per serving:

Total Calories: 88kcal, **Fats:** 3g, **Carbohydrates:** 13g, **Protein:** 2g

9. Hand Pies

Ready in: 30 mins.

Serves: 8

Difficulty: medium

Ingredients:

- ¼ cup of fresh blueberries (60 mL)

- ¼ cup of blueberry jam (60 mL)

- 1 lemon

- Flour to dust

- 1 egg

- 1 package of refrigerated pie crusts, softened (14.1-oz./399-g), 2 crusts

- 2 tbsp. of sugar (30 mL)

- Oil for spritzing

- ¼ tsp. of ground cinnamon (1 mL)

- Optional: ¼ cup of powdered sugar (60 mL)

Directions:

- In a medium dish, mix the jam and

blueberries. 1 teaspoon of lemon should be zested (5 mL). Add to bowl & thoroughly combine.

- The pie crust should be unrolled onto a gently dusted surface. From every piece of pie dough, cut 8 circles using a 3" (7.5 cm) biscuit cutter.

- Each circle should have 1 tiny tbsp. of filling on it. Add the rest of dough circles on top, sealing the borders with pressure. Use a fork to crimp the edges. Make 2 tiny venting vents in the centre of each pie.

- The egg is whisked in a small bowl. Apply the egg wash sparingly to the pies.

- Sprinkle the pies with the sugar-cinnamon mixture.

- Oil the cooking trays for the Air Fryer. Put 4 pies onto each baking sheet. Put a tray on the centre rack and another on the top rack.

- Set the timer for 14 minutes. Halfway through cooking, switch the cooking trays. The pies need to have a golden colour.

- Juice one teaspoon of lemon if desired. In a separate dish, whisk together the juice & powdered sugar until well combined. Drizzle all over the pies.

Nutritional values per serving:

Total Calories: 240kcal, Fats: 12g, Carbohydrates: 32g, Protein: 2g

10. Air Fried Oreos

Ready in: 10 mins.

Serves: 8

Difficulty: easy

Ingredients:

- 8 Oreo cookies

- 1 can of Crescents Dough

- 1-2 tbsp. of Powdered Sugar

Directions:

- Split apart the crescents and spread the dough over the Oreos, ensuring there aren't air bubbles and that the dough fully encases the Oreo.

- Set the air fryer to the bottom rack position and heat it at 170°C for 4 minutes before cooking the wrapped Oreos.

- After 3 to 4 minutes, or when the tops are slightly golden brown, flip the Oreos.

- Before serving, sprinkle powdered sugar over the finished Oreos.

Nutritional values per serving:

Total Calories: 159kcal, Fats: 8g, Carbohydrates: 21g, Protein: 2g

11. Apple Fritters

Ready in: 35 mins.

Serves: 10

Difficulty: medium

Ingredients:

- ½ tsp. of ground cinnamon

- ½ cup of sugar

- 1 cup of peeled & chopped apple (medium)

- 3 tbsp. of butter, melted

- 1 can of refrigerated Buttermilk Biscuits (10.2 oz.), 5 Count

Directions:

- Cooking parchment paper should be cut into two 8-inch circles. Put one round in the air fryer basket's bottom. Use cooking spray to spritz.

- Combine sugar and cinnamon in a small bowl. 2 tbsp. of the cinnamon-sugar mixture and apple, chunks should be well combined in a separate small dish.

- Divide the dough into 4-5 biscuits and then into 2 layers for each biscuit. Create a 4-inch circle out of each. Place one heaping tablespoon of the apples in the middle of each circle. Gently fold the sides over the filling and pinch them closed. 2 tbsp. of melted butter should be used to brush the biscuits all over.

- Arrange five of the biscuits in the air fryer basket on parchment paper, seam sides down. Cooking spray should be applied to the second parchment circle's top and bottom. Add a second parchment circle on top of the biscuits in the basket before adding the last five biscuits.

- Cooking time is 8 minutes at 150°C. Remove the top parchment circle, flip the biscuits with tongs, and arrange them in a single layer in the basket. Cook for another 4 to 6 minutes, or until thoroughly heated through & apples are soft. Roll remaining cinnamon-sugar mixture around biscuits before brushing with remaining 1 tbsp. Melted butter.

Nutritional values per serving:

Total Calories: 170kcal, Fats: 7g, Carbohydrates: 13g, Protein: 25g

12. Mini Double Cherry Eggrolls

Ready in: 16 mins.

Serves: 28

Difficulty: medium

Ingredients:

- ⅓ cup of cherry jam

- ½ package of cream cheese (8 ounces), softened

- ¼ cup of tart red cherries (dried), chopped

- Cooking spray (Nonstick) or 1 tbsp. of butter, melted

- 16 wonton wrappers (almost about 1/2-inch squares)

- ½ tsp. of ground cinnamon

- 3 tbsp. of sugar

Directions:

- Set the air fryer up to 205°C. Mix the cream cheese & cherry jam in a small bowl. Add the cherries, and stir. A wonton wrapper should be placed on the work surface with the corner facing you. With water, dampen the edges. Just below the middle of the wrapper, place a round spoonful of the cherry mixture.

- Bottom corner should be folded over the filling and tucked under on the opposite side. Roll the egg roll toward the last corner, folding side corners over the filling. Use the leftover wrappers and filling to repeat. Apply melted butter or nonstick frying spray to both sides of the egg rolls. In a small dish, mix the sugar with the cinnamon; leave it aside.

- Place egg rolls in the fryer basket in a single layer, if required, in batches. Cook for 4 to 5 minutes, until well browned. Take out of the air fryer. Roll immediately in cinnamon sugar using two forks. Cool onto a wire rack for five to ten minutes. Serve hot.

Nutritional values per serving:

Total Calories: 84 kcal, Fats: 3g, Carbohydrates: 14g, Protein: 1g

13. Cheesecake Chimichangas

Ready in: 20 mins.

Serves: 2

Difficulty: medium

Ingredients:

- 1/4 cup of sour cream or nonfat plain Greek yogurt
- 1 brick of cream cheese (8 ounces), softened to normal temperature
- 1½ tbsp. of granulated sugar
- 8 strawberries (medium), quartered
- 1 tsp. of pure vanilla extract
- 1 banana (medium), peeled & sliced
- 8 tsp. of Nutella
- 8 flour tortillas (soft), 8 inches
- 3 tbsp. of melted butter
- olive oil spray

Directions:

- Blend the Greek yoghurt (or sour cream), softened cream cheese, sugar, and vanilla in a mixing bowl.
- Split the mixture of cream cheese into two medium dishes and combine it with the cut bananas and strawberries in a bowl. Stir slowly to mix (or omit completely).
- A flour tortilla should be placed on a spotless work area. On the tortilla, place 1/4 of the mixture of strawberries immediately to the left of the centre. Add a spoonful of Nutella after that.
- To enclose the filling, fold the tortilla's left side over. Roll the burrito-style by tucking the short ends inside.
- Carry out the same procedure with the rest of the strawberry and banana mixtures.
- Light your air fryer to 175°C and mist the chimichangas with olive oil spray. Work in batches, arranging the chimichangas seam-side down in an equal layer, & air frying for 8-10 minutes, or till the tortilla is golden brown, based on the size of the air fryer.
- After they have been fried, put the chimichangas on a wire rack positioned over the rimmed baking sheet. Brush butter over all surfaces, including the nooks and crannies, then roll in a dish of cinnamon sugar. Repeat.

Nutritional values per serving:

Total Calories: 109 kcal, **Fats:** 7g, **Carbohydrates:** 10g, **Protein:** 1g

---

14. Strawberry Scones

Ready in: 17 mins.

Serves: 6

Difficulty: medium

Ingredients:

- 50 g of Butter
- 225 g of Self Raising Flour
- 28 g of Caster Sugar
- Egg Wash
- 60 ml of Whole Milk
- Olive Oil Spray
- Strawberries (Fresh)

Optional:

- Squirty Cream
- Strawberry Jam

Directions:

- Combine sugar and flour in a bowl. Add butter cubes.
- Mix the flour and lard together. Use your fingers to continue until the mixture resembles coarse breadcrumbs.
- Add milk until a soft dough forms. Then, on a floured surface, lay out the dough; aim for a thickness of at least 1.5 cm; any less will result in undersized scones.

- Cut your dough into medium-sized scones using cutters, and then set them in your air fryer basket.

- To avoid sticking, spray the scones' tops and sides with egg wash before placing them in the air fryer basket.

- Air fry for 4-5 minutes at 180°C, then for 2 more minutes at 160°C.

- Serve with cream, strawberry slices, and strawberry jam.

Nutritional values per serving:

Total Calories: 219kcal, Fats: 8g, Carbohydrates: 32g, Protein: 5g

15. Chocolate Soufflé

Ready in: 30 mins.

Serves: 2

Difficulty: medium

Ingredients:

- 2 tbsp. of Splenda

- 2 tbsp. of soft Butter, melted

- ¼ cup of Chocolate Chips, Sugar-Free

- 1 tbsp. of Flour

- 1.5 tbsp. of Butter

- ⅓ cup of Milk

- 2 Egg Whites & 1 Egg Yolk

- ½ tsp. of Vanilla Extract

- ½ tsp. of Cream of Tarter

- 1 tbsp. of Splenda

Directions:

- As part of the preparation, use the softened butter to "grease" each of the ramekins. After that, top them with the substitute's granulated sugar (1 tbsp. maximum for each ramekin).

- In order to distribute the sugar substitute more evenly, you may have to rotate the ramekin. Additionally, preheat the air fryer to a low level (155-165°C).

- The chocolate will then be melted. Stir after 30 seconds in a medium-sized microwave-safe basin to melt the ingredients. Alternately, and really better for chocolate, use the double boiler technique with a basin of boiling water below. Later stages will include adding other ingredients to the bowl that this melted chocolate is in. That 1 1/2 tbsp. of butter will now be melted over low to medium heat.

- Make use of a small skillet. Whisk in the flour after the butter has melted. While whisking, wait a few minutes for the mixture to thicken. You may turn off the heat when it begins to thicken.

- During this phase, you will be multitasking. While you whisk the egg whites, we will combine the ingredients into the dish with the melted chocolate. Use a stand mixer with the whisk attachment to combine the egg whites & cream of tartar. Return to the flour & butter mixture while egg whites are being whipped to create peaks. Melted chocolate is blended with the melted butter & flour mixture. The remaining sugar substitute, vanilla essence, and egg yolks are then added. Keep an eye on the white egg mixer. When the egg whites start to form peaks, stop whisking them and carefully fold them into the mixture of other ingredients.

- Spoon the batter into the ramekins to approximately 3/4 full. The soufflés should be cooked in 12–14 minutes of air-frying.

Nutritional values per serving:

Total Calories: 288 kcal, **Fats:** 24g, **Carbohydrates:** 5g, **Protein:** 6g

16. Lemon Slice Cookies

Ready in: 5 mins.

Serves: 24

Difficulty: easy

Ingredients:

- ½ cup of Swerve granular sweetener
- ½ cup of coconut flour
- ½ tsp. of baking soda
- ½ cup of butter (unsalted), softened
- ½ tsp. of salt
- 1 tbsp. of lemon juice
- ½ tsp. of liquid vanilla stevia
- ¼ tsp. of lemon extract, optional
- Icing
- 2 egg yolks
- ⅔ cup of Swerve confectioners sweetener
- 3 tsp. of lemon juice

Directions:

- Swerve, salt, baking soda, and coconut flour should all be mixed in a stand mixer.
- Mix the dry ingredients well after adding the melted butter, including all ingredients, excluding the egg yolks. If necessary, add alternative sweetener and/or lemon essence after tasting the batter to adjust the sweetness and lemon taste to your liking. After that, stir in the yolks until well combined.
- The batter should be put in the middle of a big piece of plastic wrap that has

been placed on the counter. Form a log with the wrap by rolling it over the dough & cutting off the excess. For 2 to 3 hours or overnight, refrigerate after firmly wrapping.

- Set the air fryer's thermostat to 155°C. The air fryer's basket should be greased. Unwrap the log, then slice half of it into cookies that are 14 inches thick. Put the leftover batter in the refrigerator. In the basket of air fryers, arrange as many cookie slices as you can into a single layer. Cook the cookies for approximately 3 to 5 minutes, or till the edges are golden. Before removing the basket to totally cool on a wire rack, give it time to cool inside the basket for two minutes. Use the leftover dough to repeat. After cooling, add frosting.
- Set the oven up to 170°C. Cut the log of cookies into 14-inch-thick pieces after unwrapping. A baking sheet pan with parchment paper should have cookies on it spaced about one inch apart. The edges should brown after 8 to 10 minutes of baking. Let cool for two to three minutes before transferring to the wire rack to finish cooling before frosting.
- In a small bowl, combine the confectioners and lemon juice. On top of the cooled cookies, drizzle.

Nutritional values per serving:

Total Calories: 66 kcal, **Fats:** 6g, **Carbohydrates:** 2g, **Protein:** 1g

17. Air Fried Brownie

Ready in: 6 mins.

Serves: 2

Difficulty: easy

Ingredients:

- 3 tbsp. of almond flour
- 1 tbsp. of butter, melted
- 1 1/2 tbsp. of monk fruit sweetener

- 1/2 tsp. of baking powder
- 1 tbsp. of cocoa powder
- , a pinch of salt
- 2 tbsp. of chocolate chips, sugar-free
- 1 egg white

Directions:

- In a small ramekin, melt the butter and stir in the sweetener, almond flour, baking soda, salt, cocoa powder, and egg white. Keep in mind that the mixture would be thick and to only stir until everything is mixed. It will be shiny, much like a brownie mix from a box. Add the chocolate chunks and stir.
- For 3 minutes, preheat your air fryer up to 155°C. Add the ramekin into the air fryer that has been warmed.
- Give 6-minute cook time: This will probably result in fudgy brownies which are fully cooked on the outside but somewhat underdone in the middle.
- 8 minutes of cooking time will probably result in brownies that are fully cooked.
- Wait one minute before eating the brownie.

Nutritional values per serving:

Total Calories: 254 kcal, Fats: 16g, Carbohydrates: 7.6g, Protein: 7.7g

18. Chocolate Air Fried Molten Lava Cakes

Ready in: 20 mins.

Serves: 4

Difficulty: medium

Ingredients:

- 1/2 cup of butter (unsalted), cubed. / cooking spray (non-stick).
- 4 oz. of good quality chocolate (unsweetened), finely chopped
- 2 eggs

- 1/4 cup of All-Purpose Pure Organic Stevia Blend
- 2 egg yolks
- Pinch of salt
- 1/2 cup of whipping cream (35%)
- 2 tbsp. of flour

Directions:

- Set your air fryer's temperature to 185°C.
- Spray or lightly grease four 4-ounce oven-safe ramekins, then put aside.
- Set up a double boiler by placing a heat-resistant bowl over boiling water. Stir the butter and chocolate into the hot water to melt them.
- In a bowl, egg yolks, whisk eggs, flour, & Pure Organic Stevia blend using an electric mixer set to medium-high speed.
- Add one pinch of salt & keep whisking until the mixture becomes thick and pale.
- Once the mixture has thickened, reduce the speed of the mixer to low & gently add the chocolate till well incorporated.
- After that, evenly pour the chocolate mixture into the ramekins that have been prepared.
- Air-fried the lava cakes for 8-10 minutes, or until they are puffy and have a thin crust around the sides.
- Check on and gently remove the ramekins using silicone oven mitts or a kitchen towel. The cakes must jiggle and be mushy in the middle for the "lava" to flow. If required, extend the time.
- Use a knife to smooth the edges of the ramekin cakes before serving the molten lava cakes. Turn the cakes over onto the serving platter and top each with a dab of whipped cream.

- Whipping cream may be used to make homemade whipped cream by beating it in a bowl till soft peaks form whilst the cakes are cooling.

- The Pure Organic Stevia Blend should then be added.

- Whip for a further minute.

Nutritional values per serving:

Total Calories: 530 kcal, **Fats:** 54g, **Carbohydrates:** 26g, **Protein:** 9g

19. Chocolate Muffins

Ready in: 14 mins.

Serves: 6

Difficulty: medium

Ingredients:

- 60 g of Milk Chocolate

- 10 Squares of Chocolate

- 30 g of Self Raising Flour

- 1 Tsp. of Butter heaped

- 15 g of Cocoa Powder

- 1 Tsp. of Honey

- 1 Tsp. of Vanilla Essence optional

- 1 Tsp. of Single Cream

Directions:

- Combine chocolate pieces, butter, and honey in the air fryer baking dish. Melt the chocolate by placing it into the air fryer & cooking it for two minutes at 120°C.

- Add single cream and stir. Now it will be smooth and gorgeous. After that, add the crushed chocolate to the dish containing the flour & cocoa powder together with the melted chocolate.

- If using vanilla, add it now. Give it a Good stirring Load into the air fryer muffin cases.

- Give it 10 minutes to cook at 160 °C.

Nutritional values per serving:

Total Calories: 97kcal, **Fats:** 6g, **Carbohydrates:** 13g, **Protein:** 2g

20. Pound Cake

Ready in: 30 mins.

Serves: 8

Difficulty: easy

Ingredients:

- ½ tsp. of Baking Powder

- 1 ¾ cup of Flour

- ½ cup of softened Butter at normal temperature

- ½ tsp. of Vanilla Extract

- ½ lb. of Splenda, 1 cup plus 2 tbsp.

Directions:

- Set your air fryer up to 170°C. Prepare the cake pan by using at least two of the following techniques: greasing, flouring, or using parchment paper that has already been cut to size.

- Combine the flour and baking powder in a mixing dish using a whisk or sifter.

- Next, combine the butter and sugar substitute in a new mixing dish.

- Add each egg 1 at a time, carefully swirling in between. The vanilla extract is then added.

- The mixture of flour from the first bowl will be added to the mixing bowl in the next step. Stir just enough to mix. Add a teaspoon, or more if necessary, of whipping cream or another dairy product if it looks too thick.

- Pour the prepared cake pan with the batter until it is approximately 1/2 to 2/3 filled. Based on size of your pan, you could have batter remaining. Place the pan into the air fryer. A toothpick inserted in the middle of the cake should come out clean after 15 to 20 minutes of baking. Based on size of the air fryer, baking times may vary. Take care while removing the pan of cake since it probably will be hot.

- Let the cake cool completely before taking it out of the pan.

Nutritional values per serving:

Total Calories: 234 kcal, **Fats:** 14g, Carbohydrates: 21g, **Protein:** 6g

21. Cinnamon Bread Twists

Ready in: 30 mins.

Serves: 6

Difficulty: easy

Ingredients:

For Bread Twists Dough:

- 1 tsp. of Baking Powder
- 1 cup of All Purpose Flour (120g)
- 2/3 cup of Greek Yogurt, Fat-Free (150g)
- 1/4 tsp. of Kosher Salt

For Brushing:

- 2 Tbsp. of Granulated Sugar (24g)
- 2 Tbsp. of Light Butter (28g)
- 1-2 tsp. of Ground Cinnamon

Directions:

- Before mixing the Greek yoghurt, combine the baking powder, flour, and salt. Everything should be combined with a fork till a crumbly dough forms. There should be some dry flour left in the bowl.

- Place the dough on a flat surface & shape it into a single, round ball. The dough should be divided into six 45-gram portions. The dough pieces should be rolled into thin, 8" long strips between your hands or on a flat surface.

- Form a shape of a ribbon by folding the end of every strip over, then place the ribbon on an oiled air fryer basket. Spray the top of the basket with cooking spray after placing all 6 bread twists within, then shut the lid.

- Air fry for 15 minutes at 170°C. (Or just bake for 25–30 minutes onto a baking sheet @ 190°C)

- Near the finish of cooking, melt the butter in the microwave, then stir in the sugar and cinnamon. When the bread twists are taken out of the air fryer, immediately brush them with the cinnamon sugar butter. Serve hot.

Nutritional values per serving:

Total Calories: 120kcal, **Fats:** 12g, Carbohydrates: 2g, **Protein:** 2g

22. Apple Chips

Ready in: 35 mins.

Serves: 10

Difficulty: easy

Ingredients:

- 3/4 tsp. of ground cinnamon
- large crisp, sweet apples
- a pinch salt

Directions:

- Start by giving your apples a good cleaning.

- When chopping apples, you have the option of leaving the seeds in or coring them. It works both ways. Use a mandolin or a sharp knife to produce rounds that are approximately 1/8 of one inch thick after they have been cleaned and cored.

- Set the air fryer up to 198°C. Combine salt and cinnamon in a medium bowl if you're using both. If not, sprinkle the apple slices with cinnamon and place them in a layer at the base of the basket. Just enough slices must be placed to create one single layer without any overlap.

- Cook the slices of apple for 8 minutes, turning them over halfway through. You may take the crisped apples out of the fryer if you find them to be just right, then cook the remaining apples as necessary.

- Increase the air fryer's cooking time a little if you need the food to be crispier. Only add 1 minute at one time till the appropriate crisp level is obtained, according to our advice.

Nutritional values per serving:

Total Calories: 65kcal, **Fats:** 0g, **Carbohydrates:** 18g, **Protein:** 0g

23. Cinnamon Apple Empanadas

Ready in: 25 mins.

Serves: 12

Difficulty: medium

Ingredients:

- 2 apples, any
- 12 thawed empanada wrappers
- 2 tbsp. of raw honey
- 1 tsp. of cinnamon
- 1 tsp. of vanilla extract
- 1/8 tsp. of nutmeg
- 1 tsp. of water
- 2 tsp. of cornstarch
- Cooking oil.
- 1 egg, beaten

Directions:

- Set a saucepan over a medium-high flame. Apples, nutmeg, cinnamon, honey, & vanilla should all be added. The apples should be tender after 2–3 minutes of stirring and cooking.

- In a small bowl, combine the water and cornstarch. Stir after adding to the pan. For 30 seconds, cook.

- Before adding the filling to the empanada wrappers, let the mixture cool for at least five minutes.

- The empanada wrappers should be placed on a level surface. In water, dunk a frying brush. Make sure the edges of each empanada wrapper are sealed with a wet brush. The crust will get softer, as a result, making rolling simpler.

- Fill each with the apple mixture. For each empanada, add 1 spoonful of the apple mixture. Never overfill. Use a spoon to spread the mixture out.

- Tuck the empanadas in. Create indentations in the crust with a fork to enclose the empanadas around the edges. Along each edge, pierce the crust with the fork.

- Spray cooking oil on the air fryer basket. Empanadas should be added to the basket of the Air Fryer. Avoid piling the empanadas. If necessary, cook in batches.

- Apply the beaten egg to the top of every empanada using a frying brush (egg wash).

- The Air Fryer should be set at 205°C. Cook until crisp, about 8 to 10 minutes.

- Before serving, cool.

Nutritional values per serving:

Total Calories: 164kcal, **Fats:** 1g, **Carbohydrates:** 0g, **Protein:** 5g

24. Air Fried Banana

Ready in: 10 mins.

Serves: 2

Difficulty: easy

Ingredients:

- 1/4 tsp. of cinnamon
- 1 banana (ripe), cut in half-inch slices
- 1/2 tsp. of brown sugar
- 1 tbsp. of Chopped nuts (toasted) to taste
- 1 tbsp. of Granola

Directions:

- Combine the brown sugar and cinnamon in a small bowl; leave aside.
- Grease a small baking pan sparingly. Slice the bananas and add them to the pan. The banana should be sprayed with oil before being dusted with cinnamon sugar. For about 4-5 minutes, air fried at 200°C.
- When serving, top the banana with some granola and almonds.

Nutritional values per serving:

Total Calories: 113kcal, **Fats:** 4g, **Carbohydrates:** 19g, **Protein:** 2g

25. Strawberry Turnovers

Ready in: 40 mins.

Serves: 12

Difficulty: easy

Ingredients:

- ¾ cup of finely chopped strawberries
- 1 pie crust (store-bought or homemade)
- 2 tbsp. of sugar
- half lemon zest
- ½ tsp. of vanilla
- 1 tbsp. of cornstarch
- Sugar for sprinkling
- 1 beaten egg

Directions:

- On a floured board, roll out pie dough to a thickness of approximately 1/4". Cut as many dough circles out as you can using the round cookie cutter. Take the leftovers and create a new ball if necessary. Once again, roll out your dough and cut out additional rounds to make a total of 12 pieces.
- In a mixing dish, combine the diced strawberries with vanilla, sugar, lemon zest, & cornstarch. On each round, spoon 1 to 2 Tbsp. of filling.
- Apply egg wash to the circular edges & fold in half. To seal the edges, use a fork. Make 3 slits on the top of turnovers with a sharp knife. The turnovers' tops

are brushed with egg wash and dusted with sugar.

- For a short while, preheat your air fryer to 170°C. Spray nonstick cooking spray on the air fryer basket. Make sure there is space between each turnover for hot air to flow. Put 5–6 turnovers in the air fryer basket and cook for 10 minutes, or till the crust is brownish golden. The pastries may be taken out with tongs and put onto a wire rack or dish to cool. Continue with the remaining pies.

Nutritional values per serving:

Total Calories: 91kcal, **Fats:** 4.7g, **Carbohydrates:** 10.7g, **Proteins:** 1.2g

Chapter 11: Healthy 28-Days Meal Plan

A healthy 28-day meal plan is given below, including all the recipes already mentioned in the previous chapters of this book. According to the recipes present in this book, an everyday meal plan is divided into 3 meals a day.

Week 1:

Day 1:

Daytime:

- Italian-Style Beef Meatballs
- Coconut Shrimp

Evening:

- Coconut Crusted Air Fried Turkey Fingers

Night time:

- Air Fried Meatloaf
- Fried Spicy Green Beans

Day 2:

Daytime:

- Lamb Meatball Kebabs
- Sweet Potato Nachos

Evening:

- Turkey Croquettes

Night time:

- Bacon Hot Dogs
- Rosemary-Garlic Brussels Sprouts

Day 3:

Daytime:

- Steak Bites
- Red Potatoes

Evening:

- Fish & Chips

Night time:

- Juicy Pork Chops

- Delicious Radishes

Day 4:

Daytime:

- Air fried Brats
- Breaded Summer Squash

Evening:

- Crusted Sweet Potato Chicken Nuggets

Night time:

- Thai Air Fried Chicken Meatballs
- Herb & Lemon Cauliflower

Day 5:

Daytime:

- Chicken Cutlets
- Air-Fried Asparagus

Evening:

- Potato Chips

Night time:

- Leg of Lamb
- Green Tomato Stacks

Day 6:

Daytime:

- Lobster Tails with Garlic-Lemon Butter
- Air-Fried Roasted Green Beans

Evening:

- Cauliflower Gnocchi & Marinara Sauce

Night time:

- Spicy Bay Scallops

Day 7:

Daytime:

- Lamb & Cauliflower Rice
- Crispy bacon

Evening:

- Bacon Wrapped Scallops

Night time:

- Crumbed Fish
- Air Fried Vegetables

Week 2:

Day 1:

Daytime:

- Meat Filled Air Fried Pita Pockets
- Crispy Garlic Croutons

Evening:

- Feta Beets

Night time:

- Lamb Spicy Curry Puffs
- Air Fried Cabbage

Day 2:

Daytime:

- Stuffed Turkey Peppers
- Jalapeño Bacon Wrapped Poppers

Evening:

- Cinnamon Apples

Night time:

- Chicken Cordon Bleu
- Air-Fried Okra

Day 3:

Daytime:

- Nashville Delicious Hot Chicken
- Crispy Chickpeas

Evening:

- Zucchini Fries

Night time:

- Mustard Honey Turkey Breast
- Air-Fried Zucchini

Day 4:

Daytime:

- Air Fried Lamb & Potatoes
- Air-Fried Plantains

Evening:

- Chicken Wings

Night time:

- Lemon Pepper Shrimp
- Air-Fried Carrots

Day 5:

Daytime:

- Crispy Parmesan Cod
- Air-Fried Eggplant

Evening:

- Bolognese Zucchini Boats

Night time:

- Paneer Tikka Fry
- Blooming Onions

Day 6:

Daytime:

- Zucchini Pizza
- Air-Fried Broccoli

Evening:

- Onion Rings

Night time:

- Stuffed Okra
- Air-Fried Spaghetti Squash

Day 7:

Daytime:

- Braised Delicious Lamb-shanks
- Crispy Chickpeas

Evening:

- Crab Rangoon

Night time:

- Jamaican Chicken Curry
- Jalapeño Bacon Wrapped Poppers

Week 3:

Day 1:

Daytime:

- Piccata Chicken Pockets
- Blooming Onions

Evening:

- Air Fried Churros

Night time:

- Pork Skewers with Sauce
- Air Fried Cabbage

Day 2:

Daytime:

- Zucchini Filled With Hamburger
- Air-Fried Okra

Evening:

- Egg Rolls

Night time:

- Frozen Pork Meatballs
- Green Tomato Stacks

Day 3:

Daytime:

- Feta Lemon Chicken
- Crispy Garlic Croutons

Evening:

- Stuffed Mushrooms

Night time:

- Healthy Chicken & Veggies
- Air-Fried Plantains

Day 4:

Daytime:

- Mushroom Egg Turkey Burgers
- Air-Fried Asparagus

Evening:

- Pretzel Bites

Night time:

- Rotisserie Chicken
- Herb & Lemon Cauliflower

Day 5:

Daytime:

- Spaghetti & Lamb meatball muffins
- Air-Fried Roasted Green Beans

Evening:

- Pretzel Dogs

Night time:

- Lamb kebab
- Crispy Bacon

Day 6:

Daytime:

- Stuffed Lamb Feta Burgers
- Breaded Summer Squash

Evening:

- Air-Fried Ravioli

Night time:

- Salmon Nuggets
- Delicious Radishes

Day 7:

Daytime:

- Chili Lime Tilapia
- Jalapeño Bacon Wrapped Poppers

Evening:

- Cheeseburger Onion Rings

Night time:

- Swordfish Steak & Mango Citrus Salsa
- Air-Fried Okra

Week 4:

Day 1:

Daytime:

- Air Fried Tofu
- Fried Spicy Green Beans

Evening:

- Sriracha Crispy Spring Rolls

Night time:

- Onion Bites
- Sweet Potato Nachos

Day 2:

Daytime:

- Tandoori Cauliflower
- Crispy Garlic Croutons

Evening:

- Air-Fried Calamari

Night time:

- Beetroot Cutlet
- Air-Fried Plantains

Day 3:

Daytime:

- Crispy Corn Fritters
- Crispy Bacon

Evening:

- Mushroom Roll-Ups
- Fried Spicy Green Beans

Day 7:

Daytime:

Night time:

- Cajun Potatoes
- Herb & Lemon Cauliflower

Day 4:

Daytime:

- Eggplant Parmesan Pasta
- Air Fried Asparagus

Evening:

- Garlic Bread

Night time:

- Kale & Sweet Potato Calzones
- Air-Fried Zucchini

Day 5:

Daytime:

- Stuffed Bitter Gourd
- Air Fried Carrots

Evening:

- Chocolate Donuts

Night time:

- Pumpkin Pie
- Coconut Shrimp

Day 6:

Daytime:

- Italian-Style Beef Meatballs
- Coconut Shrimp

Evening:

- Coconut Crusted Air Fried Turkey Fingers

Night time:

- Air Fried Meatloaf
- Lamb Meatball Kebabs
- Sweet Potato Nachos

Evening:

- Turkey Croquettes

Night time:

- Bacon Hot Dogs
- Rosemary-Garlic Brussels Sprouts

Cooking Measurement Chart

COOKING CONVERSION CHART

Measurement

CUP	ONCES	MILLILITERS	TABLESPOONS
8 cup	64 oz	1895 ml	128
6 cup	48 oz	1420 ml	96
5 cup	40 oz	1180 ml	80
4 cup	32 oz	960 ml	64
2 cup	16 oz	480 ml	32
1 cup	8 oz	240 ml	16
3/4 cup	6 oz	177 ml	12
2/3 cup	5 oz	158 ml	11
1/2 cup	4 oz	118 ml	8
3/8 cup	3 oz	90 ml	6
1/3 cup	2.5 oz	79 ml	5.5
1/4 cup	2 oz	59 ml	4
1/8 cup	1 oz	30 ml	3
1/16 cup	1/2 oz	15 ml	1

Temperature

FAHRENHEIT	CELSIUS
100 °F	37 °C
150 °F	65 °C
200 °F	93 °C
250 °F	121 °C
300 °F	150 °C
325 °F	160 °C
350 °F	180 °C
375 °F	190 °C
400 °F	200 °C
425 °F	220 °C
450 °F	230 °C
500 °F	260 °C
525 °F	274 °C
550 °F	288 °C

Weight

IMPERIAL	METRIC
1/2 oz	15 g
1 oz	29 g
2 oz	57 g
3 oz	85 g
4 oz	113 g
5 oz	141 g
6 oz	170 g
8 oz	227 g
10 oz	283 g
12 oz	340 g
13 oz	369 g
14 oz	397 g
15 oz	425 g
1 lb	453 g

Conclusion

Your body can't effectively handle and use the glucose from your diet if you have diabetes. There are several forms of diabetes, each form with its own origins, but they are all characterised by an excess of glucose in the blood. Insulin and/or medicines are used as treatments. Adopting a healthier diet may help avoid certain kinds of diabetes. You have a lot of options for preventing the onset of diabetes. But if you start to have diabetic symptoms, visit a doctor. Diabetes may be treated and controlled more effectively the earlier it is identified and treated. Your chances of living a long, healthy life increase with how well you can regulate your blood sugar level.

It's crucial to consume the correct quantity of meals each day if you have diabetes. In order to receive the proper quantity of carbohydrates in every meal or snack, the eating plan will contain information on how much to consume. You'll have to discover how to weigh your meals and count carbohydrates. It's also critical to eat at the appropriate times. To prevent having low or high blood sugar levels, you should make plans for frequent, balanced meals. It might be beneficial to have about the same quantity of carbohydrates at each meal. Your eating plan would also show you how to follow it both at home and in restaurants.

Without a doubt, a diabetic person can utilize the air fryer often to prepare healthful meals. The food you choose to cook in an appliance will have a greater impact on its suitability than the equipment itself. You have a fantastic opportunity with the air fryer to prepare healthier cuisine with fewer calories, less acrylamide generation, few Tran's fats, and better nutrient retention. Having said that, the air fryer doesn't miraculously turn harmful meals into healthful treats for our bodies. It's crucial to do an analysis of the food to learn what it contains since the decisions you make could still have an impact on you.

Book 2: Type 2 Diabetes Cookbook For Beginners

365 Days Simple & Quick Recipes with Inexpensive Ingredients to Lower Your Blood Sugar for Diabetics and Pre-Diabetics | Bonus: 28 Days Healthy Meal Plan.

TABLE OF CONTENTS

Introduction

Diabetes is a common disease which leads to metabolic disorders of carbohydrates and water balance.

As a result of that, the pancreatic functions are impaired. It is the pancreas that produces an important hormone called insulin.

Insulin regulates the level of blood sugar that is supplied with food. Without it, the body cannot convert sugar into glucose, and sugar starts accumulating in the body of a person with the disease.

Apart from the pancreas disorders, the water balance is impaired as well. As a result of that, the tissues do not retain water, and the kidneys excrete much fluid.

So what happens when a person has diabetes?

When the condition develops, the body produces too little insulin. At the same time, the level of blood sugar increases and the cells become starved for glucose, which is the main base of energy.

Types Of Diabetes

There are two types of diabetes.

Type 1 diabetes. This condition is also known as insulin-dependent. It usually affects young people under 40. Individuals with type 1 diabetes will need to take insulin injections for the rest of their lives because their body produces antibodies that destroy the beta-cells which produce the hormone.

Type 1 diabetes is hard to cure. However, it is possible to restore pancreatic functions by adhering to a healthy diet. Products with a high glycemic index such as soda, juice and sweets should be excluded.

Type 2 diabetes. this happens as a result of lack of sensitivity of the pancreas cells towards insulin because of the excess of nutrients. People with excess weight are the most susceptible to the disease.

Symptoms & Risk factors

In type 1 diabetes, the list of symptoms can be extensive with both serious and less obvious indicators. Below, I will list the most common symptoms as well as other potential complications of type 1 diabetes:

- **Excessive thirst:** Extreme thirst is one of the less noticeable indicators of type 1 diabetes. It is brought upon by high blood sugar (hyperglycemia).

- **Frequent urination:** Frequent urination is caused by your kidneys failing to process all of the glucose in your blood; this forces your body to attempt to flush out excess glucose through urinating.

- **Fatigue:** Fatigue in type 1 diabetes patients is caused by the body's inability to process glucose for energy.

- **Excessive hunger:** Those suffering from type 1 diabetes often have persistent hunger and increased appetites. This is because the body is desperate for glucose despite its inability to process it without insulin.

- **Cloudy or unclear vision:** Rapid fluctuations in blood sugar levels can lead to cloudy or blurred vision. Those suffering from untreated type 1 diabetes are unable to naturally control their blood sugar levels, making rapid fluctuations a very common occurrence.

- **Rapid weight loss:** Rapid weight loss is probably the most noticeable symptom of type 1 diabetes. As your body starves off glucose, it resorts to breaking down muscle and fat to sustain itself. This can lead to incredibly fast weight loss in type 1 diabetes cases.

- **Ketoacidosis:** Ketoacidosis is a potentially deadly complication of untreated type 1 diabetes. In response to the lack of glucose being fed into your muscles and organs, your body starts breaking down your fat and muscle into an energy source called ketones, which can be burned without the need of insulin. Ketones are usually perfectly fine in normal amounts. But, when your body is starving, it may end up flooding itself with ketones in an attempt to fuel itself; the acidification of your blood

- that follows this influx of acid molecules may lead to more serious conditions, a coma, or death.

In cases of type 2 diabetes, the symptoms tend to be slower to develop, and they tend to be mild early on. Some early symptoms mimic type 1 diabetes and may include:

- **Excessive hunger:** Similar to type 1 diabetes, those of us with type 2 diabetes will feel constant hunger. Again, this is brought on by our bodies looking for fuel because of our inability to process glucose.

- **Fatigue and mental fog:** Depending on the severity of the insulin shortage in type 2 sufferers, they may feel physical fatigue and a mental fogginess during their average day.

- **Frequent urination:** Another symptom of both type 1 and 2 diabetes. Frequent urination is simply your body's way of attempting to rid itself of excess glucose.

- **Dry mouth and constant thirst:** It are unclear what causes dry mouth in diabetic sufferers, but it is tightly linked to high blood sugar levels. Constant thirst is brought on not only by a dry mouth but also by the dehydration that frequent urination causes.

- **Itchy skin:** Itching of the skin, especially around the hands and feet, is a sign of polyneuropathy (diabetic nerve damage). As well as being a sign of potential nerve damage, itching can be a sign of high concentrations of cytokines circulating in your bloodstream; these are inflammatory molecules that can lead to itching. Cytokines are signaling proteins and hormonal regulators that are often released in high amounts before nerve damage.

SYMPTOMS OF TYPE 2 DIABETES

As type 2 diabetes progresses and becomes more serious, the symptoms can become highly uncomfortable and dangerous. Some of these advanced symptoms include:

- **Slow healing of bruises, cuts, and abrasions:** Many people suffering from type 2 diabetes have impaired immune systems due to the lack of energy available to the body. As well as a lack of energy, many diabetics have slowed circulation brought upon by high blood glucose levels. Both of these factors lead to a much slower healing process and far greater risks of infection.

- **Yeast infections:** Women with type 2 diabetes, the chances of yeast infections are far higher than in non-diabetic women. This is due to high blood sugar levels and a lowered immune system response.

- **Neuropathy or numbness:** Long-term high blood sugar levels can lead to severe nerve damage in adults with diabetes. It is believed around 70 percent of people with type 2 diabetes have some form of neuropathy (Hoskins, 2020). Diabetic neuropathy is characterized by a numbness in the extremities, specifically around the feet and fingers.

- **Dark skin patches (acanthosis nigricans):** Some people with type 2 diabetes may have far above normal levels of insulin in their blood, as their body is unable to utilize it due to insulin resistance. This rise of insulin in the bloodstream can lead to some skin cells over reproducing and cause black patches to form on the skin.

Complications

Severe complications of diabetes can be debilitating and deadly. Both type 1 & type 2 diabetes can cause serious neurological, cardiovascular, and optical conditions. Some of the most common complications of advanced diabetes are as follows:

- **Heart attacks:** Diabetes is directly linked to a higher rate of heart attacks in adults. High blood glucose levels damage the cells and nerves around the heart and blood vessels over time, which can cause a plethora of heart diseases to form.

- **Cataracts:** People with diabetes have a nearly 60 percent greater chance of developing cataracts later in life if their diabetes is left unchecked (Diabetes.co.uk, 2019a). Doctors are not sure of the real reason for cataracts forming at a higher rate in diabetes patients, but many believe it has to do with the lower amounts of glucose available to the cells powering our eyes.

- **Peripheral artery disease (PAD):** This is a very common diabetes and This causes decreased blood flow, which leads to serious issues in the lower legs, often resulting in amputation.

- **Diabetic nephropathy:** Diabetic nephropathy happens when high levels of blood glucose damage parts of your kidneys, which is responsible for filtering blood. This causes your kidneys to develop chronic kidney diseases and break down over time, leading to failure.

- **Glaucoma:** Diabetes can cause glaucoma in sufferers due to high blood sugar levels and this directly damages blood vessels in the eyes. When your body attempts to repair these vessels, it may cause glaucoma on the iris where the damage was caused.

10 Tips to Control Diabetes

- **Eat less salt:** Salt can increase your chances of having high blood pressure, which leads to increased chances of heart disease and stroke.

- **Replace sugar:** Replace sugar with zero calorie sweeteners. Cutting out sugar gives you much more control over your blood sugar levels.

- **Cut out alcohol:** Alcohol tends to be high in calories, and if drunk on an empty stomach with insulin medication, it can cause drastic drops in blood sugar.

- **Be physically active:** Physical action decreases your risk of cardiovascular issues and increases your body's natural glucose burn rate.

- **Avoid saturated fats:** Saturated fats like butter and pastries can lead to high cholesterol and blood circulation issues.

- **Use canola or olive oil:** If you need to use oil in your cooking, use canola or olive oil. Both are high in beneficial fatty acids and monounsaturated fat.

- **Drink water:** Water is by far the healthiest drink you can have. Drinking water helps to regulate blood sugar and insulin levels.

- **Make sure you get enough vitamin D:** Vitamin D is a crucial vitamin for controlling blood sugar levels. Eat food high in this vitamin or ask your doctor about supplements.

- **Avoid processed food:** Processed foods tend to be high in vegetable oils, salt, refined grains, or other unhealthy additives.

- **Drink coffee and tea:** Not only are coffee and tea great hunger suppressants for dieters, but they contain important antioxidants that help with protecting cells.

Type 1 vs Type 2 diabetes

Type 1 diabetes is an autoimmune disease. In cases of type 1 diabetes, the immune system attacks cells in the pancreas responsible for insulin production. Although we are unsure what causes this reaction, many experts believe it is brought upon by a gene deficiency or by viral infections that may trigger the disease.

Type 2 diabetes is a metabolic disorder, although research suggests it may warrant reclassification as an autoimmune disease as well. People who grieve from type 2 diabetes have a high resistance to insulin or an inability to produce enough insulin. Professionals believe that type 2 diabetes is a result of a genetic predisposition in many people, which is further aggravated by obesity and other environmental triggers.

Diagnosis

Diabetes diagnosis has come incredibly far in the last few decades. Currently, there are two primary tests for diagnosing diabetes: the fasting plasma glucose (FPG) test and the hemoglobin A1c test.

The FPG test takes your blood sugar levels after an eight-hour fasting period; this helps to show if your body is processing glucose at a healthy rate.

The A1c test shows your blood sugar levels over the last three months. It does this by testing the amount of glucose being carried by the hemoglobin of your red blood cells. Hemoglobin has a lifespan of roughly three months; this allows us to test them to see how long they have been carrying their glucose for and how much they have.

Chapter 1: How to Prevent Type 2 Diabetes

Diabetes mellitus is a disease that affects our metabolism. The predominant characteristic of diabetes is an inability to create or utilize insulin, a hormone that moves sugar from our blood cells into the rest of our bodies' cells. This is crucial for us because we rely on that blood sugar to power our body and provide energy. High blood sugar, if not treated, can lead to serious damage of our eyes, nerves, kidneys, and other major organs. There are 2 main types of diabetes, they are type 1 and type 2, with the second being the most common of the two with over 90 percent of diabetics suffering from it

Insulin resistance is the most popular cause of type 2 diabetes. Because muscle, fat, and liver cells no longer respond to insulin, the pancreas secretes a lot of it in order to keep blood sugar levels in check. Insulin resistance is exacerbated by being overweight and physically sedentary.

Prediabetes and glucose intolerance both cause insulin resistance. Prediabetes affects an estimated 79 million Americans. According to studies, decreasing 7% of your body weight and exercising regularly can reduce your risk of type 2 diabetes by 58 percent. Insulin resistance can be reduced by decreasing weight, exercising regularly, eating carbohydrates in moderation, and eating a nutritious diet once you've been diagnosed with diabetes. As a result, better blood sugar control will be achieved.

Type 2 diabetes is the most common form of the disease in adults. As we age, our cells don't use insulin as well and therefore cannot convert glucose into energy. The condition also increases your risk for serious health risks like heart disease, blindness, kidney failure, amputations and stroke.

The first step in preventing diabetes is to know what the risk factors are.

It all starts with your levels of glucose in the blood. This can be measured by two methods: fasting plasma glucose test and random plasma glucose test.

The number one cause of diabetes is family history: people who have a parent or sibling with type 1 or type 2 diabetes are likely to develop it themselves . If you want to lower your own risk, avoid early pregnancies, limit weight gain during pregnancy and breastfeed for at least two years . Also Know Your Glycemic Index To Help You Lose Weight .

The next step is to start eating right and exercising regularly.

• Eat a balanced diet. Include lean proteins (meat from chicken, fish or other lean sources). These foods provide building blocks for healthy muscles , skin and bones . Also eat a wide variety of foods. A varied diet provides the nutrients your body needs while preventing any known risk factors (such as heart disease) from occurring.

• Limit sugar to no more than 10% of your total daily calories. This limit means that you can eat foods like fruit, vegetables and other carbohydrates (like potatoes and pasta). You can also include some protein in your meals if these foods have little or no carbohydrate .

• Work out each day. The benefits are many: improved blood sugar control , weight-loss, increased energy and lower blood cholesterol levels .

• Reduce the amount of alcohol you drink . Drinking alcohol is a commonly implicated risk factor for diabetes. When alcohol is consumed, glucose levels go up because the liver must break down and store all the alcohol as fat. When this happens, insulin may be less effective at bringing glucose into the cells. This can lead to diabetes and heart disease over time.

• Take aspirin to reduce your risk of heart disease . The benefits are many: reduced blood cholesterol levels , less inflamed blood vessels , possibly fewer strokes , and even better memory . You should take a low-dose aspirin daily to reduce your risk of heart disease.

• Get regular exercise . Aerobic exercise like walking, swimming and dancing is beneficial for everyone but especially for people over 60 years old . There are many forms of aerobic exercises. Some are as simple as walking or stretching; others are more advanced. The American Diabetes Association suggests that you participate in an activity a minimum of 20 minutes three times per week (on nonconsecutive days).

• Get regular blood pressure checks .

• Stay away from tobacco . Smoking can lead to diabetes and is linked with a host of other diseases. Tobacco smoke contains more than 4,000 chemicals , many of which are known to damage a person's health. The nicotine in tobacco also gets into saliva and causes your body to absorb the more harmful chemicals even more rapidly. If you smoke, quit . The best way is to smoke a cigarette that contains only nicotine and no tobacco (such as an electronic cigarette) for a period of at least two weeks .

• Avoid heavy drinking . If you do drink alcohol, limit yourself to only one drink maximum per day (for women) or two drinks max per day (for guys).

• Learn your family history. If your family has diabetes, consult with a doctor who can help you lower your own risk by offering advice about food, physical activity and other factors that influence blood sugar levels and weight. If a parent or sibling has diabetes, it is important to talk with a doctor about whether genetic tests are recommended.

It is advisable to visit the doctor every 6 months for a check up and be aware of all the early symptoms of diabetes.

All in all, type 2 diabetes can be prevented by a balanced diet, regular exercise, weight loss and avoiding heavy drinking.

Chapter 2: Food to Eat

Vegetables

Fresh vegetables never cause harm to anyone. So, adding a meal full of vegetables is the best shot for all diabetic patients. But not all vegetables contain the same amount of macronutrients. Some vegetables contain a high amount of carbohydrates, so those are not suitable for a diabetic diet. We need to use vegetables which contain a low amount of carbohydrates.

1. Cauliflower
2. Spinach
3. Tomatoes
4. Broccoli
5. Lemons
6. Artichoke
7. Garlic
8. Asparagus
9. Spring onions
10. Onions
11. Ginger etc.

Meat

Meat is not on the red list for the diabetic diet. It is fine to have some meat every now and then for diabetic patients. However certain meat types are better than others. For instance, red meat is not a preferable option for such patients. They should consume white meat more often whether it's seafood or poultry. Healthy options in meat are:

1. All fish, i.e., salmon, halibut, trout, cod, sardine, etc.
2. Scallops
3. Mussels
4. Shrimp
5. Oysters etc.

Fruits

Not all fruits are good for diabetes. To know if the fruit is suitable for this diet, it is important to note its sugar content. Some fruits contain a high amount of sugars in the form of sucrose and fructose, and those should be readily avoided. Here is the list of popularly used fruits which can be taken on the diabetic diet:

1. Peaches
2. Nectarines
3. Avocados
4. Apples
5. Berries
6. Grapefruit
7. Kiwi Fruit
8. Bananas
9. Cherries
10. Grapes
11. Orange
12. Pears
13. Plums
14. Strawberries

Nuts and Seeds

Nuts and seeds are perhaps the most enriched edibles, and they contain such a mix of macronutrients which can never harm anyone. So diabetic patients can take the nuts and seeds in their diet without any fear of a glucose spike.

1. Pistachios
2. Sunflower seeds
3. Walnuts
4. Peanuts
5. Pecans
6. Pumpkin seeds
7. Almonds
8. Sesame seeds etc.

Grains

Diabetic patients should also be selective while choosing the right grains for their diet. The idea is to keep the amount of starch as minimum as possible. That is why you won't see any white rice in the list rather it is replaced with more fibrous brown rice.

1. Quinoa
2. Oats
3. Multigrain
4. Whole grains
5. Brown rice
6. Millet
7. Barley
8. Sorghum
9. Tapioca

Fats

Fat intake is the most debated topic as far as the diabetic diet is concerned. As there are diets like ketogenic, which are loaded with fats and still proved effective for diabetic patients. The key is the absence of carbohydrates. In any other situation, the fats are as harmful to diabetics as any normal person. Switching to unsaturated fats is a better option.

1. Sesame oil
2. Olive oil
3. Canola oil
4. Grapeseed oil
5. Other vegetable oils
6. Fats extracted from plant sources.

Diary

Any dairy product which directly or indirectly causes a glucose rise in the blood should not be taken on this diet. other than those, all products are good to use. These items include:

1. Skimmed milk
2. Low-fat cheese
3. Eggs
4. Yogurt

5. Trans fat-free margarine or butter

Sugar Alternatives

Since ordinary sugars or sweeteners are strictly forbidden on a diabetic diet. There are artificial varieties that can add sweetness without raising the level of carbohydrates in the meal. These substitutes are:

1. Stevia
2. Xylitol
3. Natvia
4. Swerve
5. Monk fruit
6. Erythritol

Make sure to substitute them with extra care. The sweetness of each sweetener is entirely different from the table sugar, so add each in accordance with the intensity of their flavor. Stevia is the sweetest of them, and it should be used with more care. In place of 1 cup of sugar, a teaspoon of stevia is enough. All other sweeteners are more or less similar to sugar in their intensity of sweetness.

Foods to Avoid

Knowing a general scheme of diet helps a lot, but it is equally important to be well familiar with the items which have to be avoided. With this list, you can make your diet a hundred% sugar-free. There are many other food items which can cause some harm to a diabetic patient as the sugars do. So, let's discuss them in some detail here.

1. Sugars

Sugar is a big NO-GO for a diabetic diet. Once you are diabetic, you would need to say goodbye to all the natural sweeteners which are loaded with carbohydrates. They contain polysaccharides which readily break into glucose after getting into our body. And the list does not only include table sugars but other items like honey and molasses should also be avoided.

1. White sugar
2. Brown sugar
3. Confectionary sugar
4. Honey
5. Molasses
6. Granulated sugar

Your mind and your body, will not accept the abrupt change. It is recommended to go for a gradual change. It means start substituting it with low carb substitutes in a small amount, day by day.

2. High Fat Dairy Products

Once you are diabetic, you may get susceptible to a number of other fatal diseases including cardiovascular ones. That is why experts strictly recommend avoiding high-fat food products, especially dairy items. The high amount of fat can make your body insulin resistant. So even when you take insulin, it won't be of any use as the body will not work on it.

3. Saturated Animal Fats

Saturated animal fats are not good for anyone, whether diabetic or normal. So, better avoid using them in general. Whenever you are cooking meat, try to trim off all the excess fat. Cooking oils made out of these saturated fats should be avoided. Keep yourself away from any of the animal origin fats.

4. High Carb Vegetables

As discussed above, vegetables with more starch are not suitable for diabetes. These veggies can increase the carbohydrate levels of food. So, omit these from the recipes and enjoy the rest of the less starchy vegetables. Some of the high carb vegetables are:

1. Potatoes
2. Sweet potatoes
3. Yams etc.

5. Cholesterol Rich ingredients

Bad cholesterol or High-density Lipoprotein has the tendency to deposit in different parts of the body. That is why food items having high bad cholesterol are not good for diabetes. Such items should be replaced with the ones with low cholesterol.

6. High Sodium Products

Sodium is related to hypertension and blood pressure. Since diabetes is already the result of a hormonal imbalance in the body, in the presence of excess sodium—another imbalance—a fluid imbalance may occur which a diabetic body cannot tolerate. It adds up to already present complications of the disease. So, avoid using food items with a high amount of sodium. Mainly store packed items, processed foods, and salt all contain sodium, and one should avoid them all. Use only the 'Unsalted' variety of food products, whether it's butter, margarine, nuts, or other items.

7. Sugary Drinks

Cola drinks or other similar beverages are filled with sugars. If you had seen different video presentations showing the amount of the sugars present in a single bottle of soda, you would know how dangerous those are for diabetic patients. They can drastically increase the amount of blood glucose level within 30 minutes of drinking. Fortunately, there are many sugar-free varieties available in the drinks which are suitable for diabetic patients.

8. Sugar Syrups and Toppings

A number of syrups available in the markets are made out of nothing but sugar. Maple syrup is one good example. For a diabetic diet, the patient should avoid such sugary syrups and also stay away from the sugar-rich toppings available in the stores. If you want to use them at all, trust yourself and prepare them at home with a sugar-free recipe.

9. Sweet Chocolate and candies

For diabetic patients, sugar-free chocolates or candies are the best way out. Other processed chocolate bars and candies are extremely damaging to their health, and all of these should be avoided. You can try and prepare healthy bars and candies at home with sugar-free recipes.

10. Alcohol

Alcohol has the tendency to reduce the rate of our metabolism and take away our appetite, which can render a diabetic patient into a very life-threatening condition. Alcohol in a very small amount cannot harm the patient, but the regular or constant intake of alcohol is bad for health and glucose levels.

The importance of insuline

Diabetes is a serious condition caused by a deficiency of insulin. Insulin is a hormone that is necessary for the proper functioning of the body. When a person develops diabetes, the cells in the body do not respond to insulin properly. The result is that the cells do not get the energy and nutrients they need, and then they start to die

Diabetes treatments differ depending on the kind, number, and severity of complications as well as the patient's overall health. Fortunately, diabetes has been studied extensively by the medical community, and as a result, there are numerous resources and treatments accessible.

For type 1 diabetes, insulin supplements are essential. Type 1 diabetics rely on daily insulin injections; some prefer a costlier but easier-to-use insulin pump. Insulin needs in type 1 diabetics will vary throughout the day as they eat and exercise. This means many type 1 diabetics will regularly test their blood sugar levels to assess whether their insulin needs are being met.

Some type 1 diabetics develop insulin resistance after years of injections. This means that oral diabetes medication such as metformin is becoming increasingly more commonly prescribed to type 1 diabetics to help prevent insulin resistance.

In some circumstances, type 2 diabetes can be managed without the need of medication. Many type 2 diabetics individuals can control their blood sugar levels by watching what they eat and doing some modest exercise. The majority of type 2 diabetics are advised to stick to low-fat, high-fiber, low-carbohydrate diets.

Medication is required for some persons with type 2 diabetes. Type 2 diabetes, unlike type 1, does not demand the use of insulin as frequently. Some type 2 diabetics, however, require insulin to complement their pancreas' production.

Metformin is the most widely given type 2 diabetic medication. This prescription medication aids in the reduction of blood glucose levels and the improvement of insulin sensitivity. Other drugs prescribed to type 2 diabetics include sulfonylureas, thiazolidinediones, and meglitinides, which all help increase insulin production or sensitivity.

Causes of Type 2 diabetes

Although some of the causes are completely unclear, even trivial viral infections are recognized, which can affect insulin-producing cells in the pancreas, such as:

- Measles.

- Cytomegalovirus.

- Epstein-Barr.

- Coxsackievirus.

For Type 2 Diabetes, however, the main risk factors are:

- Overweight and obesity.

- Genetic factors: family history increases the risk of developing type 2 diabetes.

- Ethnicity: the highest number of cases is recorded in the populations of sub-Saharan Africa and the middle east and north Africa.

- Environmental factors are especially related to incorrect lifestyles (sedentary lifestyle and obesity).

- Gestational diabetes, which is diabetes that happens during pregnancy.

- Age: type 2 diabetes increases with increasing age, especially above the age of 65.

- Diet high in fat that promotes obesity.

- Alcohol consumption.

- Sedentary lifestyle.

Chapter 3: Antidiabetic Life-Style, Develop Good Habits

We all know that healthy living is key to living well and feeling better. When it comes to diabetes, a healthy lifestyle can help control the condition and make it more manageable. What's an anti-diabetic lifestyle? It's all the things we need to do on a daily basis to keep ourselves in good health, including eating right, getting plenty of exercise, staying at a healthy weight and going easy on stress.

Diabetes is a chronic disorder of the endocrine system that occurs over time when your body cannot produce or respond to insulin. This can lead to excessive blood glucose levels.

The American Diabetes Association estimates that around 29 million Americans have diabetes, which translates into 9% of the population having diabetes.

One of the symptoms of diabetes is high blood glucose levels. This is why people with diabetes need to regularly monitor their blood glucose levels and have a healthy diet, with regular exercise.

Your doctor will recommend that you follow an antidiabetic lifestyle. It will give you stable blood glucose levels, which means fewer or no possible complications.

An anti-diabetic lifestyle consists of 4 parts: healthy food habits, physical activity pattern , monitoring blood glucose levels and self care . Following this lifestyle can help to prevent weight gain and reduce your risk for further complications from diabetes. It can also help to improve your overall health and help you live longer.

If you already have diabetes, an anti-diabetic lifestyle can help manage your blood glucose levels and prevent or delay complications. It is a healthy choice for all people with diabetes, regardless of the type.

In order to maintain this healthy lifestyle and achieve stable blood glucose levels, you will need to manage your weight, avoid unhealthy habits like smoking and alcohol abuse and follow the medical advice given by your doctor.

The following tips will prepare you for an anti-diabetic lifestyle:

Choose healthy food:

Eat a variety of foods like fruits, vegetables, whole grains, legumes and nuts that are rich in fiber.

Avoid junk food :

Choose healthy snacks and drinks like vegetables, fruits and milk.

Eat breakfast :

Breakfast is very important to stay healthy. Eat 'real' foods as often as you can . A small amount of protein at each meal has been shown to reduce the risk of heart disease in people with diabetes. Get most of your calories from carbohydrate foods (e.g., whole grain breads, cereals, pasta, potatoes) rather than fat or cholesterol-rich foods (e.g., ice cream).

Avoid excess fat:

Try to take the first meal of the day with a carbohydrate-rich food and avoid eating large amounts of fat and protein.

Avoid alcohol consumption:

If you drink alcohol, try to have it in moderation . Avoid excessive consumption of alcohol. Drinking too much can raise your blood glucose levels.

Monitor your weight:

If you are overweight, lose some weight to improve your health and lower your blood sugar. If you are underweight, try to gain some weight to reduce risk for complications from diabetes.So all it takes is living in a more natural and efficient way and you will reduce your chances of getting sick or becoming chronically ill. In fact, there are many other studies that prove not only that yoga can help cure chronic illnesses but it can also prevent them from happening in the first place. A recent study conducted by the University of Kansas looked at the untapped benefits of yoga, and found that it has 'miraculous' effects on reducing stress and disease. They added: 'Yoga is a therapeutic style that combines physical postures, controlled breathing techniques, meditation and contemplation. It is often thought to be an ancient Indian practice, but it has been included in the revised American Heritage Dictionary since the 1970s.' The NIH (National Institute of Health) and VA (Veterans Administration) have collaborated to create a series of health care resources for veterans called Warrior Yoga™. These resources are intended to help veterans manage their stress through yoga, and are credited for helping decrease instances of PTSD (Post Traumatic Stress Disorder) by 40% in the first year of participation.

Chapter 4: Appendix
Measurements Conversion

GAS MARK	DEGREE CELCIUS °C	DEGREE CELSIUS FAN °C	DEGREE FAHRENHEIT °F
1/4	110°C	100°C	225 °F
1/2	120°C	110°C	250 °F
1	140°C	120°C	275 °F
2	150°C	130°C	300 °F
3	170°C	140°C	325 °F
4	180°C	160°C	350 °F
5	190 °C	170°C	375 °F
6	200 °C	180°C	400 °F
7	220 °C	200°C	425 °F
8	230 °C	210°C	450 °F
9	240 °C	220°C	475 °F
10	260 °C	240°C	500 °F

Volume Conversions

Metric	Imperial	US Cups
250ml	8 fl oz	1 cup
180ml	6 fl oz	¾ cup
150 ml	5fl oz	⅔ cup
120ml	4 fl oz	½ cup
75ml	2 ½ fl oz	⅓ cup
60ml	2 fl oz	¼ cup
30 ml	1 fl oz	⅛ cup
15ml	½ fl oz	1 tablespoon

Grams	Pounds & Ounces
10 g	0.25 oz
20 g	0.75 oz
25 g	1 oz
40 g	1.50 oz
50 g	2 oz
60 g	2.5 oz
75 g	3 oz
110 g	4 oz
125 g	4.5 oz
150 g	5 oz
175 g	6 oz
200 g	7 oz
225 g	8 oz
250 g	9 oz
350 g	12 oz
450 g	1 lb
700 g	1 lb 8oz
900 g	2 lb
1.35 kg	3lb

Chapter 5: Recipes

Breakfast Recipes

1. Bacon and Chicken Garlic Wrap

Preparation Time: 15 minutes

Cooking Time: 10 minutes

Servings: 4

Ingredients

- 1 chicken fillet, cut into small cubes
- 8-9 thin slices bacon, cut to fit cubes
- 6 garlic cloves, minced

Directions:

1. Preheat your oven to 400 degrees F
2. Line a baking tray with aluminum foil
3. Add minced garlic to a bowl and rub each chicken piece with it
4. Wrap bacon piece around each garlic chicken bite
5. Secure with toothpick
6. Transfer bites to the baking sheet, keeping a little bit of space between them
7. Bake for about 15-20 minutes until crispy
8. Serve and enjoy!

Nutrition: Calories: 260 Fat: 19g Carbs: 5g Protein: 22g Sugar: 12g; Fiber: 3g; Sodium: 187mg

2. Salty Macadamia Chocolate Smoothie

Preparation Time: 5 minutes

Cooking Time: Nil

Servings: 1

Ingredients

- 2 tablespoons macadamia nuts, salted
- 1/3 cup chocolate whey protein powder, low carb

- 1 cup almond milk, unsweetened

Directions:

1. Add the listed ingredients to your blender and blend until you have a smooth mixture
2. Chill and enjoy it!

Nutrition: Calories: 165 Fat: 2g Carbs: 1g Protein: 12g Sugar: 8 g; Fiber: 4g; Sodium: 192mg

3. Buckwheat grouts breakfast bowl

Preparation time: 5 minutes, plus overnight to soak

Cooking time: 10 to 12 minutes

Servings: 4

Ingredients:

- 3 cups skim milk
- 1 cup buckwheat grouts
- ¼ cup chia seeds
- 2 teaspoons vanilla extract
- 1/2 teaspoon ground cinnamon
- Pinch salt
- 1 cup water
- 1/2 cup unsalted pistachios
- 2 cups sliced fresh strawberries
- ¼ cup cacao nibs (optional)

Directions:

1. In a large bowl, stir together the milk, groats, chia seeds, vanilla, cinnamon, and salt. Cover and refrigerate overnight.
2. The next morning, transfer the soaked mixture to a medium pot and add the water. Bring to a boil over medium-high heat, reduce the heat to maintain a simmer, and cook for 10 to 12 minutes, until the buckwheat is tender and thickened.

3. Transfer to bowls and serve, topped with the pistachios, strawberries, and cacao nibs (if using).

Nutrition: Calories: 340; Fat: 8g; Carbs: 52g; Protein: 15g; Sugar: 14g; Fiber: 10g; Sodium: 140mg

4. Peach muesli bake

Preparation time: 10 minutes

Cooking time: 40 minutes

Servings: 4

Ingredients:

- Nonstick cooking spray
- 2 cups skim milk
- 1 1/2 cups rolled oats
- 1/2 cup chopped walnuts
- 1 large egg
- 2 tablespoons maple syrup
- 1 teaspoon ground cinnamon
- 1 teaspoon baking powder
- 1/2 teaspoon salt
- 2 to 3 peaches, sliced

Directions:

1. Preheat the oven to 375f. Spray a 9-inch square baking dish with cooking spray. Set aside.

2. In a large bowl, stir together the milk, oats, walnuts, egg, maple syrup, cinnamon, baking powder, and salt. Spread half the mixture in the prepared baking dish.

3. Place half the peaches in a single layer across the oat mixture.

4. Spread the remaining oat mixture over the top. Add the remaining peaches in a thin layer over the oats. Bake for 35 to 40 minutes, uncovered, until thickened and browned.

5. Cut into 8 squares and serve warm.

Nutrition: Calories: 138; Fat: 3g; Protein: 6g; Carbs: 22g; Sugar: 10g; Fiber: 3g; Sodium: 191mg

5. Steel-cut oatmeal bowl with fruit and nuts

Preparation time: 5 minutes

Cooking time: 20 minutes

Servings: 4

Ingredients:

- 1 cup steel-cut oats
- 2 cups almond milk
- ¾ cup water
- 1 teaspoon ground cinnamon
- ¼ teaspoon salt
- 2 cups chopped fresh fruit, such as blueberries, strawberries, raspberries, or peaches
- 1/2 cup chopped walnuts
- ¼ cup chia seeds

Directions:

1. In a medium saucepan over medium-high heat, combine the oats, almond milk, water, cinnamon, and salt. Bring to a boil, reduce the heat to low, and simmer for 15 to 20 minutes, until the oats are softened and thickened.

2. Top each bowl with 1/2 cup of fresh fruit, 2 tablespoons of walnuts, and 1 tablespoon of chia seeds before serving.

Nutrition: Calories: 288; Fat: 11g; Protein: 10g; Carbs: 38g; Sugar: 7g; Fiber: 10g; Sodium: 329mg

6. Whole-grain dutch baby pancake

Preparation time: 5 minutes

Cooking time: 25 minutes

Servings: 4

Ingredients:

- 2 tablespoons coconut oil

- 1/2 cup whole-wheat flour
- ¼ cup skim milk
- 3 large eggs
- 1 teaspoon vanilla extract
- 1/2 teaspoon baking powder
- ¼ teaspoon salt
- ¼ teaspoon ground cinnamon
- Powdered sugar, for dusting

Directions:

1. Preheat the oven to 400f.
2. Put the coconut oil in a medium oven-safe skillet, and place the skillet in the oven to melt the oil while it preheats.
3. In a blender, combine the flour, milk, eggs, vanilla, baking powder, salt, and cinnamon. Process until smooth.
4. Carefully remove the skillet from the oven and tilt to spread the oil around evenly.
5. Pour the batter into the skillet and return it to the oven for 23 to 25 minutes, until the pancake puffs and lightly browns.
6. Remove, dust lightly with powdered sugar, cut into 4 wedges, and serve.

Nutrition: Calories: 195; Fat: 11g; Protein: 8g; Carbs: 16g; Sugar: 1g; Fiber: 2g; Sodium: 209mg

7. Mushroom, zucchini, and onion frittata

Preparation time: 10 minutes

Cooking time: 20 minutes

Servings: 4

Ingredients:

- 1 tablespoon extra-virgin olive oil
- 1/2 onion, chopped
- 1 medium zucchini, chopped
- 1 1/2 cups sliced mushrooms

- 6 large eggs, beaten
- 2 tablespoons skim milk
- Salt
- Freshly ground black pepper
- 1 ounce feta cheese, crumbled

Directions:

1. Preheat the oven to 400f.
2. In a medium oven-safe skillet over medium-high heat, heat the olive oil.
3. Add the onion and sauté for 3 to 5 minutes, until translucent.
4. Add the zucchini and mushrooms, and cook for 3 to 5 more minutes, until the vegetables are tender.
5. Meanwhile, in a small bowl, whisk the eggs, milk, salt, and pepper. Pour the mixture into the skillet, stirring to combine, and transfer the skillet to the oven. Cook for 7 to 9 minutes, until set.
6. Sprinkle with the feta cheese, and cook for 1 to 2 minutes more, until heated through.
7. Remove, cut into 4 wedges, and serve.

Nutrition: Calories: 178; Fat: 13g; Protein: 12g; Carbs: 5g; Sugar: 3g; Fiber: 1g; Sodium: 234mg

8. Berry-oat breakfast bars

Preparation time: 10 minutes

Cooking time: 25 minutes

Servings: 2

Ingredients:

- 2 cups fresh raspberries or blueberries
- 2 tablespoons sugar
- 2 tablespoons freshly squeezed lemon juice
- 1 tablespoon cornstarch
- 1 1/2 cups rolled oats
- 1/2 cup whole-wheat flour

- 1/2 cup walnuts
- ¼ cup chia seeds
- ¼ cup extra-virgin olive oil
- ¼ cup honey
- 1 large egg

Directions:

1. Preheat the oven to 350f.

2. In a small saucepan over medium heat, stir together the berries, sugar, lemon juice, and cornstarch. Bring to a simmer. Reduce the heat and simmer for 2 to 3 minutes, until the mixture thickens.

3. In a food processor or high-speed blender, combine the oats, flour, walnuts, and chia seeds. Process until powdered. Add the olive oil, honey, and egg. Pulse a few more times, until well combined. Press half of the mixture into a 9-inch square baking dish.

4. Spread the berry filling over the oat mixture. Add the remaining oat mixture on top of the berries. Bake for 25 minutes, until browned.

5. Let cool completely, cut into 12 pieces, and serve. Store in a covered container for up to 5 days.

Nutrition: Calories: 201; Fat: 10g; Protein: 5g; Carbs: 26g; Sugar: 9g; Fiber: 5g; Sodium: 8mg

9. Spinach and cheese quiche

Preparation time: 10 minutes, plus 10 minutes to rest

Cooking time: 50 minutes

Servings: 4

Ingredients:

- Nonstick cooking spray
- 8 ounces yukon gold potatoes, shredded
- 1 tablespoon plus 2 teaspoons extra-virgin olive oil, divided
- 1 teaspoon salt, divided
- Freshly ground black pepper
- 1 onion, finely chopped
- 1 (10-ounce) bag fresh spinach
- 4 large eggs
- 1/2 cup skim milk
- 1 ounce gruyère cheese, shredded

Directions:

1. Preheat the oven to 350f. Spray a 9-inch pie dish with cooking spray. Set aside.

2. In a small bowl, toss the potatoes with 2 teaspoons of olive oil, 1/2 teaspoon of salt, and season with pepper. Press the potatoes into the bottom and sides of the pie dish to form a thin, even layer. Bake for 20 minutes, until golden brown. Remove from the oven and set aside to cool.

3. In a large skillet over medium-high heat, heat the remaining 1 tablespoon of olive oil.

4. Add the onion and sauté for 3 to 5 minutes, until softened.

5. By handfuls, add the spinach, stirring between each addition, until it just starts to wilt before adding more. Cook for about 1 minute, until it cooks down.

6. In a medium bowl, whisk the eggs and milk. Add the gruyère, and season with the remaining 1/2 teaspoon of salt and some pepper. Fold the eggs into the spinach. Pour the mixture into the pie dish and bake for 25 minutes, until the eggs are set.

7. Let rest for 10 minutes before serving.

Nutrition: Calories: 445; Fat: 14g; Protein: 19g; Carbs: 68g; Sugar: 6g; Fiber: 7g; Sodium: 773mg

10. Spicy Jalapeno Popper Deviled Eggs

Preparation Time: 5 minutes

Cooking Time: 5 minutes

Servings: 4

Ingredients

- 4 large whole eggs, hardboiled
- 2 tablespoons Keto-Friendly mayonnaise
- ¼ cup cheddar cheese, grated
- 2 slices bacon, cooked and crumbled
- 1 jalapeno, sliced

Directions:

1. Cut eggs in half, remove the yolk and put them in bowl
2. Lay egg whites on a platter
3. Mix in remaining ingredients and mash them with the egg yolks
4. Transfer yolk mix back to the egg whites
5. Serve and enjoy!

Nutrition: Calories: 176 Fat: 14g Carbs: 0.7g Protein: 10g Sugar: 10g; Fiber: 7g; Sodium: 653mg

11. Blueberry breakfast cake

Preparation time: 15 minutes

Cooking time: 45 minutes

Servings: 4

Ingredients:

For the topping

- ¼ cup finely chopped walnuts
- 1/2 teaspoon ground cinnamon
- 2 tablespoons butter, chopped into small pieces
- 2 tablespoons sugar

For the cake

- Nonstick cooking spray
- 1 cup whole-wheat pastry flour
- 1 cup oat flour
- ¼ cup sugar
- 2 teaspoons baking powder
- 1 large egg, beaten
- 1/2 cup skim milk
- 2 tablespoons butter, melted
- 1 teaspoon grated lemon peel
- 2 cups fresh or frozen blueberries

Directions:

To make the topping

In a small bowl, stir together the walnuts, cinnamon, butter, and sugar. Set aside.

To make the cake

1. Preheat the oven to 350f. Spray a 9-inch square pan with cooking spray. Set aside.
2. In a large bowl, stir together the pastry flour, oat flour, sugar, and baking powder.
3. Add the egg, milk, butter, and lemon peel, and stir until there are no dry spots.
4. Stir in the blueberries, and gently mix until incorporated. Press the batter into the prepared pan, using a spoon to flatten it into the dish.
5. Sprinkle the topping over the cake.
6. Bake for 40 to 45 minutes, until a toothpick inserted into the cake comes out clean, and serve.

Nutrition: Calories: 177; Fat: 7g; Protein: 4g; Carbs: 26g; Sugar: 9g; Fiber: 3g; Sodium: 39mg

12. Lovely Porridge

Preparation Time: 15 minutes

Cooking Time: Nil

Servings: 2

Ingredients

- 2 tablespoons coconut flour
- 2 tablespoons vanilla protein powder
- 3 tablespoons Golden Flaxseed meal
- 1 and 1/2 cups almond milk, unsweetened
- Powdered erythritol

Directions:

1. Take a bowl and mix in flaxseed meal, protein powder, coconut flour and mix well
2. Add mix to the saucepan (placed over medium heat)
3. Add almond milk and stir, let the mixture thicken
4. Add your desired amount of sweetener and serve
5. Enjoy!

Nutrition: Calories: 259 Fat: 13g Carbs: 5g Protein: 16g Sugar: 14g; Fiber: 10g; Sodium: 140mg

13. Basil and Tomato Baked Eggs

Preparation Time: 10 minutes

Cooking Time: 15 minutes

Servings: 4

Ingredients

- 1 garlic clove, minced
- 1 cup canned tomatoes
- ¼ cup fresh basil leaves, roughly chopped
- 1/2 teaspoon chili powder
- 1 tablespoon olive oil
- 4 whole eggs
- Salt and pepper to taste

Directions:

1. Preheat your oven to 375 degrees F
2. Take a small baking dish and grease with olive oil

3. Add garlic, basil, tomatoes chili, olive oil into a dish and stir
4. Crackdown eggs into a dish, keeping space between the two
5. Sprinkle the whole dish with salt and pepper
6. Place in oven and cook for 12 minutes until eggs are set and tomatoes are bubbling
7. Serve with basil on top
8. Enjoy!

Nutrition: Calories: 235 Fat: 16g Carbs: 7g Protein: 14g Sugar: 18g; Fiber: 13g; Sodium: 142mg

14. Whole-grain pancakes

Preparation time: 10 minutes

Cooking time: 15 minutes

Servings: 4

Ingredients:

- 2 cups whole-wheat pastry flour
- 4 teaspoons baking powder
- 2 teaspoons ground cinnamon
- 1/2 teaspoon salt
- 2 cups skim milk, plus more as needed
- 2 large eggs
- 1 tablespoon honey
- Nonstick cooking spray
- Maple syrup, for serving
- Fresh fruit, for serving

Directions:

1. In a large bowl, stir together the flour, baking powder, cinnamon, and salt.
2. Add the milk, eggs, and honey, and stir well to combine. If needed, add more milk, 1 tablespoon at a time, until there are no dry spots and you has a pourable batter.

3. Heat a large skillet over medium-high heat, and spray it with cooking spray.

4. Using a ¼-cup measuring cup, scoop 2 or 3 pancakes into the skillet at a time. Cook for a couple of minutes, until bubbles form on the surface of the pancakes, flip, and cook for 1 to 2 minutes more, until golden brown and cooked through. Repeat with the remaining batter.

5. Serve topped with maple syrup or fresh fruit.

Nutrition: Calories: 392; Fat: 4g; Protein: 15g; Carbs: 71g; Sugar: 11g; Fiber: 9g; Sodium: 396mg

15. Whole-grain breakfast cookies

Preparation time: 20 minutes

Cooking time: 10 minutes

Servings: 18 cookies

Ingredients:

- 2 cups rolled oats
- 1/2 cup whole-wheat flour
- ¼ cup ground flaxseed
- 1 teaspoon baking powder
- 1 cup unsweetened applesauce
- 2 large eggs
- 2 tablespoons vegetable oil
- 2 teaspoons vanilla extract
- 1 teaspoon ground cinnamon
- 1/2 cup dried cherries
- ¼ cup unsweetened shredded coconut
- 2 ounces dark chocolate, chopped

Directions:

1. Preheat the oven to 350f.

2. In a large bowl, combine the oats, flour, flaxseed, and baking powder. Stir well to mix.

3. In a medium bowl, whisk the applesauce, eggs, vegetable oil, vanilla, and cinnamon. Pour the wet mixture into the dry mixture, and stir until just combined.

4. Fold in the cherries, coconut, and chocolate. Drop tablespoon-size balls of dough onto a baking sheet. Bake for 10 to 12 minutes, until browned and cooked through.

5. Let cool for about 3 minutes, remove from the baking sheet, and cool completely before serving. Store in an airtight container for up to 1 week.

Nutrition: Calories: 136; Fat: 7g; Protein: 4g; Carbs: 14g; Sugar: 4g; Fiber: 3g; Sodium: 11mg

16. Cinnamon and Coconut Porridge

Preparation Time: 5 minutes

Cooking Time: 5 minutes

Servings: 4

Ingredients

- 2 cups of water
- 1 cup 36% heavy cream
- 1/2 cup unsweetened dried coconut, shredded
- 2 tablespoons flaxseed meal
- 1 tablespoon butter
- 1 and 1/2 teaspoon stevia
- 1 teaspoon cinnamon
- Salt to taste
- Toppings as blueberries

Directions:

1. Add the listed ingredients to a small pot, mix well

2. Transfer pot to stove and place it over medium-low heat

3. Bring to mix to a slow boil

4. Stir well and remove the heat

5. Divide the mix into equal servings and let them sit for 10 minutes

6. Top with your desired toppings and enjoy!

Nutrition: Calories: 171 Fat: 16g Carbs: 6g Protein: 2g Sugar: 14g; Fiber: 10g; Sodium: 140mg

17. An Omelet of Swiss chard

Preparation Time: 5 minutes

Cooking Time: 5 minutes

Servings: 4

Ingredients

- 4 eggs, lightly beaten
- 4 cups Swiss chard, sliced
- 2 tablespoons butter
- 1/2 teaspoon garlic salt
- Fresh pepper

Directions:

1. Take a non-stick frying pan and place it over medium-low heat

2. Once the butter melts, add Swiss chard and stir cook for 2 minutes

3. Pour egg into the pan and gently stir them into Swiss chard

4. Season with garlic salt and pepper

5. Cook for 2 minutes

6. Serve and enjoy!

Nutrition: Calories: 260 Fat: 21g Carbs: 4g Protein: 14g Sugar: 12g; Fiber: 8g; Sodium: 137mg

18. Cheesy Low-Carb Omelet

Preparation Time: 5 minutes

Cooking Time: 5 minutes

Servings: 3

Ingredients

- 2 whole eggs
- 1 tablespoon water

- 1 tablespoon butter
- 3 thin slices salami
- 5 fresh basil leaves
- 5 thin slices, fresh ripe tomatoes
- 2 ounces fresh mozzarella cheese
- Salt and pepper as needed

Directions:

1. Take a small bowl and whisk in eggs and water

2. Take a non-stick Sauté pan and place it over medium heat, add butter and let it melt

3. Pour egg mixture and cook for 30 seconds

4. Spread salami slices on half of egg mix and top with cheese, tomatoes, basil slices

5. Season with salt and pepper according to your taste

6. Cook for 2 minutes and fold the egg with the empty half

7. Cover and cook on LOW for 1 minute

8. Serve and enjoy!

Nutrition: Calories: 451 Fat: 36g Carbs: 3g Protein:33g Sugar: 11g; Fiber: 14g; Sodium: 134mg

19. Yogurt and Kale Smoothie

Preparation Time: 10 minutes

Servings: 1

Ingredients:

- 1 cup whole milk yogurt
- 1 cup baby kale greens
- 1 pack stevia
- 1 tablespoon MCT oil
- 1 tablespoon sunflower seeds
- 1 cup of water

Directions:

1. Add listed ingredients to the blender
2. Blend until you have a smooth and creamy texture
3. Serve chilled and enjoy!

Nutrition: Calories: 329 Fat: 26g Carbs: 15g Protein: 11g Sugar: 10g; Fiber: 15g; Sodium: 144mg

20.   Grilled Chicken Platter

Preparation Time: 5 minutes

Cooking Time: 10 minutes

Servings: 3

Ingredients

- 3 large chicken breast, sliced half lengthwise
- 10-ounce spinach, frozen and drained
- 3-ounce mozzarella cheese, part-skim
- 1/2 a cup of roasted red peppers, cut in long strips
- 1 teaspoon of olive oil
- 2 garlic cloves, minced
- Salt and pepper as needed

Directions:

1. Preheat your oven to 400 degrees Fahrenheit
2. Slice 3 chicken breast lengthwise
3. Take a non-stick pan and grease with cooking spray
4. Bake for 2-3 minutes each side
5. Take another skillet and cook spinach and garlic in oil for 3 minutes
6. Place chicken on an oven pan and top with spinach, roasted peppers, and mozzarella
7. Bake until the cheese melted
8. Enjoy!

Nutrition: Calories: 195 Fat: 7g Protein: 30g Sugar: 14g; Fiber: 10g; Sodium: 140mg

21.   Parsley Chicken Breast

Preparation Time: 10 minutes

Cooking Time: 40 minutes

Servings: 4

Ingredients

- 1 tablespoon dry parsley
- 1 tablespoon dry basil
- 4 chicken breast halves, boneless and skinless
- 1/2 teaspoon salt
- 1/2 teaspoon red pepper flakes, crushed
- 2 tomatoes, sliced

Directions:

1. Preheat your oven to 350 degrees F
2. Take a 9x13 inch baking dish and grease it up with cooking spray
3. Sprinkle 1 tablespoon of parsley, 1 teaspoon of basil and spread the mixture over your baking dish
4. Arrange the chicken breast halves over the dish and sprinkle garlic slices on top
5. Take a small bowl and add 1 teaspoon parsley, 1 teaspoon of basil, salt, basil, red pepper and mix well. Pour the mixture over the chicken breast
6. Top with tomato slices and cover, bake for 25 minutes
7. Remove the cover and bake for 15 minutes more
8. Serve and enjoy!

Nutrition: Calories: 150 Fat: 4g Carbs: 4g Protein: 25g Sugar: 17g; Fiber: 7g; Sodium: 133mg

22.   Mustard Chicken

Preparation Time: 10 minutes

Cooking Time: 40 minutes

Servings: 2

Ingredients

- 4 chicken breasts
- 1/2 cup chicken broth
- 3-4 tablespoons mustard
- 3 tablespoons olive oil
- 1 teaspoon paprika
- 1 teaspoon chili powder
- 1 teaspoon garlic powder

Directions:

1. Take a small bowl and mix mustard, olive oil, paprika, chicken broth, garlic powder, chicken broth, and chili
2. Add chicken breast and marinate for 30 minutes
3. Take a lined baking sheet and arrange the chicken
4. Bake for 35 minutes at 375 degrees Fahrenheit
5. Serve and enjoy!

Nutrition: Calories: 531 Fat: 23g Carbs: 10g Protein: 64g Sugar: 14g; Fiber: 12g; Sodium: 148mg

23.   Balsamic Chicken

Preparation Time: 10 minutes

Cooking Time: 25 minutes

Servings: 3

Ingredients

- 6 chicken breast halves, skinless and boneless
- 1 teaspoon garlic salt
- Ground black pepper
- 2 tablespoons olive oil
- 1 onion, thinly sliced
- 14 and 1/2 ounces tomatoes, diced
- 1/2 cup balsamic vinegar

- 1 teaspoon dried basil
- 1 teaspoon dried oregano
- 1 teaspoon dried rosemary
- 1/2 teaspoon dried thyme

Directions:

1. Season both sides of your chicken breasts thoroughly with pepper and garlic salt
2. Take a skillet and place it over medium heat
3. Add some oil and cook your seasoned chicken for 3-4 minutes per side until the breasts are nicely browned
4. Add some onion and cook for another 3-4 minutes until the onions are browned
5. Pour the diced up tomatoes and balsamic vinegar over your chicken and season with some rosemary, basil, thyme, and rosemary
6. Simmer the chicken for about 15 minutes until they are no longer pink
7. Take an instant-read thermometer and check if the internal temperature gives a reading of 165 degrees Fahrenheit
8. If yes, then you are good to go!

Nutrition: Calories: 196 Fat: 7g Carbs: 7g Protein: 23g Sugar: 10g; Fiber: 12g; Sodium: 142mg

24.   Greek Chicken Breast

Preparation Time: 10 minutes

Cooking Time: 25 minutes

Servings: 4

Ingredients

- 4 chicken breast halves, skinless and boneless
- 1 cup extra virgin olive oil
- 1 lemon, juiced
- 2 teaspoons garlic, crushed

- 1 and 1/2 teaspoons black pepper
- 1/3 teaspoon paprika

Directions:

1. Cut 3 slits in the chicken breast
2. Take a small bowl and whisk in olive oil, salt, lemon juice, garlic, paprika, pepper and whisk for 30 seconds
3. Place chicken in a large bowl and pour marinade
4. Rub the marinade all over using your hand
5. Refrigerate overnight
6. Pre-heat grill to medium heat and oil the grate
7. Cook chicken in the grill until center is no longer pink
8. Serve and enjoy!

Nutrition: Calories: 644 Fat: 57g Carbs: 2g Protein: 27g Sugar: 14g; Fiber: 10g; Sodium: 140mg

25. Chipotle Lettuce Chicken

Preparation Time: 10 minutes

Cooking Time: 25 minutes

Servings: 3

Ingredients

- 1 pound chicken breast, cut into strips
- Splash of olive oil
- 1 red onion, finely sliced
- 14 ounces tomatoes
- 1 teaspoon chipotle, chopped
- 1/2 teaspoon cumin
- Pinch of sugar
- Lettuce as needed
- Fresh coriander leaves
- Jalapeno chilies, sliced
- Fresh tomato slices for garnish

- Lime wedges

Directions:

1. Take a non-stick frying pan and place it over medium heat
2. Add oil and heat it up
3. Add chicken and cook until brown
4. Keep the chicken on the side
5. Add tomatoes, sugar, chipotle, cumin to the same pan and simmer for 25 minutes until you have a nice sauce
6. Add chicken into the sauce and cook for 5 minutes
7. Transfer the mix to another place
8. Use lettuce wraps to take a portion of the mixture and serve with a squeeze of lemon
9. Enjoy!

Nutrition: Calories: 332 Fat: 15g Carbs: 13g Protein: 34g Sugar: 12g; Fiber: 10g; Sodium: 140mg

26. Stylish Chicken-Bacon Wrap

Preparation Time: 5 minutes

Cooking Time: 50 minutes

Servings: 3

Ingredients

- 8 ounces lean chicken breast
- 6 bacon slices
- 3 ounces shredded cheese
- 4 slices ham

Directions:

1. Cut chicken breast into bite-sized portions
2. Transfer shredded cheese onto ham slices
3. Roll up chicken breast and ham slices in bacon slices

4. Take a skillet and place it over medium heat

5. Add olive oil and brown bacon for a while

6. Remove rolls and transfer to your oven

7. Bake for 45 minutes at 325 degrees F

8. Serve and enjoy!

Nutrition: Calories: 275 Fat: 11g Carbs: 0.5g Protein: 40g Sugar: 14g; Fiber: 10g; Sodium: 138mg

27. Healthy Cottage Cheese Pancakes

Preparation Time: 10 minutes

Cooking Time: 15

Servings: 1

Ingredients:

- 1/2 cup of Cottage cheese (low-fat)
- 1/3 cup (approx. 2 egg whites) Egg whites
- ¼ cup of Oats
- 1 teaspoon of Vanilla extract
- Olive oil cooking spray
- 1 tablespoon of Stevia (raw)
- Berries or sugar-free jam (optional)

Directions:

1. Begin by taking a food blender and adding in the egg whites and cottage cheese. Also add in the vanilla extract, a pinch of stevia, and oats. Palpitate until the consistency is well smooth.

2. Get a nonstick pan and oil it nicely with the cooking spray. Position the pan on low heat.

3. After it has been heated, scoop out half of the batter and pour it on the pan. Cook for about 21/2 minutes on each side.

4. Position the cooked pancakes on a serving plate and cover with sugar-free jam or berries.

Nutrition: Calories: 205 Fat: 1.5 g, Protein: 24.5 g, Carbs: 19 g Sugar: 14g; Fiber: 10g; Sodium: 140mg

28. Avocado Lemon Toast

Preparation Time: 10 minutes

Cooking Time: 13 minutes

Servings: 2

Ingredients:

- Whole-grain bread: 2 slices
- Fresh cilantro (chopped): 2 tablespoons
- Lemon zest: ¼ teaspoon
- Fine sea salt: 1 pinch

Directions:

1. Begin by getting a medium-sized mixing bowl and adding in the avocado. Make use of a fork to crush it properly.

2. Then, add in the cilantro, lemon zest, lemon juice, sea salt, and cayenne pepper. Mix well until combined.

3. Toast the bread slices in a toaster until golden brown. It should take about 3 minutes.

4. Top the toasted bread slices with the avocado mixture and finalize by drizzling with chia seeds.

Nutrition: Calories: 72 Protein: 3.6 g Fat: 1.2 g Carbs: 11.6 g Sugar: 12g; Fiber: 8g; Sodium: 139mg

29. Healthy Baked Eggs

Preparation Time: 10 minutes

Cooking Time: 1 hour

Servings: 3

Ingredients:

- Olive oil: 1 tablespoon
- Garlic: 2 cloves
- Eggs: 8 large
- Sea salt: 1/2 teaspoon

- Shredded mozzarella cheese (medium-fat): 3 cups
- Olive oil spray
- Onion (chopped): 1 medium
- Spinach leaves: 8 ounces
- Half-and-half: 1 cup
- Black pepper: 1 teaspoon
- Feta cheese: 1/2 cup

Directions:

1. Begin by heating the oven to 375F.

2. Get a glass baking dish and grease it with olive oil spray. Arrange aside.

3. Now take a nonstick pan and pour in the olive oil. Position the pan on allows heat and allows it heat.

4. Immediately you are done, toss in the garlic, spinach, and onion. Prepare for about 5 minutes. Arrange aside.

5. You can now Get a large mixing bowl and add in the half, eggs, pepper, and salt. Whisk thoroughly to combine.

6. Put in the feta cheese and chopped mozzarella cheese (reserve 1/2 cup of mozzarella cheese for later).

7. Put the egg mixture and prepared spinach to the prepared glass baking dish. Blend well to combine. Drizzle the reserved cheese over the top.

8. Bake the egg mix for about 45 minutes.

9. Extract the baking dish from the oven and allow it to stand for 10 minutes.

10. Dice and serve!

Nutrition: Calories: 323 Fat: 22.3 g Protein: 22.6 g Carbs: 7.9 g Sugar: 14g; Fiber: 12g; Sodium: 144mg

30.   Quick Low-Carb Oatmeal

Preparation Time: 10 minutes

Cooking Time: 15 minutes

Servings: 2

Ingredients:

- Almond flour: 1/2 cup
- Flax meal: 2 tablespoons
- Cinnamon (ground): 1 teaspoon
- Almond milk (unsweetened): 1 1/2 cups
- Salt: as per taste
- Chia seeds: 2 tablespoons
- Liquid stevia: 10: 15 drops
- Vanilla extract: 1 teaspoon

Directions:

1. Begin by taking a large mixing bowl and adding in the coconut flour, almond flour, ground cinnamon, flax seed powder, and chia seeds. Mix properly to combine.

2. Position a stockpot on a low heat and add in the dry ingredients. Also add in the liquid stevia, vanilla extract, and almond milk. Mix well to combine.

3. Prepare the flour and almond milk for about 4 minutes. Add salt if needed.

4. Move the oatmeal to a serving bowl and top with nuts, seeds, and pure and neat berries.

Nutrition: Calories: Protein: 11.7 g Fat: 24.3 g Carbs: 16.7 g Sugar: 13g; Fiber: 12g; Sodium: 135mg

31.   Tofu and Vegetable Scramble

Preparation Time: 10 minutes

Cooking Time: 15 minutes

Servings: 2

Ingredients:

- Firm tofu (drained): 16 ounces
- Sea salt: 1/2 teaspoon
- Garlic powder: 1 teaspoon
- Fresh coriander: for garnishing
- Red onion: 1/2 medium

- Cumin powder: 1 teaspoon
- Lemon juice: for topping
- Green bell pepper: 1 medium
- Garlic powder: 1 teaspoon
- Fresh coriander: for garnishing
- Red onion: 1/2 medium
- Cumin powder: 1 teaspoon
- Lemon juice: for topping

Directions:

1. Begin by preparing the ingredients. For this, you are to extract the seeds of the tomato and green bell pepper. Shred the onion, bell pepper, and tomato into small cubes.

2. Get a small mixing bowl and position the fairly hard tofu inside it. Make use of your hands to break the fairly hard tofu. Arrange aside.

3. Get a nonstick pan and add in the onion, tomato, and bell pepper. Mix and cook for about 3 minutes.

4. Put the somewhat hard crumbled tofu to the pan and combine well.

5. Get a small bowl and put in the water, turmeric, garlic powder, cumin powder, and chili powder. Combine well and stream it over the tofu and vegetable mixture.

6. Allow the tofu and vegetable crumble cook with seasoning for 5 minutes. Continuously stir so that the pan is not holding the ingredients.

7. Drizzle the tofu scramble with chili flakes and salt. Combine well.

8. Transfer the prepared scramble to a serving bowl and give it a proper spray of lemon juice.

9. Finalize by garnishing with pure and neat coriander. Serve while hot!

Nutrition: Calories: 238 Carbs: 16.6 g Fat: 11 g Sugar: 13g; Fiber: 11g; Sodium: 142mg

32. Breakfast Smoothie Bowl with Fresh Berries

Preparation Time: 10 minutes

Cooking Time: 5 minutes

Servings: 2

Ingredients

- 1 heaping cup organic frozen mixed berries
- 1 small ripe banana (sliced and frozen)
- 2-3 Tbsp light coconut or **almond milk**

Directions:

1. Begin by taking a blender and adding in the mashed ice cubes. Allow them to rest for about 30 seconds.

2. Then put in the almond milk, shredded strawberries, pea protein powder, psyllium husk powder, coconut oil, and liquid stevia. Blend well until it turns into a smooth and creamy puree.

3. Vacant the prepared smoothie into 2 glasses.

4. Cover with coconut flakes and pure and neat strawberries.

Nutrition: Calories: 166 Fat: 9.2 g Carbs: 4.1 g Protein: 17.6 g Sugar: 11g; Fiber: 13g; Sodium: 136mg

33. Chia and Coconut Pudding

Preparation Time: 10 minutes

Cooking Time: 5 minutes

Servings: 2

Ingredients:

- Light coconut milk: 7 ounces
- Liquid stevia: 3 to 4 drops
- Kiwi: 1
- Chia seeds: ¼ cup

- Clementine: 1
- Shredded coconut (unsweetened)

Directions:

1. Begin by getting a mixing bowl and putting in the light coconut milk. Set in the liquid stevia to sweeten the milk. Combine well.

2. Put the chia seeds to the milk and whisk until well-combined. Arrange aside.

3. Scrape the clementine and carefully extract the skin from the wedges. Leave aside.

4. Also, scrape the kiwi and dice it into small pieces.

5. Get a glass vessel and gather the pudding. For this, position the fruits at the bottom of the jar; then put a dollop of chia pudding. Then spray the fruits and then put another layer of chia pudding.

6. Finalize by garnishing with the rest of the fruits and chopped coconut.

Nutrition: Calories: 201 Protein: 5.4 g Fat: 10 g Carbs: 22.8 g Sugar: 14g; Fiber: 10g; Sodium: 140mg

34.   Tomato and Zucchini Sauté

Preparation Time: 10 minutes

Cooking Time: 43 minutes

Servings: 3

Ingredients:

- Vegetable oil: 1 tablespoon
- Tomatoes (chopped): 2
- Green bell pepper (chopped): 1
- Black pepper (freshly ground): as per taste
- Onion (sliced): 1
- Zucchini (peeled): 2 pounds and cut into 1-inch-thick slices
- Salt: as per taste

- Uncooked white rice: ¼ cup

Directions:

1. Begin by getting a nonstick pan and putting it over low heat. Stream in the oil and allow it to heat through.

Put in the onions and sauté for about 3 minutes.

2. Then pour in the zucchini and green peppers. Mix well and spice with black pepper and salt.

3. Reduce the heat and cover the pan with a lid. Allow the veggies cook on low for 5 minutes.

4. While you're done, put in the water and rice. Place the lid back on and cook on low for 20 minutes.

Nutrition: Calories: 94 Fat: 2.8 g Protein: 3.2 g Carbs: 16.1 g Sugar: 16g; Fiber: 9g; Sodium: 133mg

35.   Steamed Kale with Mediterranean Dressing

Preparation Time: 10 minutes

Cooking Time: 25 minutes

Servings: 3

Ingredients:

- Kale (chopped): 12 cups
- Olive oil: 1 tablespoon
- Soy sauce: 1 teaspoon
- Pepper (freshly ground): as per taste
- Lemon juice: 2 tablespoons
- Garlic (minced): 1 tablespoon
- Salt: as per taste

Directions:

1. Get a gas steamer or an electric steamer and fill the bottom pan with water. If making use of a gas steamer, position it on high heat. Making use of an electric steamer, place it on the highest setting.

2. Immediately the water comes to a boil, put in the shredded kale and cover with

a lid. Boil for about 8 minutes. The kale should be tender by now.

3. During the kale is boiling, take a big mixing bowl and put in the olive oil, lemon juice, soy sauce, garlic, pepper, and salt. Whisk well to mix.

4. Now toss in the steamed kale and carefully enclose into the dressing. Be assured the kale is well-coated.

5. Serve while it's hot!

Nutrition: Calories: 91 Fat: 3.5 g Protein: 4.6 g Carbs: 14.5 g Sugar: 14.2g; Fiber: 12.5g; Sodium: 139mg

Lunch Recipes

36. Cauliflower Rice with Chicken

Preparation Time: 15 Minutes

Cooking Time: 15 Minutes

Servings: 4

Ingredients

- 1/2 large cauliflower
- 3/4 cup cooked meat
- 1/2 bell pepper
- 1 carrot
- 2 ribs celery
- 1 tbsp. stir fry sauce (low carb)
- 1 tbsp. extra virgin olive oil
- Salt and pepper to taste

Directions

1. Chop cauliflower in a processor to "rice." Place in a bowl.

2. Properly chop all vegetables in a food processor into thin slices.

3. Add cauliflower and other plants to WOK with heated oil. Fry until all veggies are tender.

4. Add chopped meat and sauce to the wok and fry 10 Minutes.

5. Serve.

6. This dish is very mouth-watering!

Nutrition: Calories 200 Protein 10 g Fat 12 g Carbs 10 g Sugar: 14g; Fiber: 12g; Sodium: 143mg

37. Turkey with Fried Eggs

Preparation Time: 10 Minutes

Cooking Time: 20 Minutes Servings: 4

Ingredients

- 4 large potatoes
- 1 cooked turkey thigh
- 1 large onion (about 2 cups diced)
- butter
- Chile flakes
- 4 eggs
- salt to taste
- pepper to taste

Directions

1. Rub the cold boiled potatoes on the coarsest holes of a box grater. Dice the turkey.

2. Cook the onion in as much unsalted butter as you feel comfortable with until it's just fragrant and translucent.

3. Add the rubbed potatoes and a cup of diced cooked turkey, salt and pepper to taste, and cook 20 Minutes.

4. Top each with a fried egg. Yummy!

Nutrition: Calories 170 Protein 19 g Fat 7 g Carbs 6 g Sugar: 11g; Fiber: 13g; Sodium: 128mg

38.   Sweet Potato, Kale, and White Bean Stew

Preparation time: 15 minutes

Cooking time: 25 minutes

Servings: 4

Ingredients:

- 1 (15-ounce) can low-sodium cannellini beans, rinsed and drained, divided
- 1 tablespoon olive oil
- 1 medium onion, chopped
- 2 garlic cloves, minced
- 2 celery stalks, chopped
- 3 medium carrots, chopped
- 2 cups low-sodium vegetable broth
- 1 teaspoon apple cider vinegar
- 2 medium sweet potatoes (about 1¼ pounds)
- 2 cups chopped kale
- 1 cup shelled edamame
- ¼ cup quinoa
- 1 teaspoon dried thyme
- 1/2 teaspoon cayenne pepper
- 1/2 teaspoon salt
- ¼ teaspoon freshly ground black pepper

Directions:

1. Put half the beans into a blender and blend until smooth. Set aside.
2. In a large soup pot over medium heat, heat the oil. When the oil is shining, include the onion and garlic, and cook until the onion softens and the garlic is sweet, about 3 minutes. Add the celery and carrots, and continue cooking until the vegetables soften, about 5 minutes.
3. Add the broth, vinegar, sweet potatoes, unblended beans, kale, edamame, and quinoa, and bring the mixture to a boil. Reduce the heat and simmer until the vegetables soften, about 10 minutes.
4. Add the blended beans, thyme, cayenne, salt, and black pepper, increase the heat to medium-high, and bring the mixture to a boil. Reduce the heat and simmer, uncovered, until the flavors combine, about 5 minutes.
5. Into each of 4 containers, scoop 1¾ cups of stew.

Nutrition: Calories: 373; Fat: 7g; Protein: 15g; Carbs: 65g; Fiber: 15g; Sugar: 13g; Sodium: 540mg

39.   Slow Cooker Two-Bean Sloppy Joes

Preparation time: 10 minutes

Cooking time: 6 hours

Servings: 4

Ingredients:

- 1 (15-ounce) can low-sodium black beans
- 1 (15-ounce) can low-sodium pinto beans
- 1 (15-ounce) can no-salt-added diced tomatoes
- 1 medium green bell pepper, cored, seeded, and chopped
- 1 medium yellow onion, chopped
- ¼ cup low-sodium vegetable broth
- 2 garlic cloves, minced
- 2 servings (¼ cup) meal prep barbecue sauce or bottled barbecue sauce
- ¼ teaspoon salt
- ¼ teaspoon freshly ground black pepper
- 4 whole-wheat buns

Directions:

1. In a slow cooker, combine the black beans, pinto beans, diced tomatoes, bell pepper, onion, broth, garlic, meal prep barbecue sauce, salt, and black pepper. Stir the ingredients, then cover and cook on low for 6 hours.

2. Into each of 4 containers, spoon 1¼ cups of sloppy joe mix. Serve with 1 whole-wheat bun.

3. Storage: place airtight containers in the refrigerator for up to 1 week. To freeze, place freezer-safe containers in the freezer for up to 2 months. To defrost, refrigerate overnight. To reheat individual portions, microwave uncovered on high for 2 to 21/2 minutes. Alternatively, reheat the entire dish in a saucepan on the stove top. Bring the sloppy joes to a boil, then reduce the heat and simmer until heated through, 10 to 15 minutes. Serve with a whole-wheat bun.

Nutrition: Calories: 392; Fat: 3g; Protein: 17g; Carbs: 79g; Fiber: 19g; Sugar: 15g; Sodium: 759mg

40.   Lighter Eggplant Parmesan

Preparation time: 15 minutes

Cooking time: 35 minutes

Servings: 4

Ingredients:

- Nonstick cooking spray

- 3 eggs, beaten

- 1 tablespoon dried parsley

- 2 teaspoons ground oregano

- 1/8 teaspoon freshly ground black pepper

- 1 cup panko bread crumbs, preferably whole-wheat

- 1 large eggplant (about 2 pounds)

- 5 servings (21/2 cups) chunky tomato sauce or jarred low-sodium tomato sauce

- 1 cup part-skim mozzarella cheese

- ¼ cup grated parmesan cheese

Directions:

1. Preheat the oven to 450f. Coat a baking sheet with cooking spray.

2. In a medium bowl, whisk together the eggs, parsley, oregano, and pepper.

3. Pour the panko into a separate medium bowl.

4. Slice the eggplant into ¼-inch-thick slices. Dip each slice of eggplant into the egg mixture, shaking off the excess. Then dredge both sides of the eggplant in the panko bread crumbs. Place the coated eggplant on the prepared baking sheet, leaving a 1/2-inch space between each slice.

5. Bake for about 15 minutes until soft and golden brown. Remove from the oven and set aside to slightly cool.

6. Pour 1/2 cup of chunky tomato sauce on the bottom of an 8-by-15-inch baking dish. Using a spatula or the back of a spoon spread the tomato sauce evenly. Place half the slices of cooked eggplant, slightly overlapping, in the dish, and top with 1 cup of chunky tomato sauce, 1/2 cup of mozzarella and 2 tablespoons of grated parmesan. Repeat the layer, ending with the cheese.

7. Bake uncovered for 20 minutes until the cheese is bubbling and slightly browned.

8. Remove from the oven and allow cooling for 15 minutes before dividing the eggplant equally into 4 separate containers.

Nutrition: Calories: 333; Fat: 14g; Protein: 20g; Carbs: 35g; Fiber: 11g; Sugar: 15g; Sodium: 994mg

41. Coconut-Lentil Curry

Preparation time: 15 minutes

Cooking time: 35 minutes

Servings: 4

Ingredients:

- 1 tablespoon olive oil
- 1 medium yellow onion, chopped
- 1 garlic clove, minced
- 1 medium red bell pepper, diced
- 1 (15-ounce) can green or brown lentils, rinsed and drained
- 2 medium sweet potatoes, washed, peeled, and cut into bite-size chunks (about 1¼ pounds)
- 1 (15-ounce) can no-salt-added diced tomatoes
- 2 tablespoons tomato paste
- 4 teaspoons curry powder
- 1/8 teaspoon ground cloves
- 1 (15-ounce) can light coconut milk
- ¼ teaspoon salt
- 2 pieces whole-wheat naan bread, halved, or 4 slices crusty bread

Directions:

1. In a large saucepan over medium heat, heat the olive oil. When the oil is shimmering, add both the onion and garlic and cook until the onion softens and the garlic is sweet, for about 3 minutes.

2. Add the bell pepper and continue cooking until it softens, about 5 minutes more. Add the lentils, sweet potatoes, tomatoes, tomato paste, curry powder, and cloves, and bring the mixture to a boil. Reduce the heat to medium-low, cover, and simmer until the potatoes are softened, about 20 minutes.

3. Add the coconut milk and salt, and return to a boil. Reduce the heat and simmer until the flavors combine, about 5 minutes.

4. Into each of 4 containers, spoon 2 cups of curry.

5. Enjoy each serving with half of a piece of naan bread or 1 slice of crusty bread.

Nutrition: Calories: 559; Fat: 16g; Protein: 16g; Carbs: 86g; Fiber: 16g; Sugar: 18g; Sodium: 819mg

42. Stuffed Portobello with Cheese

Preparation time: 15 minutes

Cooking time: 25 minutes

Servings: 4

Ingredients:

- 4 Portobello mushroom caps
- 1 tablespoon olive oil
- 1/2 teaspoon salt, divided
- ¼ teaspoon freshly ground black pepper, divided
- 1 cup baby spinach, chopped
- 1 1/2 cups part-skim ricotta cheese
- 1/2 cup part-skim shredded mozzarella cheese
- ¼ cup grated parmesan cheese
- 1 garlic clove, minced
- 1 tablespoon dried parsley
- 2 teaspoons dried oregano
- 4 teaspoons unseasoned bread crumbs, divided
- 4 servings (4 cups) roasted broccoli with shallots

Directions:

1. Preheat the oven to 375f. Line a baking sheet with aluminum foil.

2. Brush the mushroom caps with the olive oil, and sprinkle with ¼ teaspoon salt and 1/8 teaspoon pepper. Put the

mushroom caps on the prepared baking sheet and bake until soft, about 12 minutes.

3. In a medium bowl, mix together the spinach, ricotta, mozzarella, parmesan, garlic, parsley, oregano, and the remaining ¼ teaspoon of salt and 1/8 teaspoon of pepper.

4. Spoon 1/2 cup of cheese mixture into each mushroom cap, and sprinkle each with 1 teaspoon of bread crumbs. Return the mushrooms to the oven for an additional 8 to 10 minutes until warmed through.

5. Remove from the oven and allow the mushrooms to cool for about 10 minutes before placing each in an individual container. Add 1 cup of roasted broccoli with shallots to each container.

Nutrition: Calories: 419; Fat: 30g; Protein: 23g; Carbs: 19g; Fiber: 2g; Sugar: 3g; Sodium: 790mg

43.   Lighter Shrimp Scampi

Preparation time: 15 minutes

Cooking time: 15 minutes

Servings: 4

Ingredients:

- 1 1/2 pounds large peeled and deveined shrimp

- ¼ teaspoon salt

- 1/8 teaspoon freshly ground black pepper

- 2 tablespoons olive oil

- 1 shallot, chopped

- 2 garlic cloves, minced

- ¼ cup cooking white wine

- Juice of 1/2 lemon (1 tablespoon)

- 1/2 teaspoon sriracha

- 2 tablespoons unsalted butter, at room temperature

- ¼ cup chopped fresh parsley

- 4 servings (6 cups) zucchini noodles with lemon vinaigrette

Directions:

1. Season the shrimp with the salt and pepper.

2. In a medium saucepan over medium heat, heat the oil. Add the shallot and garlic, and cook until the shallot softens and the garlic is fragrant, about 3 minutes. Add the shrimp, cover, and cook until opaque, 2 to 3 minutes on each side. Using a slotted spoon, transfer the shrimp to a large plate.

3. Add the wine, lemon juice, and sriracha to the saucepan, and stir to combine. Bring the mixture to a boil, then reduce the heat and simmer until the liquid is reduced by about half, 3 minutes. Add the butter and stir until melted, about 3 minutes. Return the shrimp to the saucepan and toss to coat. Add the parsley and stir to combine.

4. Into each of 4 containers, place 1 1/2 cups of zucchini noodles with lemon vinaigrette, and top with ¾ cup of scampi.

Nutrition: Calories: 364; Fat: 21g; Protein: 37g; Carbs: 10g; Fiber: 2g; Sugar: 6g; Sodium: 557mg

44.   Maple-Mustard Salmon

Preparation time: 10 minutes, plus 30 minutes marinating time

Cooking time: 20 minutes

Servings: 4

Ingredients:

- Nonstick cooking spray

- 1/2 cup 100% maple syrup

- 2 tablespoons Dijon mustard

- ¼ teaspoon salt

- 4 (5-ounce) salmon fillets
- 4 servings (4 cups) roasted broccoli with shallots
- 4 servings (2 cups) parleyed whole-wheat couscous

Directions:

1. Preheat the oven to 400f. Line a baking sheet with aluminum foil and coat with cooking spray.
2. In a medium bowl, whisk together the maple syrup, mustard, and salt until smooth.
3. Put the salmon fillets into the bowl and toss to coat. Cover and place in the refrigerator to marinate for at least 30 minutes and up to overnight.
4. Shake off excess marinade from the salmon fillets and place them on the prepared baking sheet, leaving a 1-inch space between each fillet. Discard the extra marinade.
5. Bake for about 20 minutes until the salmon is opaque and a thermometer inserted in the thickest part of a fillet reads 145f.
6. Into each of 4 resealable containers, place 1 salmon fillet, 1 cup of roasted broccoli with shallots, and 1/2 cup of parleyed whole-wheat couscous.

Nutrition: Calories: 601; Fat: 29g; Protein: 36g; Carbs: 51g; Fiber: 3g; Sugar: 23g; Sodium: 610mg

45. Chicken Salad with Grapes and Pecans

Preparation Time: 15 Minutes

Cooking Time: 5 Minutes

Servings: 4

Ingredients:

- 1/3 cup unsalted pecans, chopped
- 10 ounces cooked skinless, boneless chicken breast or rotisserie chicken, finely chopped
- 1/2 medium yellow onion, finely chopped
- 1 celery stalk, finely chopped
- ¾ cup red or green seedless grapes, halved
- ¼ cup light mayonnaise
- ¼ cup nonfat plain Greek yogurt
- 1 tablespoon Dijon mustard
- 1 tablespoon dried parsley
- ¼ teaspoon salt
- 1/8 teaspoon freshly ground black pepper
- 1 cup shredded romaine lettuce
- 4 (8-inch) whole-wheat pitas

Directions:

1. Heat a small skillet over medium-low heat to toast the pecans. Cook the pecans until fragrant, about 3 minutes. Remove from the heat and set aside to cool.
2. In a medium bowl, mix the chicken, onion, celery, pecans, and grapes.
3. In a small bowl, whisk together the mayonnaise, yogurt, mustard, parsley, salt, and pepper. Spoon the sauce over the chicken mixture and stir until well combined.
4. Into each of 4 containers, place ¼ cup of lettuce and top with 1 cup of chicken salad. Store the pitas separately until ready to serve.
5. When ready to eat, stuff the serving of salad and lettuce into 1 pita.

Nutrition: Calories 163 Fat 4.2 g Carbs 22.5 g Fiber 6.3 g Sugar 2.3 g Protein 9.2 g Sodium 861 mg

46.   Roasted Vegetables

Preparation time: 14 minutes

Cooking time: 17 minutes

Servings: 3

Ingredients:

- 4 Tbsp. olive oil, reserve some for greasing
- 2 heads, large garlic, tops sliced off
- 2 large eggplants/aubergine, tops removed, cubed
- 2 large shallots, peeled, quartered
- 1 large carrot, peeled, cubed
- 1 large parsnips, peeled, cubed
- 1 small green bell pepper, deseeded, ribbed, cubed
- 1 small red bell pepper, deseeded, ribbed, cubed
- ½ pound Brussels sprouts, halved, do not remove cores
- 1 sprig, large thyme, leaves picked
- sea salt, coarse-grained

For garnish

- 1 large lemon, halved, ½ squeezed, ½ sliced into smaller wedges
- ⅛ cup fennel bulb, minced

Directions:

1. From 425°F or 220°C preheat oven for at least 5 minutes before using.

2. Line deep roasting pan with aluminum foil; lightly grease with oil. Tumble in bell peppers, Brussels sprouts, carrots, eggplants, garlic, parsnips, rosemary leaves, shallots, and thyme. Add a pinch of sea salt; drizzle in remaining oil and lemon juice. Toss well to combine.

3. Cover roasting pan with a sheet of aluminum foil. Place this on middle rack of oven. Bake for 20 to 30 minutes. Remove aluminum foil. Roast, for another 5 to 10 minutes, or until some vegetables brown at the edges. Remove roasting pan from oven. Cool slightly before ladling equal portions into plates.

4. Garnish with fennel and a wedge of lemon. Squeeze lemon juice on top of dish before eating.

Nutrition: Calories: 270 Fat: 8g Carbs: 42g Fiber: 5g Sugar: 3g Protein: 6g Sodium 320 mg

47.   Millet Pilaf

Preparation time: 10 minutes

Cooking time: 15 minutes

Servings: 4

Ingredients:

- 1 cup millet
- 2 tomatoes, rinsed, seeded, and chopped
- 1¾ cups filtered water
- 2 tablespoons extra-virgin olive oil
- ¼ cup chopped dried apricot
- Zest of 1 lemon
- Juice of 1 lemon
- ½ cup fresh parsley, rinsed and chopped
- Himalayan pink salt
- Freshly ground black pepper

Directions:

1. In an electric pressure cooker, combine the millet, tomatoes, and water. Lock the lid into place, select Manual and High Pressure, and cook for 7 minutes.

2. When the beep sounds, quick release the pressure by pressing Cancel and twisting the steam valve to the Venting position. Carefully remove the lid.

3. Stir in the olive oil, apricot, lemon zest, lemon juice, and parsley. Taste, season with salt and pepper, and serve.

Nutrition: Calories 203 Fat 41.2 g Carbs 29.5 g Fiber 16.3 g Sugar 29.3 g Protein 19.2 g Sodium 154mg

48.   Sweet and Sour Onions

Preparation time: 10 minutes

Cooking time: 11 minutes

Servings: 4

Ingredients:

- 4 large onions, halved
- 2 garlic cloves, crushed
- 3 cups vegetable stock
- 1 ½ tablespoon balsamic vinegar
- ½ teaspoon Dijon mustard
- 1 tablespoon sugar

Directions:

1. Combine onions and garlic in a pan. Fry for 3 minutes, or till softened.
2. Pour stock, vinegar, Dijon mustard, and sugar. Bring to a boil.
3. Reduce heat. Cover and let the combination simmer for 10 minutes.
4. Get rid of from heat. Continue stirring until the liquid is reduced and the onions are brown. Serve.

Nutrition: Calories 343 Fat 51.2 g Carbs 22.5 g Fiber 6.3 g Sugar 2.3 g Protein 9.2 g Sodium 135mg

49.   Sautéed Apples and Onions

Preparation time: 14 minutes

Cooking time: 16 minutes

Servings: 3

Ingredients:

- 2 cups dry cider
- 1 large onion, halved
- 2 cups vegetable stock
- 4 apples, sliced into wedges
- Pinch of salt
- Pinch of pepper

Directions:

1. Combine cider and onion in a saucepan. Bring to a boil until the onions are cooked and liquid almost gone.
2. Pour the stock and the apples. Season with salt and pepper. Stir occasionally. Cook for about 10 minutes or until the apples are tender but not mushy. Serve.

Nutrition: Calories 163 Fat 4.2 g Carbs 22.5 g Fiber 6.3 g Sugar 2.3 g Protein 9.2 g Sodium 112mg

50.   Zucchini Noodles with Portabella Mushrooms

Preparation time: 14 minutes

Cooking time: 16 minutes

Servings: 3

Ingredients:

- 1 zucchini, processed into spaghetti-like noodles
- 3 garlic cloves, minced
- 2 white onions, thinly sliced
- 1 thumb-sized ginger, julienned
- 1 lb. chicken thighs
- 1 lb. portabella mushrooms, sliced into thick slivers
- 2 cups chicken stock
- 3 cups water
- Pinch of sea salt, add more if needed
- Pinch of black pepper, add more if needed
- 2 tsp. sesame oil
- 4 Tbsp. coconut oil, divided
- ¼ cup fresh chives, minced, for garnish

Directions:

1. Pour 2 tablespoons of coconut oil into a large saucepan. Fry mushroom slivers in batches for 5 minutes or until seared brown. Set aside. Transfer these to a plate.

2. Sauté the onion, garlic, and ginger for 3 minutes or until tender. Add in chicken thighs, cooked mushrooms, chicken stock, water, salt, and pepper stir mixture well. Bring to a boil.

3. Decrease gradually the heat and allow simmering for 20 minutes or until the chicken is forking tender. Tip in sesame oil.

4. Serve by placing an equal amount of zucchini noodles into bowls. Ladle soup and garnish with chives.

Nutrition: Calories 163 Fat 4.2 g Carbs 22.5 g Fiber 6.3 g Sugar 2.3 g Protein 9.2 g Sodium 130mg

51. Grilled Tempeh with Pineapple

Preparation time: 12 minutes

Cooking time: 16 minutes

Servings: 3

Ingredients:

- 10 oz. tempeh, sliced
- 1 red bell pepper, quartered
- 1/4 pineapple, sliced into rings
- 6 oz. green beans
- 1 tbsp. coconut aminos
- 2 1/2 tbsp. orange juice, freshly squeeze
- 1 1/2 tbsp. lemon juice, freshly squeezed
- 1 tbsp. extra virgin olive oil
- 1/4 cup hoisin sauce

Directions:

1. Blend together the olive oil, orange and lemon juices, coconut aminos or soy sauce, and hoisin sauce in a bowl. Add the diced tempeh and set aside.

2. Heat up the grill or place a grill pan over medium high flame. Once hot, lift the marinated tempeh from the bowl with a pair of tongs and transfer them to the grill or pan.

3. Grille for 2 to 3 minutes, or until browned all over.

4. Grill the sliced pineapples alongside the tempeh, then transfer them directly onto the serving platter.

5. Place the grilled tempeh beside the grilled pineapple and cover with aluminum foil to keep warm.

6. Meanwhile, place the green beans and bell peppers in a bowl and add just enough of the marinade to coat.

7. Prepare the grill pan and add the vegetables. Grill until fork tender and slightly charred.

8. Transfer the grilled vegetables to the serving platter and arrange artfully with the tempeh and pineapple. Serve at once.

Nutrition: Calories 173 Fat 9.2 g Carbs 22.5 g Fiber 6.3 g Sugar 2.3 g Protein 9.2 g Sodium 105mg

52. Courgettes In Cider Sauce

Preparation time: 13 minutes

Cooking time: 17 minutes

Servings: 3

Ingredients:

- 2 cups baby courgettes
- 3 tablespoons vegetable stock
- 2 tablespoons apple cider vinegar
- 1 tablespoon light brown sugar
- 4 spring onions, finely sliced

- 1 piece fresh gingerroot, grated
- 1 teaspoon corn flour
- 2 teaspoons water

Directions:

1. Bring a pan with salted water to a boil. Add courgettes. Bring to a boil for 5 minutes.

2. Meanwhile, in a pan, combine vegetable stock, apple cider vinegar, brown sugar, onions, gingerroot, lemon juice and rind, and orange juice and rind. Take to a boil. Lower the heat and allow simmering for 3 minutes.

3. Mix the corn flour with water. Stir well. Pour into the sauce. Continue stirring until the sauce thickens.

4. Drain courgettes. Transfer to the serving dish. Spoon over the sauce. Toss to coat courgettes. Serve.

Nutrition: Calories 343 Fat 4.2 g Carbs 22.5 g Fiber 6.3 g Sugar 2.3 g Protein 9.2 g Sodium 135mg

53.   Baked Mixed Mushrooms

Preparation time: 8 minutes

Cooking time: 20 minutes

Servings: 3

Ingredients:

- 2 cups mixed wild mushrooms
- 1 cup chestnut mushrooms
- 2 cups dried porcini
- 2 shallots
- 4 garlic cloves
- 3 cups raw pecans
- ½ bunch fresh thyme
- 1 bunch flat-leaf parsley
- 2 tablespoons olive oil
- 2 fresh bay leaves
- 1 ½ cups stale bread

Directions:

1. Remove skin and finely chop garlic and shallots. Roughly chop the wild mushrooms and chestnut mushrooms. Pick the leaves of the thyme and tear the bread into small pieces. Put inside the pressure cooker.

2. Place the pecans and roughly chop the nuts. Pick the parsley leaves and roughly chop.

3. Place the porcini in a bowl then add 300ml of boiling water. Set aside until needed.

4. Heat oil in the pressure cooker. Add the garlic and shallots. Cook for 3 minutes while stirring occasionally.

5. Drain porcini and reserve the liquid. Add the porcini into the pressure cooker together with the wild mushrooms and chestnut mushrooms. Add the bay leaves and thyme.

6. Position the lid and lock in place. Put to high heat and bring to high pressure. Adjust heat to stabilize. Cook for 10 minutes. Adjust taste if necessary.

7. Transfer the mushroom mixture into a bowl and set aside to cool completely.

8. Once the mushrooms are completely cool, add the bread, pecans, a pinch of black pepper and sea salt, and half of the reserved liquid into the bowl. Mix well. Add more reserved liquid if the mixture seems dry.

9. Add more than half of the parsley into the bowl and stir. Transfer the mixture into a 20cm x 25cm lightly greased baking dish and cover with tin foil.

10. Bake in the oven for 35 minutes. Then, get rid of the foil and cook for another 10 minutes. Once done, sprinkle the remaining parsley on top and serve with bread or crackers. Serve.

Nutrition: Calories 163 Fat 4.2 g Carbs 22.5 g Fiber 6.3 g Sugar 2.3 g Protein 9.2 g Sodium 143mg

54. Spiced Okra

Preparation time: 14 minutes

Cooking time: 16 minutes

Servings: 3

Ingredients:

- 2 cups okra
- ¼ teaspoon stevia
- 1 teaspoon chilli powder
- ½ teaspoon ground turmeric
- 1 tablespoon ground coriander
- 2 tablespoons fresh coriander, chopped
- 1 tablespoon ground cumin
- ¼ teaspoon salt
- 1 tablespoon desiccated coconut
- 3 tablespoons vegetable oil
- ½ teaspoon black mustard seeds
- ½ teaspoon cumin seeds
- Fresh tomatoes, to garnish

Directions:

1. Trim okra. Wash and dry.
2. Combine stevia, chilli powder, turmeric, ground coriander, fresh coriander, cumin, salt, and desiccated coconut in a bowl.
3. Heat the oil in a pan. Cook mustard and cumin seeds for 3 minutes. Stir continuously. Add okra. Tip in the spice mixture. Cook on low heat for 8 minutes.
4. Transfer to a serving dish. Garnish with fresh tomatoes.

Nutrition: Calories 131 Protein 12 Fat 1 g Carbs 19 g Sugar: 6g; Fiber: 7g; Sodium: 173mg

55. Lemony Salmon Burgers

Preparation Time: 10 Minutes

Cooking Time: 10 Minutes

Servings: 4

Ingredients

- 2 (3-oz) cans boneless, skinless pink salmon
- 1/4 cup panko breadcrumbs
- 4 tsp. lemon juice
- 1/4 cup red bell pepper
- 1/4 cup sugar-free yogurt
- 1 egg
- 2 (1.5-oz) whole wheat hamburger toasted buns

Directions

1. Mix drained and flaked salmon, finely-chopped bell pepper, panko breadcrumbs.
2. Combine 2 tbsp. cup sugar-free yogurt, 3 tsp. fresh lemon juice, and egg in a bowl. Shape mixture into 2 (3-inch) patties, bake on the skillet over medium heat 4 to 5 Minutes per side.
3. Stir together 2 tbsp. sugar-free yogurt and 1 tsp. lemon juice; spread over bottom halves of buns.
4. Top each with 1 patty, and cover with bun tops.
5. This dish is very mouth-watering!

Nutrition: Calories 180 Protein 7 g Fat 4 g Carbs 20 g Sugar: 6g; Fiber: 9g; Sodium: 395mg

56. Caprese Turkey Burgers

Preparation Time 10 Minutes

Cooking Time: 10 Minutes

Servings: 4

Ingredients

- 1/2 lb. 93% lean ground turkey
- 2 (1,5-oz) whole wheat hamburger buns (toasted)
- 1/4 cup shredded mozzarella cheese (part-skim)
- 1 egg
- 1 big tomato
- 1 small clove garlic
- 4 large basil leaves
- 1/8 tsp. salt
- 1/8 tsp. pepper

Directions

1. Combine turkey, white egg, Minced garlic, salt, and pepper (mix until combined);
2. Shape into 2 cutlets. Put cutlets into a skillet; cook 5 to 7 Minutes per side.
3. Top cutlets properly with cheese and sliced tomato at the end of cooking.
4. Put 1 cutlet on the bottom of each bun.
5. Top each patty with 2 basil leaves. Cover with bun tops.

My guests enjoy this dish every time they visit my home.

Nutrition: Calories 200 Protein 15 g Fat 3 g Carbs 6 g Sugar: 6g; Fiber: 5g; Sodium: 583mg

57. Pasta Salad

Preparation Time: 15 Minutes

Cooking Time: 15 Minutes

Servings: 4

Ingredients

- 8 oz. whole-wheat pasta
- 2 tomatoes
- 1 (5-oz) pkg spring mix
- 9 slices bacon
- 1/3 cup mayonnaise (reduced-fat)
- 1 tbsp. Dijon mustard
- 3 tbsp. apple cider vinegar
- 1/4 tsp. salt
- 1/2 tsp. pepper

Directions

1. Cook pasta.
2. Chilled pasta, chopped tomatoes and spring mix in a bowl.
3. Crumble cooked bacon over pasta.
4. Combine mayonnaise, mustard, vinegar, salt and pepper in a small bowl.
5. Pour dressing over pasta, stirring to coat.

Understanding diabetes is the first step in curing.

Nutrition: Calories 150 Protein 15 g Fat 10 g Carbs 5 g Sugar: 6g; Fiber: 7g; Sodium: 489mg

58. Chicken, Strawberry, And Avocado Salad

Preparation Time: 10 Minutes

Cooking Time: 5 Minutes

Ingredients

- 1,5 cups chicken (skin removed)
- 1/4 cup almonds
- 2 (5-oz) pkg salad greens
- 1 (16-oz) pkg strawberries
- 1 avocado
- 1/4 cup green onion
- 1/4 cup lime juice
- 3 tbsp. extra virgin olive oil
- 2 tbsp. honey
- 1/4 tsp. salt
- 1/4 tsp. pepper

Directions

1. Toast almonds until golden and fragrant.
2. Mix lime juice, oil, honey, salt, and pepper.
3. Mix greens, sliced strawberries, chicken, diced avocado, and sliced green onion and sliced almonds; drizzle with dressing. Toss to coat.
4. Yummy!

Nutrition: Calories 40 Protein 10 g Fat 6 g Carbs 2 g Sugar: 6g; Fiber: 7g; Sodium: 773mg

59.   Lemon-Thyme Eggs

Preparation Time: 10 Minutes

Cooking Time: 5 Minutes

Servings: 4

Ingredients

- 7 large eggs
- 1/4 cup mayonnaise (reduced-fat)
- 2 tsp. lemon juice
- 1 tsp. Dijon mustard
- 1 tsp. chopped fresh thyme
- 1/8 tsp. cayenne pepper

Directions

1. Bring eggs to a boil.
2. Peel and cut each egg in half lengthwise.
3. Remove yolks to a bowl. Add mayonnaise, lemon juice, mustard, thyme, and cayenne to egg yolks; mash to blend. Fill egg white halves with yolk mixture.
4. Chill until ready to serve.
5. Please your family with a delicious meal.

Nutrition: Calories 110 Protein 6 g Fat 2 g Carbs 1 g Sugar: 8g; Fiber: 10g; Sodium: 709mg

60.   Spinach Salad with Bacon

Preparation Time: 15 Minutes

Cooking Time: 0 Minutes

Servings: 4

Ingredients

- 8 slices center-cut bacon
- 3 tbsp. extra virgin olive oil
- 1 (5-oz) pkg baby spinach
- 1 tbsp. apple cider vinegar
- 1 tsp. Dijon mustard
- 1/2 tsp. honey
- 1/4 tsp. salt
- 1/2 tsp. pepper

Directions

1. Mix vinegar, mustard, honey, salt and pepper in a bowl.
2. Whisk in oil. Place spinach in a serving bowl; drizzle with dressing, and toss to coat.
3. Sprinkle with cooked and crumbled bacon.

Nutrition: Calories 110 Protein 6 g Fat 2 g Carbs 1 g

61.   Pea and Collards Soup

Preparation Time: 10 Minutes

Cooking Time: 50 Minutes

Servings: 4

Ingredients

- 1/2 (16-oz) pkg black-eyed peas
- 1 onion
- 2 carrots
- 1,5 cups ham (low-sodium)
- 1 (1-lb) bunch collard greens (trimmed)
- 1 tbsp. extra virgin olive oil

- 2 cloves garlic
- 1/2 tsp. black pepper
- Hot sauce

Directions

1. Cook chopped onion and carrots 10 Minutes.
2. Add peas, diced ham, collards, and Minced garlic. Cook 5 Minutes.
3. Add broth, 3 cups water, and pepper. Bring to a boil; simmer 35 Minutes, adding water if needed.
4. Serve with favorite sauce.

Nutrition: Calories 200 Protein 10 g Fat 20 g Carbs 1 g Sugar: 8g; Fiber: 7g; Sodium: 546mg

62.   Spanish Stew

Preparation Time: 10 Minutes

Cooking Time: 25 Minutes

Servings: 4

Ingredients

- 1.1/2 (12-oz) pkg smoked chicken sausage links
- 1 (5-oz) pkg baby spinach
- 1 (15-oz) can chickpeas
- 1 (14.5-oz) can tomatoes with basil, garlic, and oregano
- 1/2 tsp. smoked paprika
- 1/2 tsp. cumin
- 3/4 cup onions
- 1 tbsp. extra virgin olive oil

Directions

1. Cook sliced the sausage in hot oil until browned. Remove from pot.
2. Add chopped onions; cook until tender.
3. Add sausage, drained and rinsed chickpeas, diced tomatoes, paprika, and ground cumin. Cook 15 Minutes.
4. Add in spinach; cook 1 to 2 Minutes.

5. This dish is ideal for every day and for a festive table.

Nutrition: Calories 60 Protein 3 g Fat 1 g Carbs 8 g Sugar: 6g; Fiber: 7g; Sodium: 773mg

63.   Creamy Taco Soup

Preparation Time: 10 Minutes

Cooking Time: 20 Minutes

Servings: 4

Ingredients

- 3/4 lb. ground sirloin
- 1/2 (8-oz) cream cheese
- 1/2 onion
- 1 clove garlic
- 1 (10-oz) can tomatoes and green chiles
- 1 (14.5-oz) can beef broth
- 1/4 cup heavy cream
- 1,5 tsp. cumin
- 1/2 tsp. chili powder

Directions

1. Cook beef, chopped onion, and Minced garlic until meat is browned and crumbly; drain and return to pot.
2. Add ground cumin, chili powder, and cream cheese cut into small pieces and softened, stirring until cheese is melted.
3. Add diced tomatoes, broth, and cream; bring to a boil, and simmer 10 Minutes. Season with pepper and salt to taste.
4. You've got to give someone the recipe for this soup dish!

Nutrition: Calories 210 Protein 28 g Fat 17 g Carbs 0, 1 g Sugar: 5g; Fiber: 8g; Sodium: 674mg

64. Chicken with Caprese Salsa

Preparation Time: 15 Minutes

Cooking Time: 5 Minutes

Servings: 4

Ingredients

- 3/4 lb. boneless, skinless chicken breasts
- 2 big tomatoes
- 1/2 (8-oz) ball fresh mozzarella cheese
- 1/4 cup red onion
- 2 tbsp. fresh basil
- 1 tbsp. balsamic vinegar
- 2 tbsp. extra virgin olive oil (divided)
- 1/2 tsp. salt (divided)
- 1/4 tsp. pepper (divided)

Directions

1. Sprinkle cut in half lengthwise chicken with 1/4 tsp. salt and 1/8 tsp. pepper.
2. Heat 1 tbsp. olive oil, cook chicken 5 Minutes.
3. Meanwhile, mix chopped tomatoes, diced cheese, finely chopped onion, chopped basil, vinegar, 1 tbsp. oil, and 1/4 tsp. salt and 1/8 tsp. pepper.
4. Spoon salsa over chicken.
5. Chicken with Caprese Salsa is a nutritious, simple and very tasty dish that can be prepared in a few Minutes.

Nutrition: Calories 27 Protein 3 g Fat 0, 3 g Carbs 4 g Sugar: 11g; Fiber: 9g; Sodium: 644mg

65. Balsamic-Roasted Broccoli

Preparation Time: 10 Minutes

Cooking Time: 15 Minutes

Servings: 4

Ingredients

- 1 lb. broccoli
- 1 tbsp. extra virgin olive oil
- 1 tbsp. balsamic vinegar
- 1 clove garlic
- 1/8 tsp. salt
- Pepper to taste

Directions

1. Preheat oven to 450F.
2. Combine broccoli, olive oil, vinegar, Minced garlic, salt, and pepper; toss.
3. Spread broccoli on a baking sheet.
4. Bake 12 to 15 Minutes.
5. Really good!

Nutrition: Calories 170 Protein 17 g Fat 8 g Carbs 3 g Sugar: 6g; Fiber: 10g; Sodium: 681mg

66. Hearty Beef and Vegetable Soup

Preparation Time: 10 Minutes

Cooking Time: 30 Minutes

Servings: 4

Ingredients

- 1/2 lb. lean ground beef
- 2 cups beef broth
- 1,5 tbsp. vegetable oil (divided)
- 1 cup green bell pepper
- 1/2 cup red onion
- 1 cup green cabbage
- 1 cup frozen mixed vegetables
- 1/2 can tomatoes
- 1,5 tsp. Worcestershire sauce
- 1 small bay leaf
- 1,8 tsp. pepper
- 2 tbsp. ketchup

Directions

1. Cook beef in 1/2 tbsp. hot oil 2 Minutes.
2. Stir in chopped bell pepper and chopped onion; cook 4 Minutes.
3. Add chopped cabbage, mixed vegetables, stewed tomatoes, broth, Worcestershire sauce, bay leaf, and pepper; bring to a boil.
4. Reduce heat to medium; cover, and cook 15 Minutes.
5. Stir in ketchup and 1 tbsp. oil, and remove from heat. Let stand 10 Minutes.
6. The right diet is excellent diabetes remedy.

Nutrition: Calories 116 Protein 10 g Fat 7 g Carbs 3 g Sugar: 9g; Fiber: 17g; Sodium: 549mg

67. Cauliflower Muffin

Preparation Time: 15 Minutes

Cooking Time: 30 Minutes

Servings: 4

Ingredients

- 2,5 cup cauliflower
- 2/3 cup ham
- 2,5 cups of cheese
- 2/3 cup champignon
- 1,5 tbsp. flaxseed
- 3 eggs
- 1/4 tsp. salt
- 1/8 tsp. pepper

Directions

1. 1. Preheat oven to 375 F.
2. Put muffin liners in a 12-muffin tin.
3. Combine diced cauliflower, ground flaxseed, beaten eggs, cup diced ham, grated cheese, and diced mushrooms, salt, pepper.

4. Divide mixture rightly between muffin liners.
5. Bake 30 Minutes.
6. This is a great lunch for the whole family.

Nutrition: Calories 180 Protein 13 g Fat 13 g Carbs 2 g Sugar: 6g; Fiber: 7g; Sodium: 773mg g

68. Ham and Egg Cups

Preparation Time: 10 Minutes

Cooking Time: 15 Minutes

Servings: 4

Ingredients

- 5 slices ham
- 4 tbsp. cheese
- 1,5 tbsp. cream
- 3 egg whites
- 1,5 tbsp. pepper (green)
- 1 tsp. salt
- pepper to taste

Directions

1. Preheat oven to 350 F.
2. Arrange each slice of thinly sliced ham into 4 muffin tin.
3. Put 1/4 of grated cheese into ham cup.
4. Mix eggs, cream, salt and pepper and divide it into 2 tins.
5. Bake in oven 15 Minutes; after baking, sprinkle with green onions.
6. If you want to keep your current shape, also pay attention to this dish.

Nutrition: Calories: 1124 Fat: 72g Carbs: 59g Protein: 49g Sugar: 11g Fiber: 10g; Sodium: 140mg

69.   Bacon BBQ

Preparation time: 2 minutes

Cooking time: 8 minutes

Servings: 2

Ingredients:

- 13g dark brown sugar
- 5g chili powder
- 1g ground cumin
- 1g cayenne pepper
- 4 slices of bacon, cut in half

Directions:

1. Mix seasonings until well combined.
2. Dip the bacon in the dressing until it is completely covered. Leave aside.
3. Preheat the air fryer, set it to 160C.
4. Place the bacon in the preheated air fryer
5. Select Bacon and press Start/Pause.

Nutrition: Calories: 340 Fat: 15g Carbs: 32g Protein: 15g Sugar: 0g Fiber: 12g; Sodium: 128mg

70.   Misto Quente

Preparation time: 5 minutes

Cooking time: 10 minutes

Servings: 4

Ingredients:

- 4 slices of bread without shell
- 4 slices of turkey breast
- 4 slices of cheese
- 2 tbsp. cream cheese
- 2 spoons of butter

Directions:

1. Preheat the air fryer. Set the timer of 5 minutes and the temperature to 200C.

2. Pass the butter on one side of the slice of bread, and on the other side of the slice, the cream cheese.
3. Mount the sandwiches placing two slices of turkey breast and two slices cheese between the breads, with the cream cheese inside and the side with butter.
4. Place the sandwiches in the basket of the air fryer. Set the timer of the air fryer for 5 minutes and press the power button.

Nutrition: Calories: 294 Fat: 23g Carbs: 7g Proteins: 11g Sugar: 14g; Fiber: 12g; Sodium: 143mg

Dinner Recipes

71.   Cauliflower Mac & Cheese

Preparation Time: 5 Minutes

Cooking Time: 25 Minutes

Effort: Easy

Serving Size: 4

Ingredients:

- 1 Cauliflower Head, torn into florets
- Salt & Black Pepper, as needed
- ¼ cup Almond Milk, unsweetened
- ¼ cup Heavy Cream
- 3 tbsp. Butter, preferably grass-fed
- 1 cup Cheddar Cheese, shredded

Directions:

1. Preheat the oven to 450 F.
2. Melt the butter in a small microwave-safe bowl and heat it for 30 seconds.
3. Pour the melted butter over the cauliflower florets along with salt and pepper. Toss them well.
4. Place the cauliflower florets in a parchment paper-covered large baking sheet.
5. Bake them for 15 minutes or until the cauliflower is crisp-tender.

6. Once baked, mix the heavy cream, cheddar cheese, almond milk, and the remaining butter in a large microwave-safe bowl and heat it on high heat for 2 minutes or until the cheese mixture is smooth. Repeat the procedure until the cheese has melted.

7. Finally, stir in the cauliflower to the sauce mixture and coat well.

Nutrition: Calories: 294 Fat: 23g Carbs: 7g Proteins: 11g Sugar: 14g; Fiber: 12g; Sodium: 143mg

72. Easy Egg Salad

Preparation Time: 5 Minutes

Cooking Time: 15 to 20 Minutes

Effort: Easy

Servings: 4

Ingredients:

- 6 Eggs, preferably free-range
- ¼ tsp. Salt
- 2 tbsp. Mayonnaise
- 1 tsp. Lemon juice
- 1 tsp. Dijon mustard
- Pepper, to taste
- Lettuce leaves, to serve

Directions:

1. Keep the eggs in a saucepan of water and pour cold water until it covers the egg by another 1 inch.

2. Bring to a boil and then remove the eggs from heat.

3. Peel the eggs under cold running water.

4. Transfer the cooked eggs into a food processor and pulse them until chopped.

5. Stir in the mayonnaise, lemon juice, salt, Dijon mustard, and pepper and mix them well.

6. Taste for seasoning and add more if required.

7. Serve in the lettuce leaves.

Nutrition: Calories: 166 Fat: 14g Carbs - 0.85g Proteins: 10g Sodium: 132mg Sugar: 14g; Fiber: 12g;

73. Baked Chicken Legs

Preparation Time: 10 Minutes

Cooking Time: 40 Minutes

Effort: Easy

Servings: 6

Ingredients:

- 6 Chicken Legs
- ¼ tsp. Black Pepper
- ¼ cup Butter
- 1/2 tsp. Sea Salt
- 1/2 tsp. Smoked Paprika
- 1/2 tsp. Garlic Powder

Directions:

1. Preheat the oven to 425 F.

2. Pat the chicken legs with a paper towel to absorb any excess moisture.

3. Marinate the chicken pieces by first applying the butter over them and then with the seasoning. Set it aside for a few minutes.

4. Bake them for 25 minutes. Turnover and bake for further 10 minutes or until the internal temperature reaches 165 F.

5. Serve them hot.

Nutrition: Calories: 236 Fat16g Carbs: 0g Protein: 22g Sodium: 314mg Sugar: 10g; Fiber: 5g;

74. Creamed Spinach

Preparation Time: 5 Minutes

Cooking Time: 10 Minutes

Effort: Easy

Servings: 4

Ingredients:

- 3 tbsp. Butter
- ¼ tsp. Black Pepper
- 4 cloves of Garlic, minced
- ¼ tsp. Sea Salt
- 10 oz. Baby Spinach, chopped
- 1 tsp. Italian Seasoning
- 1/2 cup Heavy Cream
- 3 oz. Cream Cheese

Directions:

1. Melt butter in a large sauté pan over medium heat.
2. Once the butter has melted, spoon in the garlic and sauté for 30 seconds or until aromatic.
3. Spoon in the spinach and cook for 3 to 4 minutes or until wilted.
4. Add all the remaining ingredients to it and continuously stir until the cream cheese melts and the mixture gets thickened.
5. Serve hot

Nutrition: Calories: 274 Fat27g Carbs: 4g Protein: 4g Sodium: 114mg Sugar: 10g; Fiber: 9g;

75.   Stuffed Mushrooms

Preparation Time: 10 Minutes

Cooking Time: 20 Minutes

Servings: 4

Ingredients:

- 4 Portobello Mushrooms, large
- 1/2 cup Mozzarella Cheese, shredded
- 1/2 cup Marinara, low-sugar
- Olive Oil Spray

Directions:

1. Preheat the oven to 375 F.

2. Take out the dark gills from the mushrooms with the help of a spoon.
3. Keep the mushroom stem upside down and spoon it with two tablespoons of marinara sauce and mozzarella cheese.
4. Bake for 18 minutes or until the cheese is bubbly.

Nutrition: Calories: 113 Fat6g Carbs: 4g Protein: 7g Sodium: 14mg Sugar: 11g; Fiber: 8g;

76.   Vegetable Soup

Preparation Time: 10 Minutes

Cooking Time: 30 Minutes

Servings: 5

Ingredients:

- 8 cups Vegetable Broth
- 2 tbsp. Olive Oil
- 1 tbsp. Italian Seasoning
- 1 Onion, large & diced
- 2 Bay Leaves, dried
- 2 Bell Pepper, large & diced
- Sea Salt & Black Pepper, as needed
- 4 cloves of Garlic, minced
- 28 oz. Tomatoes, diced
- 1 Cauliflower head, medium & torn into florets
- 2 cups Green Beans, trimmed & chopped

Directions:

1. Heat oil in a Dutch oven over medium heat.
2. Once the oil becomes hot, stir in the onions and pepper.
3. Cook for 10 minutes or until the onion is softened and browned.
4. Spoon in the garlic and sauté for a minute or until fragrant.
5. Add all the remaining ingredients to it. Mix until everything comes together.

6. Bring the mixture to a boil. Lower the heat and cook for further 20 minutes or until the vegetables have softened.

7. Serve hot.

Nutrition: Calories: 79 Fat 2g Carbs: 8g Protein: 2g Sugar: 14g; Fiber: 12g; Sodium: 143mg

77.   Pork Chop Diane

Preparation Time: 10 minutes

Cooking Time: 20 minutes

Serving: 4

Ingredients:

- ¼ cup low-sodium chicken broth
- 1 tablespoon freshly squeezed lemon juice
- 2 teaspoons Worcestershire sauce
- 2 teaspoons Dijon mustard
- 4 (5-ounce) boneless pork top loin chops
- 1 teaspoon extra-virgin olive oil
- 1 teaspoon lemon zest
- 1 teaspoon butter
- 2 teaspoons chopped fresh chives

Direction:

1. Blend together the chicken broth, lemon juice, Worcestershire sauce, and Dijon mustard and set it aside.

2. Season the pork chops lightly.

3. Situate large skillet over medium-high heat and add the olive oil.

4. Cook the pork chops, turning once, until they are no longer pink, about 8 minutes per side.

5. Put aside the chops.

6. Pour the broth mixture into the skillet and cook until warmed through and thickened, about 2 minutes.

7. Blend lemon zest, butter, and chives.

8. Garnish with a generous spoonful of sauce.

Nutrition: Calories 200 Fat 8g Carbs 1g Sugar: 12g; Fiber: 10g; Sodium: 138mg

78.   Autumn Pork Chops with Red Cabbage and Apples

Preparation Time: 15 minutes

Cooking Time: 30 minutes

Serving: 4

Ingredients:

- ¼ cup apple cider vinegar
- 2 tablespoons granulated sweetener
- 4 (4-ounce) pork chops, about 1 inch thick
- 1 tablespoon extra-virgin olive oil
- ½ red cabbage, finely shredded
- 1 sweet onion, thinly sliced
- 1 apple, peeled, cored, and sliced
- 1 teaspoon chopped fresh thyme

Direction:

1. Scourge together the vinegar and sweetener. Set it aside.

2. Season the pork with salt and pepper.

3. Position huge skillet over medium-high heat and add the olive oil.

4. Cook the pork chops until no longer pink, turning once, about 8 minutes per side.

5. Put chops aside.

6. Add the cabbage and onion to the skillet and sauté until the vegetables have softened, about 5 minutes.

7. Add the vinegar mixture and the apple slices to the skillet and bring the mixture to a boil.

8. Adjust heat to low and simmer, covered, for 5 additional minutes.

9. Return the pork chops to the skillet, along with any accumulated juices and thyme, cover, and cook for 5 more minutes.

Nutrition: Calories 223 Carbs 12g Fiber 3g Protein: 15g; Sugar: 11g; Sodium: 396mg

79. Chipotle Chili Pork Chops

Preparation Time: 4 hours

Cooking Time: 20 minutes

Serving: 4

Ingredients:

- Juice and zest of 1 lime
- 1 tablespoon extra-virgin olive oil
- 1 tablespoon chipotle chili powder
- 2 teaspoons minced garlic
- 1 teaspoon ground cinnamon
- Pinch sea salt
- 4 (5-ounce) pork chops

Direction:

1. Combine the lime juice and zest, oil, chipotle chili powder, garlic, cinnamon, and salt in a resealable plastic bag. Add the pork chops. Remove as much air as possible and seal the bag.
2. Marinate the chops in the refrigerator for at least 4 hours, and up to 24 hours, turning them several times.
3. Ready the oven to 400°F and set a rack on a baking sheet. Let the chops rest at room temperature for 15 minutes, then arrange them on the rack and discard the remaining marinade.
4. Roast the chops until cooked through, turning once, about 10 minutes per side.
5. Serve with lime wedges.

Nutrition: Calories 204 Carbs 1g Sugar 1g Protein: 15g; Fiber: 11g; Sodium: 420mg

80. Orange-Marinated Pork Tenderloin

Preparation Time: 2 hours

Cooking Time: 30 minutes

Serving: 4

Ingredients:

- ¼ cup freshly squeezed orange juice
- 2 teaspoons orange zest
- 2 teaspoons minced garlic
- 1 teaspoon low-sodium soy sauce
- 1 teaspoon grated fresh ginger
- 1 teaspoon honey
- 1½ pounds pork tenderloin roast
- 1 tablespoon extra-virgin olive oil

Direction:

1. Blend together the orange juice, zest, garlic, soy sauce, ginger, and honey.
2. Pour the marinade into a resealable plastic bag and add the pork tenderloin.
3. Remove as much air as possible and seal the bag. Marinate the pork in the refrigerator, turning the bag a few times, for 2 hours.
4. Preheat the oven to 400°F.
5. Pull out tenderloin from the marinade and discard the marinade.
6. Position big ovenproof skillet over medium-high heat and add the oil.
7. Sear the pork tenderloin on all sides, about 5 minutes in total.
8. Position skillet to the oven and roast for 25 minutes.
9. Put aside for 10 minutes before serving.

Nutrition: Calories 228 Carbs 4g Sugar 3g Protein: 15g; Fiber: 9g; Sodium: 345mg

81. Homestyle Herb Meatballs

Preparation Time: 10 minutes

Cooking Time: 15 minutes

Serving: 4

Ingredients:

- ½ pound lean ground pork
- ½ pound lean ground beef
- 1 sweet onion, finely chopped
- ¼ cup bread crumbs
- 2 tablespoons chopped fresh basil
- 2 teaspoons minced garlic
- 1 egg

Direction:

1. Preheat the oven to 350°F.
2. Ready baking tray with parchment paper and set it aside.
3. In a large bowl, mix together the pork, beef, onion, bread crumbs, basil, garlic, egg, salt, and pepper until very well mixed.
4. Roll the meat mixture into 2-inch meatballs.
5. Transfer the meatballs to the baking sheet and bake until they are browned and cooked through, about 15 minutes.
6. Serve the meatballs with your favorite marinara sauce and some steamed green beans.

Nutrition: Calories 332 Carbs 13g Sugar 3g Protein: 15g; Carbs: 71g; Fiber: 9g; Sodium: 396mg

82. Lime-Parsley Lamb Cutlets

Preparation Time: 4 hours

Cooking Time: 10 minutes

Serving: 4

Ingredients:

- ¼ cup extra-virgin olive oil
- ¼ cup freshly squeezed lime juice
- 2 tablespoons lime zest
- 2 tablespoons chopped fresh parsley
- 12 lamb cutlets (about 1½ pounds total)

Direction:

1. Scourge the oil, lime juice, zest, parsley, salt, and pepper.
2. Pour marinade to a resealable plastic bag.
3. Add the cutlets to the bag and remove as much air as possible before sealing.
4. Marinate the lamb in the refrigerator for about 4 hours, turning the bag several times.
5. Preheat the oven to broil.
6. Remove the chops from the bag and arrange them on an aluminum foil–lined baking sheet. Discard the marinade.
7. Broil the chops for 4 minutes per side for medium doneness.
8. Let the chops rest for 5 minutes before serving.

Nutrition: Calories 413 Carbs 31g Protein: 15g; Sugar: 11g; Fiber: 12g; Sodium: 228mg

83. Mediterranean Steak Sandwiches

Preparation Time: 1 hour

Cooking Time: 10 minutes

Serving: 4

Ingredients:

- 2 tablespoons extra-virgin olive oil
- 2 tablespoons balsamic vinegar
- 2 teaspoons garlic
- 2 teaspoons lemon juice
- 2 teaspoons fresh oregano
- 1 teaspoon fresh parsley

- 1-pound flank steak
- 4 whole-wheat pitas
- 2 cups shredded lettuce
- 1 red onion, thinly sliced
- 1 tomato, chopped
- 1 ounce low-sodium feta cheese

Direction:

1. Scourge olive oil, balsamic vinegar, garlic, lemon juice, oregano, and parsley.
2. Add the steak to the bowl, turning to coat it completely.
3. Marinate the steak for 1 hour in the refrigerator, turning it over several times.
4. Preheat the broiler. Line a baking sheet with aluminum foil.
5. Put steak out of the bowl and discard the marinade.
6. Situate steak on the baking sheet and broil for 5 minutes per side for medium.
7. Set aside for 10 minutes before slicing.
8. Stuff the pitas with the sliced steak, lettuce, onion, tomato, and feta.

Nutrition: Calories 344 Carbs 22g Fiber 3g Sodium: 396mg Protein: 15g; Carbs: 71g; Sugar: 11g;

84. Roasted Beef with Peppercorn Sauce

Preparation Time: 10 minutes

Cooking Time: 90 minutes

Serving: 4

Ingredients:

- 1½ pounds top rump beef roast
- 3 teaspoons extra-virgin olive oil
- 3 shallots, minced
- 2 teaspoons minced garlic

- 1 tablespoon green peppercorns
- 2 tablespoons dry sherry
- 2 tablespoons all-purpose flour
- 1 cup sodium-free beef broth

Direction:

1. Heat the oven to 300°F.
2. Season the roast with salt and pepper.
3. Position huge skillet over medium-high heat and add 2 teaspoons of olive oil.
4. Brown the beef on all sides, about 10 minutes in total, and transfer the roast to a baking dish.
5. Roast until desired doneness, about 1½ hours for medium. When the roast has been in the oven for 1 hour, start the sauce.
6. In a medium saucepan over medium-high heat, sauté the shallots in the remaining 1 teaspoon of olive oil until translucent, about 4 minutes.
7. Stir in the garlic and peppercorns, and cook for another minute. Whisk in the sherry to deglaze the pan.
8. Whisk in the flour to form a thick paste, cooking for 1 minute and stirring constantly.
9. Fill in the beef broth and whisk for 4 minutes. Season the sauce.
10. Serve the beef with a generous spoonful of sauce.

Nutrition: Calories 330 Carbs 4g Protein 36g Carbs: 71g; Sugar: 11g; Fiber: 9g; Sodium: 286mg

85. Coffee-and-Herb-Marinated Steak

Preparation Time: 2 hours

Cooking Time: 10 minutes

Serving: 3

Ingredients:

- ¼ cup whole coffee beans

- 2 teaspoons garlic
- 2 teaspoons rosemary
- 2 teaspoons thyme
- 1 teaspoon black pepper
- 2 tablespoons apple cider vinegar
- 2 tablespoons extra-virgin olive oil
- 1-pound flank steak, trimmed of visible fat

Direction:

1. Place the coffee beans, garlic, rosemary, thyme, and black pepper in a coffee grinder or food processor and pulse until coarsely ground.
2. Transfer the coffee mixture to a resealable plastic bag and add the vinegar and oil. Shake to combine.
3. Add the flank steak and squeeze the excess air out of the bag. Seal it. Marinate the steak in the refrigerator for at least 2 hours, occasionally turning the bag over.
4. Preheat the broiler. Line a baking sheet with aluminum foil.
5. Pull the steak out and discard the marinade.
6. Position steak on the baking sheet and broil until it is done to your liking.
7. Put aside for 10 minutes before cutting it.
8. Serve with your favorite side dish.

Nutrition: Calories 313 Fat 31g Protein 20g Carbs: 68g; Sugar: 9g; Fiber: 9g; Sodium: 277mg

86. Traditional Beef Stroganoff

Preparation Time: 10 minutes

Cooking Time: 30 minutes

Serving: 4

Ingredients:

- 1 teaspoon extra-virgin olive oil

- 1-pound top sirloin, cut into thin strips
- 1 cup sliced button mushrooms
- ½ sweet onion, finely chopped
- 1 teaspoon minced garlic
- 1 tablespoon whole-wheat flour
- ½ cup low-sodium beef broth
- ¼ cup dry sherry
- ½ cup fat-free sour cream
- 1 tablespoon chopped fresh parsley

Direction:

1. Position the skillet over medium-high heat and add the oil.
2. Sauté the beef until browned, about 10 minutes, then remove the beef with a slotted spoon to a plate and set it aside.
3. Add the mushrooms, onion, and garlic to the skillet and sauté until lightly browned, about 5 minutes.
4. Whisk in the flour and then whisk in the beef broth and sherry.
5. Return the sirloin to the skillet and bring the mixture to a boil.
6. Reduce the heat to low and simmer until the beef is tender, about 10 minutes.
7. Stir in the sour cream and parsley. Season with salt and pepper.

Nutrition: Calories 257 Carbs 6g Fiber 1g Protein: 15g; Sugar: 11g; Sodium: 346mg

87. Chicken and Roasted Vegetable Wraps

Preparation Time: 10 minutes

Cooking Time: 20 minutes

Serving: 4

Ingredients:

- ½ small eggplant
- 1 red bell pepper
- 1 medium zucchini

- ½ small red onion, sliced
- 1 tablespoon extra-virgin olive oil
- 2 (8-ounce) cooked chicken breasts, sliced
- 4 whole-wheat tortilla wraps

Direction:

1. Preheat the oven to 400°F.
2. Wrap baking sheet with foil and set it aside.
3. In a large bowl, toss the eggplant, bell pepper, zucchini, and red onion with the olive oil.
4. Transfer the vegetables to the baking sheet and lightly season with salt and pepper.
5. Roast the vegetables until soft and slightly charred, about 20 minutes.
6. Divide the vegetables and chicken into four portions.
7. Wrap 1 tortilla around each portion of chicken and grilled vegetables, and serve.

Nutrition: Calories 483 Carbs 45g Fiber 3g Sodium: 396mg Protein: 15g; Sugar: 11g;

88.   Spicy Chicken Cacciatore

Preparation Time: 20 minutes

Cooking Time: 1 hour

Serving: 6

Ingredients:

- 1 (2-pound) chicken
- ¼ cup all-purpose flour
- 2 tablespoons extra-virgin olive oil
- 3 slices bacon
- 1 sweet onion
- 2 teaspoons minced garlic
- 4 ounces button mushrooms, halved

- 1 (28-ounce) can low-sodium stewed tomatoes
- ½ cup red wine
- 2 teaspoons chopped fresh oregano

Direction:

1. Cut the chicken into pieces: 2 drumsticks, 2 thighs, 2 wings, and 4 breast pieces.
2. Dredge the chicken pieces in the flour and season each piece with salt and pepper.
3. Place a large skillet over medium-high heat and add the olive oil.
4. Brown the chicken pieces on all sides, about 20 minutes in total. Transfer the chicken to a plate.
5. Cook chopped bacon to the skillet for 5 minutes. With a slotted spoon, transfer the cooked bacon to the same plate as the chicken.
6. Pour off most of the oil from the skillet, leaving just a light coating. Sauté the onion, garlic, and mushrooms in the skillet until tender, about 4 minutes.
7. Stir in the tomatoes, wine, oregano, and red pepper flakes.
8. Bring the sauce to a boil. Return the chicken and bacon, plus any accumulated juices from the plate, to the skillet.
9. Reduce the heat to low and simmer until the chicken is tender, about 30 minutes.

Nutrition: Calories 230 Carbs 14g Fiber 2g Protein: 15g; Sugar: 11g; Sodium: 327mg

89.   Scallion Sandwich

Preparation Time: 10 minutes

Cooking Time: 10 minutes

Servings: 1

Ingredients:

- 2 slices wheat bread
- 2 teaspoons butter, low fat

- 2 scallions, sliced thinly
- 1 tablespoon of parmesan cheese, grated
- 3/4 cup of cheddar cheese, reduced fat, grated

Directions:

1. Preheat the Air fryer to 356 degrees.
2. Spread butter on a slice of bread. Place inside the cooking basket with the butter side facing down.
3. Place cheese and scallions on top. Spread the rest of the butter on the other slice of bread Put it on top of the sandwich and sprinkle with parmesan cheese.
4. Cook for 10 minutes.

Nutrition: Calorie: 154 Carbs: 9g Fat: 2.5g Protein: 8.6g Fiber: 2.4g Protein: 15g; Sugar: 21g; Sodium: 276mg

90. Lean Lamb and Turkey Meatballs with Yogurt

Preparation Time: 10 minutes

Servings: 4

Cooking Time: 8 minutes

Ingredients:

- 1 egg white
- 4 ounces ground lean turkey
- 1 pound of ground lean lamb
- 1 teaspoon each of cayenne pepper, ground coriander, red chili pastes, salt, and ground cumin
- 2 garlic cloves, minced
- 1 1/2 tablespoons parsley, chopped
- 1 tablespoon mint, chopped
- 1/4 cup of olive oil

For the yogurt

- 2 tablespoons of buttermilk
- 1 garlic clove, minced

- 1/4 cup mint, chopped
- 1/2 cup of Greek yogurt, non-fat
- Salt to taste

Directions:

1. Set the Air Fryer to 390 degrees.
2. Mix all the ingredients for the meatballs in a bowl. Roll and mold them into golf-size round pieces. Arrange in the cooking basket. Cook for 8 minutes.
3. While waiting, combine all the ingredients for the mint yogurt in a bowl. Mix well.
4. Serve the meatballs with the mint yogurt. Top with olives and fresh mint.

Nutrition: Calorie: 154 Carbohydrate: 9g Fat: 2.5g Protein: 8.6g Fiber: 2.4g

91. Air Fried Section and Tomato

Preparation Time: 10 minutes

Cooking Time: 5 minutes

Servings: 2

Ingredients:

- 1 aubergine, sliced thickly into 4 disks
- 1 tomato, sliced into 2 thick disks
- 2 tsp. feta cheese, reduced fat
- 2 fresh basil leaves, minced
- 2 balls, small buffalo mozzarella, reduced fat, roughly torn
- Pinch of salt
- Pinch of black pepper

Directions:

1. Preheat Air Fryer to 330 degrees F.
2. Spray small amount of oil into the Air fryer basket. Fry aubergine slices for 5 minutes or until golden brown on both sides. Transfer to a plate.
3. Fry tomato slices in batches for 5 minutes or until seared on both sides.

4. To serve, stack salad starting with an aborigine base, buffalo mozzarella, basil leaves, tomato slice, and 1/2-teaspoon feta cheese.

5. Top of with another slice of aborigine and 1/2 tsp. feta cheese. Serve.

Nutrition: Calorie: 140.3 Carbs: 26.6 Fat: 3.4g Protein: 4.2g Fiber: 7.3g Sugar: 11g; Sodium: 343mg

92. Cheesy Salmon Fillets

Preparation Time: 15 minutes

Cooking Time: 20 minutes

Servings: 2-3

Ingredients:

For the salmon fillets

- 2 pieces, 4 oz. each salmon fillets, choose even cuts
- 1/2 cup sour cream, reduced fat
- ¼ cup cottage cheese, reduced fat
- ¼ cup Parmigiano-Reggiano cheese, freshly grated

Garnish:

- Spanish paprika
- 1/2 piece lemon, cut into wedges

Directions:

1. Preheat Air Fryer to 330 degrees F.

2. To make the salmon fillets, mix sour cream, cottage cheese, and Parmigiano-Reggiano cheese in a bowl.

3. Layer salmon fillets in the Air fryer basket. Fry for 20 minutes or until cheese turns golden brown.

4. To assemble, place a salmon fillet and sprinkle paprika. Garnish with lemon wedges and squeeze lemon juice on top. Serve.

Nutrition: Calorie: 274 Carbs: 1g Fat: 19g Protein: 24g Fiber: 0.5g Sugar: 11g; Sodium: 368mg

93. Salmon with Asparagus

Preparation Time: 5 Minutes

Cooking Time: 10 Minutes

Servings: 3

Ingredients:

- 1 lb. Salmon, sliced into fillets
- 1 tbsp. Olive Oil
- Salt & Pepper, as needed
- 1 bunch of Asparagus, trimmed
- 2 cloves of Garlic, minced
- Zest & Juice of 1/2 Lemon
- 1 tbsp. Butter, salted

Directions:

1. Spoon in the butter and olive oil into a large pan and heat it over medium-high heat.

2. Once it becomes hot, place the salmon and season it with salt and pepper.

3. Cook for 4 minutes per side and then cook the other side.

4. Stir in the garlic and lemon zest to it.

5. Cook for further 2 minutes or until slightly browned.

6. Off the heat and squeeze the lemon juice over it.

7. Serve it hot.

Nutrition: Calories: 409 Carbs: 2.7g Proteins: 32.8g Fat: 28.8g Sugar: 11g; Fiber: 9g; Sodium: 497mg

94. Shrimp in Garlic Butter

Preparation Time: 5 Minutes

Cooking Time: 20 Minutes

Servings: 4

Ingredients:

- 1 lb. Shrimp, peeled & deveined
- ¼ tsp. Red Pepper Flakes

- 6 tbsp. Butter, divided
- 1/2 cup Chicken Stock
- Salt & Pepper, as needed
- 2 tbsp. Parsley, minced
- 5 cloves of Garlic, minced
- 2 tbsp. Lemon Juice

Directions:

1. Heat a large bottomed skillet over medium-high heat.
2. Spoon in two tablespoons of the butter and melt it. Add the shrimp.
3. Season it with salt and pepper. Sear for 4 minutes or until shrimp gets cooked.
4. Transfer the shrimp to a plate and stir in the garlic.
5. Sauté for 30 seconds or until aromatic.
6. Pour the chicken stock and whisk it well. Allow it to simmer for 5 to 10 minutes or until it has reduced to half.
7. Spoon the remaining butter, red pepper, and lemon juice to the sauce. Mix.
8. Continue cooking for another 2 minutes.
9. Take off the pan from the heat and add the cooked shrimp to it.
10. Garnish with parsley and transfer to the serving bowl.
11. Enjoy.

Nutrition: Calories: 307 Carbs: 3g Proteins: 27g Fat: 20g Sugar: 14g; Fiber: 7g; Sodium: 522mg

95.   Cobb Salad

Keto & Under 30 Minutes

Preparation Time: 5 Minutes

Cooking Time: 5 Minutes

Servings: 1

Ingredients:

- 4 Cherry Tomatoes, chopped

- ¼ cup Bacon, cooked & crumbled
- 1/2 of 1 Avocado, chopped
- 2 oz. Chicken Breast, shredded
- 1 Egg, hardboiled
- 2 cups Mixed Green salad
- 1 oz. Feta Cheese, crumbled

Directions:

1. Toss all the ingredients for the Cobb salad in a large mixing bowl and toss well.
2. Serve and enjoy it.

Nutrition: Calories: 307 Carbs: 3g Proteins: 27g Fat: 20g Sugar: 11g; Fiber: 11g; Sodium: 522mg

96.   Beef Chili

Preparation Time: 10 Minutes

Cooking Time: 20 Minutes

Serving Size: 4

Ingredients:

- 1/2 tsp. Garlic Powder
- 1 tsp. Coriander, grounded
- 1 lb. Beef, grounded
- 1/2 tsp. Sea Salt
- 1/2 tsp. Cayenne Pepper
- 1 tsp. Cumin, grounded
- 1/2 tsp. Pepper, grounded
- 1/2 cup Salsa, low-carb & no-sugar

Directions:

1. Heat a large-sized pan over medium-high heat and cook the beef in it until browned.
2. Stir in all the spices and cook them for 7 minutes or until everything is combined.
3. When the beef gets cooked, spoon in the salsa.

4. Bring the mixture to a simmer and cook for another 8 minutes or until everything comes together.

5. Take it from heat and transfer to a serving bowl.

Nutrition: Calories: 229 Fat: 10g Carbs: 2g Proteins: 33g Sugar: 11g; Fiber: 9g; Sodium: 675mg

97.   Greek Broccoli Salad

Preparation Time: 10 Minutes

Cooking Time: 15 Minutes

Servings: 4

Ingredients:

- 1 ¼ lb. Broccoli, sliced into small bites
- ¼ cup Almonds, sliced
- 1/3 cup Sun-dried Tomatoes
- ¼ cup Feta Cheese, crumbled
- ¼ cup Red Onion, sliced

For the dressing:

- 1/4 cup Olive Oil
- Dash of Red Pepper Flakes
- 1 Garlic clove, minced
- ¼ tsp. Salt
- 2 tbsp. Lemon Juice
- 1/2 tsp. Dijon Mustard
- 1 tsp. Low Carb Sweetener Syrup
- 1/2 tsp. Oregano, dried

Directions:

1. Mix broccoli, onion, almonds and sun-dried tomatoes in a large mixing bowl.

2. In another small-sized bowl, combine all the dressing ingredients until emulsified.

3. Spoon the dressing over the broccoli salad.

4. Allow the salad to rest for half an hour before serving.

Nutrition: Calories: 272 Carbs: 11.9g Proteins: 8g Fat: 21.6g Sugar: 11g; Fiber: 9g; Sodium: 321mg

98.   Cheesy Cauliflower Gratin

Preparation Time: 5 Minutes

Cooking Time: 25 Minutes

Servings: 6

Ingredients:

- 6 deli slices Pepper Jack Cheese
- 4 cups Cauliflower florets
- Salt and Pepper, as needed
- 4 tbsp. Butter
- 1/3 cup Heavy Whipping Cream

Directions:

1. Mix the cauliflower, cream, butter, salt, and pepper in a safe microwave bowl and combine well.

2. Microwave the cauliflower mixture for 25 minutes on high until it becomes soft and tender.

3. Remove the ingredients from the bowl and mash with the help of a fork.

4. Taste for seasonings and spoon in salt and pepper as required.

5. Arrange the slices of pepper jack cheese on top of the cauliflower mixture and microwave for 3 minutes until the cheese starts melting.

6. Serve warm.

Nutrition: Calories: 421 Carbs: 3g Proteins: 19g Fat: 37g Sugar: 11g; Fiber: 11g; Sodium: 111mg

99.   Strawberry Spinach Salad

Preparation Time: 5 Minutes

Cooking Time: 10 Minutes

Servings: 4

Ingredients:

- 4 oz. Feta Cheese, crumbled

- 8 Strawberries, sliced
- 2 oz. Almonds
- 6 Slices Bacon, thick-cut, crispy and crumbled
- 10 oz. Spinach leaves, fresh
- 2 Roma Tomatoes, diced
- 2 oz. Red Onion, sliced thinly

Directions:

1. For making this healthy salad, mix all the ingredients needed to make the salad in a large-sized bowl and toss them well.

Nutrition: Calories: 255kcal Fat: 16g Carbohydrates: 8g Proteins: 14g Sodium: 27mg

100. Garlic Bread

Preparation time: 10 minutes

Cooking time: 15 minutes

Servings: 4-5

Ingredients:

- 2 stale French rolls
- 4 tbsp. crushed or crumpled garlic
- 1 cup of mayonnaise
- Powdered grated Parmesan
- 1 tbsp. olive oil

Directions:

1. Preheat the air fryer. Set the time of 5 minutes and the temperature to 2000C.
2. Mix mayonnaise with garlic and set aside.
3. Cut the baguettes into slices, but without separating them completely.
4. Fill the cavities of equals. Brush with olive oil and sprinkle with grated cheese.
5. Place in the basket of the air fryer. Set the timer to 10 minutes, adjust the temperature to 1800C and press the power button.

Nutrition: Calories: 340 Fat: 15g Carbs: 32g Protein: 15g Sugar: 0g Fiber: 9g; Sodium: 396mg

101. Bruschetta

Preparation time: 5 minutes

Cooking time: 10 minutes

Servings: 2

Ingredients:

- 4 slices of Italian bread
- 1 cup chopped tomato tea
- 1 cup grated mozzarella tea
- Olive oil
- Oregano, salt, and pepper
- 4 fresh basil leaves

Directions:

1. Preheat the air fryer. Set the timer of 5 minutes and the temperature to 2000C.
2. Sprinkle the slices of Italian bread with olive oil. Divide the chopped tomatoes and mozzarella between the slices. Season with salt, pepper, and oregano.
3. Put oil in the filling. Place a basil leaf on top of each slice.
4. Put the bruschetta in the basket of the air fryer being careful not to spill the filling. Set the timer of 5 minutes, set the temperature to 180C, and press the power button.
5. Transfer the bruschetta to a plate and serve.

Nutrition: Calories: 434 Fat: 14g Carbs: 63g Protein: 11g Sugar: 8g Fiber: 9g; Sodium: 276mg

102. Cream Buns with Strawberries

Preparation time: 10 minutes

Cooking time: 12 minutes

Servings: 6

Ingredients:

- 240g all-purpose flour
- 50g granulated sugar
- 8g baking powder
- 1g of salt
- 85g chopped cold butter
- 84g chopped fresh strawberries
- 120 ml whipping cream
- 2 large eggs
- 10 ml vanilla extract
- 5 ml of water

Directions:

1. Sift flour, sugar, baking powder and salt in a large bowl. Put the butter with the flour with the use of a blender or your hands until the mixture resembles thick crumbs.

2. Mix the strawberries in the flour mixture. Set aside for the mixture to stand. Beat the whipping cream, 1 egg and the vanilla extract in a separate bowl.

3. Put the cream mixture in the flour mixture until they are homogeneous, and then spread the mixture to a thickness of 38 mm.

4. Use a round cookie cutter to cut the buns. Spread the buns with a combination of egg and water. Set aside

5. Preheat the air fryer, set it to 180C.

6. Place baking paper in the preheated inner basket.

7. Place the buns on top of the baking paper and cook for 12 minutes at 180C, until golden brown.

Nutrition: Calories: 150Fat: 14g Carbs: 3g Protein: 11g Sugar: 8g Fiber: 12g; Sodium: 396mg

103.   Blueberry Buns

Preparation time: 10 minutes

Cooking time: 12 minutes

Servings: 6

Ingredients:

- 240g all-purpose flour
- 50g granulated sugar
- 8g baking powder
- 2g of salt
- 85g chopped cold butter
- 85g of fresh blueberries
- 3g grated fresh ginger
- 113 ml whipping cream
- 2 large eggs
- 4 ml vanilla extract
- 5 ml of water

Directions:

1. Put sugar, flour, baking powder and salt in a large bowl.

2. Put the butter with the flour using a blender or your hands until the mixture resembles thick crumbs.

3. Mix the blueberries and ginger in the flour mixture and set aside

4. Mix the whipping cream, 1 egg and the vanilla extract in a different container.

5. Put the cream mixture with the flour mixture until combined.

6. Shape the dough until it reaches a thickness of approximately 38 mm and cut it into eighths.

7. Spread the buns with a combination of egg and water. Set aside Preheat the air fryer set it to 180C.

8. Place baking paper in the preheated inner basket and place the buns on top of the paper. Cook for 12 minutes at 180C, until golden brown

Nutrition: Calories: 105 Fat: 1.64g Carbs: 20.09g Protein: 2.43g Sugar: 2.1g Fiber: 9g; Sodium: 344mg

104.   Cauliflower Potato Mash

Preparation Time: 30 minutes Servings: 4

Cooking Time: 5 minutes

Ingredients:

- 2 cups potatoes, peeled and cubed
- 2 tbsp. butter
- ¼ cup milk
- 10 oz. cauliflower florets
- ¾ tsp. salt

Directions:

1. Add water to the saucepan and bring to boil.
2. Reduce heat and simmer for 10 minutes.
3. Drain vegetables well. Transfer vegetables, butter, milk, and salt in a blender and blend until smooth.
4. Serve and enjoy.

Nutrition: Calories 128 Fat 6.2 g, Sugar 3.3 g, Protein 3.2 g, Fiber: 9g; Sodium: 354mg

Meat & Chicken Recipes

105.   Roasted Pork & Apples

Preparation Time: 15 minutes

Cooking Time: 30 minutes

Servings: 4

Ingredients:

- Salt and pepper to taste
- 1/2 teaspoon dried, crushed
- 1 lb. pork tenderloin
- 1 tablespoon canola oil
- 1 onion, sliced into wedges
- 3 cooking apples, sliced into wedges

- 2/3 cup apple cider
- Sprigs fresh sage

Directions:

1. In a bowl, mix salt, pepper and sage.
2. Season both sides of pork with this mixture.
3. Place a pan over medium heat.
4. Brown both sides.
5. Transfer to a roasting pan.
6. Add the onion on top and around the pork.
7. Drizzle oil on top of the pork and apples.
8. Roast in the oven at 425 degrees F for 10 minutes.
9. Add the apples, roast for another 15 minutes.
10. In a pan, boil the apple cider and then simmer for 10 minutes.
11. Pour the apple cider sauce over the pork before serving.

Nutrition: Calories 239 Fat 6 g Sodium 209 mg Carbs 22 g Fiber 3 g Sugars 16 g Protein 24 g

106.   Pork with Cranberry Relish

Preparation Time: 30 minutes

Cooking Time: 30 minutes

Servings: 4

Ingredients:

- 12 oz. pork tenderloin, fat trimmed and sliced crosswise
- Salt and pepper to taste
- ¼ cup all-purpose flour
- 2 tablespoons olive oil
- 1 onion, sliced thinly
- ¼ cup dried cranberries
- ¼ cup low-sodium chicken broth
- 1 tablespoon balsamic vinegar

Directions:

1. Flatten each slice of pork using a mallet.
2. In a dish, mix the salt, pepper and flour.
3. Dip each pork slice into the flour mixture.
4. Add oil to a pan over medium high heat.
5. Cook pork for 3 minutes per side or until golden crispy.
6. Transfer to a serving plate and cover with foil.
7. Cook the onion in the pan for 4 minutes.
8. Stir in the rest of the ingredients.
9. Simmer until the sauce has thickened.

Nutrition: Calories 211 Fat 9 g Sodium 116 mg Carbs 15 g Fiber 1 g Sugars 6 g Protein 18 g Potassium 378 mg

107.   Sesame Pork with Mustard Sauce

Preparation Time: 25 minutes

Cooking Time: 25 minutes

Servings: 4

Ingredients:

- 2 tablespoons low-sodium teriyaki sauce
- ¼ cup chili sauce
- 2 cloves garlic, minced
- 2 teaspoons ginger, grated
- 2 pork tenderloins
- 2 teaspoons sesame seeds
- ¼ cup low fat sour cream
- 1 teaspoon Dijon mustard
- Salt to taste
- 1 scallion, chopped

Directions:

1. Preheat your oven to 425 degrees F.

2. Mix the teriyaki sauce, chili sauce, garlic and ginger.
3. Put the pork on a roasting pan.
4. Brush the sauce on both sides of the pork.
5. Bake in the oven for 15 minutes.
6. Brush with more sauce.
7. Top with sesame seeds.
8. Roast for 10 more minutes.
9. Mix the rest of the ingredients.
10. Serve the pork with mustard sauce.

Nutrition: Calories 135 Fat 3 g Carbs 7 g Fiber 1 g Sugars 15 g Protein 20 g Sodium 255 mg

108.   Steak with Mushroom Sauce

Preparation Time: 20 minutes

Cooking Time: 5 minutes

Servings: 4

Ingredients:

- 12 oz. sirloin steak, sliced and trimmed
- 2 teaspoons grilling seasoning
- 2 teaspoons oil
- 6 oz. broccoli, trimmed
- 2 cups frozen peas
- 3 cups fresh mushrooms, sliced
- 1 cup beef broth (unsalted)
- 1 tablespoon mustard
- 2 teaspoons cornstarch
- Salt to taste

Directions:

1. Preheat your oven to 350 degrees F.
2. Season meat with grilling seasoning.
3. In a pan over medium high heat, cook the meat and broccoli for 4 minutes.
4. Sprinkle the peas around the steak.

5. Put the pan inside the oven and bake for 8 minutes.

6. Remove both meat and vegetables from the pan.

7. Add the mushrooms to the pan.

8. Cook for 3 minutes.

9. Mix the broth, mustard, salt and cornstarch.

10. Add to the mushrooms.

11. Cook for 1 minute.

12. Pour sauce over meat and vegetables before serving.

Nutrition: Calories 226 Fat 6 g   Sodium 356 mg Carbs 16 g Fiber 5 g Sugars 6 g Protein 26 g

109.   Steak with Tomato & Herbs

Preparation Time: 30 minutes

Cooking Time: 30 minutes

Servings: 2

Ingredients:

- 8 oz. beef loin steak, sliced in half

- Salt and pepper to taste

- Cooking spray

- 1 teaspoon fresh basil, snipped

- ¼ cup green onion, sliced

- 1/2 cup tomato, chopped

Directions:

1. Season the steak with salt and pepper.

2. Spray oil on your pan.

3. Put the pan over medium high heat.

4. Once hot, add the steaks.

5. Reduce heat to medium.

6. Cook for 10 to 13 minutes for medium, turning once.

7. Add the basil and green onion.

8. Cook for 2 minutes.

9. Add the tomato.

10. Cook for 1 minute.

11. Let cool a little before slicing.

Nutrition: Calories 170 Fat 6 g   Sodium 207 mg Carbs 3 g Fiber 1 g Sugars 5 g Protein 25 g

110.   Barbecue Beef Brisket

Preparation Time: 25 minutes

Cooking Time: 10 hours

Servings: 10

Ingredients:

- 4 lb. beef brisket (boneless), trimmed and sliced

- 1 bay leaf

- 2 onions, sliced into rings

- 1/2 teaspoon dried thyme, crushed

- ¼ cup chili sauce

- 1 clove garlic, minced

- Salt and pepper to taste

- 2 tablespoons light brown sugar

- 2 tablespoons cornstarch

- 2 tablespoons cold water

Directions:

1. Put the meat in a slow cooker.

2. Add the bay leaf and onion.

3. In a bowl, mix the thyme, chili sauce, salt, pepper and sugar.

4. Pour the sauce over the meat.

5. Mix well.

6. Seal the pot and cook on low heat for 10 hours.

7. Discard the bay leaf.

8. Pour cooking liquid in a pan.

9. Add the mixed water and cornstarch.

10. Simmer until the sauce has thickened.

11. Pour the sauce over the meat.

Nutrition: Calories 182 Fat 6 g Sodium 217 mg Sugars 4 g Protein 20 g Potassium 383 mg

111.   Beef & Asparagus

Preparation Time: 15 minutes

Cooking Time: 10 minutes

Servings: 4

Ingredients:

- 2 teaspoons olive oil
- 1 lb. lean beef sirloin, trimmed and sliced
- 1 carrot, shredded
- Salt and pepper to taste
- 12 oz. asparagus, trimmed and sliced
- 1 teaspoon dried herbes de Provence, crushed
- 1/2 cup Marsala
- ¼ teaspoon lemon zest

Directions:

1. Pour oil in a pan over medium heat.
2. Add the beef and carrot.
3. Season with salt and pepper.
4. Cook for 3 minutes.
5. Add the asparagus and herbs.
6. Cook for 2 minutes.
7. Add the Marsala and lemon zest.
8. Cook for 5 minutes, stirring frequently.

Nutrition: Calories 327 Fat 7 g Sodium 209 mg Carbs 29 g Fiber 2 g Sugars 3 g Protein 28 g

112.   Pork Chops with Grape Sauce

Preparation Time: 15 minutes

Cooking Time: 25 minutes

Servings: 4

Ingredients:

- Cooking spray
- 4 pork chops
- ¼ cup onion, sliced
- 1 clove garlic, minced
- 1/2 cup low-sodium chicken broth
- ¾ cup apple juice
- 1 tablespoon cornstarch
- 1 tablespoon balsamic vinegar
- 1 teaspoon honey
- 1 cup seedless red grapes, sliced in half

Directions:

1. Spray oil on your pan.
2. Put it over medium heat.
3. Add the pork chops to the pan.
4. Cook for 5 minutes per side.
5. Remove and set aside.
6. Add onion and garlic.
7. Cook for 2 minutes.
8. Pour in the broth and apple juice.
9. Bring to a boil.
10. Reduce heat to simmer.
11. Put the pork chops back to the skillet.
12. Simmer for 4 minutes.
13. In a bowl, mix the cornstarch, vinegar and honey.
14. Add to the pan.
15. Cook until the sauce has thickened.
16. Add the grapes.
17. Pour sauce over the pork chops before serving.

Nutrition: Calories 188 Fat 4 g   Sodium 117 mg Carbs 18 g Fiber 1 g Sugars 13 g Protein 19 g

113.   Italian Beef

Preparation Time: 20 minutes

Cooking Time: 1 hour and 20 minutes

Servings: 4

Ingredients:

- Cooking spray
- 1 lb. beef round steak, trimmed and sliced
- 1 cup onion, chopped
- 2 cloves garlic, minced
- 1 cup green bell pepper, chopped
- 1/2 cup celery, chopped
- 2 cups mushrooms, sliced
- 14 1/2 oz. canned diced tomatoes
- 1/2 teaspoon dried basil
- ¼ teaspoon dried oregano
- 1/8 teaspoon crushed red pepper
- 2 tablespoons Parmesan cheese, grated

Directions:

1. Spray oil on the pan over medium heat.
2. Cook the meat until brown on both sides.
3. Transfer meat to a plate.
4. Add the onion, garlic, bell pepper, celery and mushroom to the pan.
5. Cook until tender.
6. Add the tomatoes, herbs, and pepper.
7. Put the meat back to the pan.
8. Simmer while covered for 1 hour and 15 minutes.
9. Stir occasionally.
10. Sprinkle Parmesan cheese on top of the dish before serving.

Nutrition: Calories 212 Fat 4 g Sodium 296 mg Sugars 6 g Protein 30 g Potassium 876 mg

114. Lamb with Broccoli & Carrots

Preparation Time: 20 minutes

Cooking Time: 10 minutes

Servings: 4

Ingredients:

- 2 cloves garlic, minced
- 1 tablespoon fresh ginger, grated
- ¼ teaspoon red pepper, crushed
- 2 tablespoons low-sodium soy sauce
- 1 tablespoon white vinegar
- 1 tablespoon cornstarch
- 12 oz. lamb meat, trimmed and sliced
- 2 teaspoons cooking oil
- 1 lb. broccoli, sliced into florets
- 2 carrots, sliced into strips
- ¾ cup low-sodium beef broth
- 4 green onions, chopped
- 2 cups cooked spaghetti squash pasta

Directions:

1. Combine the garlic, ginger, red pepper, soy sauce, vinegar and cornstarch in a bowl.
2. Add lamb to the marinade.
3. Marinate for 10 minutes.
4. Discard marinade.
5. In a pan over medium heat, add the oil.
6. Add the lamb and cook for 3 minutes.
7. Transfer lamb to a plate.
8. Add the broccoli and carrots.
9. Cook for 1 minute.
10. Pour in the beef broth.
11. Cook for 5 minutes.
12. Put the meat back to the pan.

13. Sprinkle with green onion and serve on top of spaghetti squash.

Nutrition: Calories 205 Fat 6 g Sodium 659 mg Carbohydrate 17 g

115.   Rosemary Lamb

Preparation Time: 15 minutes

Cooking Time: 2 hours

Servings: 14

Ingredients:

- Salt and pepper to taste

- 2 teaspoons fresh rosemary, snipped

- 5 lb. whole leg of lamb, trimmed and cut with slits on all sides

- 3 cloves garlic, slivered

- 1 cup water

Directions:

1. Preheat your oven to 375 degrees F.

2. Mix salt, pepper and rosemary in a bowl.

3. Sprinkle mixture all over the lamb.

4. Insert slivers of garlic into the slits.

5. Put the lamb on a roasting pan.

6. Add water to the pan.

7. Roast for 2 hours.

Nutrition: Calories 136 Fat 4 g Sodium 218 mg Protein 23 g Potassium 248 mg

116.   Mediterranean   Lamb Meatballs

Preparation Time: 10 minutes

Cooking Time: 20 minutes

Servings: 8

Ingredients:

- 12 oz. roasted red peppers

- 1 1/2 cups whole wheat breadcrumbs

- 2 eggs, beaten

- 1/3 cup tomato sauce

- 1/2 cup fresh basil

- ¼ cup parsley, snipped

- Salt and pepper to taste

- 2 lb. lean ground lamb

Directions:

1. Preheat your oven to 350 degrees F.

2. In a bowl, mix all the ingredients and then form into meatballs.

3. Put the meatballs on a baking pan.

4. Bake in the oven for 20 minutes.

Nutrition: Calories 94 Fat 3 g Sodium 170 mg Total Carbohydrate 2 g Fiber 1 g Sugars 0 g

117.   Beef and Red Bean Chili

Preparation Time: 10 minutes

Cooking Time: 6 hours

Serving: 4

Ingredients

- 1 cup dry red beans

- 1 tablespoon olive oil

- 2 pounds boneless beef chuck

- 1 large onion, coarsely chopped

- 1 (14 ounce) can beef broth

- 2 chipotle chili peppers in adobo sauce

- 2 teaspoons dried oregano, crushed

- 1 teaspoon ground cumin

- ½ teaspoon salt

- 1 (14.5 ounce) can tomatoes with mild green chilis

- 1 (15 ounce) can tomato sauce

- ¼ cup snipped fresh cilantro

- 1 medium red sweet pepper

Direction

1. Rinse out the beans and place them into a Dutch oven or big saucepan, then add in water enough to cover them. Allow the beans to boil then drop the heat down. Simmer the beans without a cover for 10 minutes. Take off the heat and keep covered for an hour.

2. In a big frypan, heat up the oil upon medium-high heat, then cook onion and half the beef until they brown a bit over medium-high heat. Move into a 3 1/2- or 4-quart crockery cooker. Do this again with what's left of the beef. Add in tomato sauce, tomatoes (not drained), salt, cumin, oregano, adobo sauce, chipotle peppers, and broth, stirring to blend. Strain out and rinse beans and stir in the cooker.

3. Cook while covered on a low setting for around 10-12 hours or on high setting for 5-6 hours. Spoon the chili into bowls or mugs and top with sweet pepper and cilantro.

Nutrition: Calories 288 Carbs 24g Sugar 5g Protein: 15g; Fiber: 9g; Sodium: 396mg

118.   Berry Apple Cider

Preparation Time: 15 minutes

Cooking Time: 3 hours

Serving: 3

Ingredients

- 4 cinnamon sticks, cut into 1-inch pieces
- 1½ teaspoons whole cloves
- 4 cups apple cider
- 4 cups low-calorie cranberry-raspberry juice drink
- 1 medium apple

Direction

1. To make the spice bag, cut out a 6-inch square from double thick, pure cotton cheesecloth. Put in the cloves and cinnamon, then bring the corners up, tie it closed using a clean kitchen string that is pure cotton.

2. In a 3 1/2- 5-quart slow cooker, combine cranberry-raspberry juice, apple cider, and the spice bag.

3. Cook while covered over low heat setting for around 4-6 hours or on a high heat setting for 2-2 1/2 hours.

4. Throw out the spice bag. Serve right away or keep it warm while covered on warm or low-heat setting up to 2 hours, occasionally stirring. Garnish each serving with apples (thinly sliced).

Nutrition: Calories 89 Carbs 22g Sugar 19g Protein: 15g; Fiber: 9g; Sodium: 256mg

119.   Brunswick Stew

Preparation Time: 10 minutes

Cooking Time: 45 minutes

Serving: 3

Ingredients

- 4 ounces diced salt pork
- 2 pounds chicken parts
- 8 cups water
- 3 potatoes, cubed
- 3 onions, chopped
- 1 (28 ounce) can whole peeled tomatoes
- 2 cups canned whole kernel corn
- 1 (10 ounce) package frozen lima beans
- 1 tablespoon Worcestershire sauce
- 1/2 teaspoon salt
- 1/4 teaspoon ground black pepper

Direction

1. Mix and boil water, chicken and salt pork in a big pot on high heat. Lower heat to low. Cover then simmer until chicken is tender for 45 minutes.

2. Take out chicken. Let cool until easily handled. Take meat out. Throw out

bones and skin. Chop meat to bite-sized pieces. Put back in the soup.

3. Add ground black pepper, salt, Worcestershire sauce, lima beans, corn, tomatoes, onions and potatoes. Mix well. Stir well and simmer for 1 hour, uncovered.

Nutrition: Calories 368 Carbs 27.9g Protein 25.9g Sugar: 15g; Fiber: 8g; Sodium: 375mg

120. Buffalo Chicken Salads

Preparation Time: 7 minutes

Cooking Time: 3 hours

Serving: 5

Ingredients

- 1½ pounds chicken breast halves
- ½ cup Wing Time® Buffalo chicken sauce
- 4 teaspoons cider vinegar
- 1 teaspoon Worcestershire sauce
- 1 teaspoon paprika
- 1/3 cup light mayonnaise
- 2 tablespoons fat-free milk
- 2 tablespoons crumbled blue cheese
- 2 romaine hearts, chopped
- 1 cup whole grain croutons
- ½ cup very thinly sliced red onion

Direction

1. Place chicken in a 2-quarts slow cooker. Mix together Worcestershire sauce, 2 teaspoons of vinegar and Buffalo sauce in a small bowl; pour over chicken. Dust with paprika. Close and cook for 3 hours on low-heat setting.

2. Mix the leftover 2 teaspoons of vinegar with milk and light mayonnaise together in a small bowl at serving time; mix in blue cheese. While chicken is still in the slow cooker, pull meat into bite-sized pieces using two forks.

3. Split the romaine among 6 dishes. Spoon sauce and chicken over lettuce. Pour with blue cheese dressing then add red onion slices and croutons on top.

Nutrition: Calories 274 Carbs 11g Fiber 2g Protein: 15g; Sugar: 11g; Sodium: 286mg

121. Cacciatore Style Chicken

Preparation Time: 10 minutes

Cooking Time: 4 hours

Serving: 6

Ingredients

- 2 cups sliced fresh mushrooms
- 1 cup sliced celery
- 1 cup chopped carrot
- 2 medium onions, cut into wedges
- 1 green, yellow, or red sweet peppers
- 4 cloves garlic, minced
- 12 chicken drumsticks
- ½ cup chicken broth
- ¼ cup dry white wine
- 2 tablespoons quick-cooking tapioca
- 2 bay leaves
- 1 teaspoon dried oregano, crushed
- 1 teaspoon sugar
- ½ teaspoon salt
- ¼ teaspoon pepper
- 1 (14.5 ounce) can diced tomatoes
- 1/3 cup tomato paste
- Hot cooked pasta or rice

Direction

1. Mix garlic, sweet pepper, onions, carrot, celery and mushrooms in a 5- or 6-qt. slow cooker. Cover veggies with the chicken. Add pepper, salt, sugar, oregano, bay leaves, tapioca, wine and broth.

2. Cover. Cook for 3–3 1/2 hours on high-heat setting.

3. Take chicken out; keep warm. Discard bay leaves. Turn to high-heat setting if using low-heat setting. Mix tomato paste and undrained tomatoes in. Cover. Cook on high-heat setting for 15 more minutes. Serving: Put veggie mixture on top of pasta and chicken.

Nutrition: Calories 324 Sugar: 7g Carbs 35g Protein: 15g; Fiber: 9g; Sodium: 358mg

122. Carnitas Tacos

Preparation Time: 10 minutes

Cooking Time: 5 hours

Serving: 4

Ingredients

- 3 to 3½-pound bone-in pork shoulder roast
- ½ cup chopped onion
- 1/3 cup orange juice
- 1 tablespoon ground cumin
- 1½ teaspoons kosher salt
- 1 teaspoon dried oregano, crushed
- ¼ teaspoon cayenne pepper
- 1 lime
- 2 (5.3 ounce) containers plain low-fat Greek yogurt
- 1 pinch kosher salt
- 16 (6 inch) soft yellow corn tortillas, such as Mission® brand
- 4 leaves green cabbage, quartered
- 1 cup very thinly sliced red onion
- 1 cup salsa (optional)

Direction

1. Take off meat from the bone; throw away bone. Trim meat fat. Slice meat into 2 to 3-inch pieces; put in a slow cooker of 3 1/2 or 4-quart in size. Mix in cayenne, oregano, salt, cumin, orange juice and onion.

2. Cover and cook for 4 to 5 hours on high. Take out meat from the cooker. Shred meat with two forks. Mix in enough cooking liquid to moisten.

3. Take out 1 teaspoon zest (put aside) for lime crema, then squeeze 2 tablespoons lime juice. Mix dash salt, yogurt, and lime juice in a small bowl.

4. Serve lime crema, salsa (if wished), red onion and cabbage with meat in tortillas. Scatter with lime zest.

Nutrition: Calories 301 Carbs 28g Sugar 7g Protein: 15g; Fiber: 9g; Sodium: 351mg

123. Chicken Chili

Preparation Time: 6 minutes

Cooking Time: 1 hour

Serving: 4

Ingredients

- 3 tablespoons vegetable oil
- 2 cloves garlic, minced
- 1 green bell pepper, chopped
- 1 onion, chopped
- 1 stalk celery, sliced
- 1/4-pound mushrooms, chopped
- 1-pound chicken breast
- 1 tablespoon chili powder
- 1 teaspoon dried oregano
- 1 teaspoon ground cumin
- 1/2 teaspoon paprika
- 1/2 teaspoon cocoa powder
- 1/4 teaspoon salt
- 1 pinch crushed red pepper flakes
- 1 pinch ground black pepper
- 1 (14.5 oz) can tomatoes with juice

- 1 (19 oz) can kidney beans

Direction

1. Fill 2 tablespoons of oil into a big skillet and heat it at moderate heat. Add mushrooms, celery, onion, bell pepper and garlic, sautéing for 5 minutes. Put it to one side.

2. Insert the leftover 1 tablespoon of oil into the skillet. At high heat, cook the chicken until browned and its exterior turns firm. Transfer the vegetable mixture back into skillet.

3. Stir in ground black pepper, hot pepper flakes, salt, cocoa powder, paprika, oregano, cumin and chili powder. Continue stirring for several minutes to avoid burning. Pour in the beans and tomatoes and lead the entire mixture to boiling point then adjust the setting to low heat. Place a lid on the skillet and leave it simmering for 15 minutes. Uncover the skillet and leave it simmering for another 15 minutes.

Nutrition: Calories 308 Carbs 25.9g Protein 29g Sugar: 13g; Fiber: 9g; Sodium: 254mg

124.   Chicken Vera Cruz

Preparation Time: 7 minutes

Cooking Time: 10 hours

Serving: 5

Ingredients

- 1 medium onion, cut into wedges
- 1-pound yellow-skin potatoes
- 6 skinless, boneless chicken thighs
- 2 (14.5 oz.) cans no-salt-added diced tomatoes
- 1 fresh jalapeño chili pepper
- 2 tablespoons Worcestershire sauce
- 1 tablespoon chopped garlic
- 1 teaspoon dried oregano, crushed
- ¼ teaspoon ground cinnamon
- 1/8 teaspoon ground cloves
- ½ cup snipped fresh parsley
- ¼ cup chopped pimiento-stuffed green olives

Direction

1. Put onion in a 3 1/2- or 4-quart slow cooker. Place chicken thighs and potatoes on top. Drain and discard juices from a can of tomatoes. Stir undrained and drained tomatoes, cloves, cinnamon, oregano, garlic, Worcestershire sauce and jalapeño pepper together in a bowl. Pour over all in the cooker.

2. Cook with a cover for 10 hours on low-heat setting.

3. To make the topping: Stir chopped pimiento-stuffed green olives and snipped fresh parsley together in a small bowl. Drizzle the topping over each serving of chicken.

Nutrition: Calories 228 Sugar 9g Carbs 25g Protein: 15g; Fiber 9g; Sodium: 396mg

125.   Chicken and Cornmeal Dumplings

Preparation Time: 8 minutes

Cooking Time: 8 hours

Serving: 4

Ingredients

Chicken and Vegetable Filling

- 2 medium carrots, thinly sliced
- 1 stalk celery, thinly sliced
- 1/3 cup corn kernels
- ½ of a medium onion, thinly sliced
- 2 cloves garlic, minced
- 1 teaspoon snipped fresh rosemary
- ¼ teaspoon ground black pepper
- 2 chicken thighs, skinned
- 1 cup reduced sodium chicken broth

- ½ cup fat-free milk
- 1 tablespoon all-purpose flour

Cornmeal Dumplings

- ¼ cup flour
- ¼ cup cornmeal
- ½ teaspoon baking powder
- 1 egg white
- 1 tablespoon fat-free milk
- 1 tablespoon canola oil

Direction

1. Mix 1/4 teaspoon pepper, carrots, garlic, celery, rosemary, corn, and onion in a 1 1/2 or 2-quart slow cooker. Place chicken on top. Pour the broth atop mixture in the cooker.

2. Close and cook on low-heat for 7 to 8 hours.

3. If cooking with the low-heat setting, switch to high-heat setting (or if heat setting is not available, continue to cook). Place the chicken onto a cutting board and let to cool slightly. Once cool enough to handle, chop off chicken from bones and get rid of the bones. Chop the chicken and place back into the mixture in cooker. Mix flour and milk in a small bowl until smooth. Stir into the mixture in cooker.

4. Drop the Cornmeal Dumplings dough into 4 mounds atop hot chicken mixture using two spoons. Cover and cook for 20 to 25 minutes more or until a toothpick come out clean when inserted into a dumpling. (Avoid lifting lid when cooking.) Sprinkle each of the serving with coarse pepper if desired.

5. Mix together 1/2 teaspoon baking powder, 1/4 cup flour, a dash of salt and 1/4 cup cornmeal in a medium bowl. Mix 1 tablespoon canola oil, 1 egg white and 1 tablespoon fat-free milk in a small bowl. Pour the egg mixture into the flour mixture. Mix just until moistened.

Nutrition: Calories 369 Sugar 47g Carbs 9g Protein: 15g; Fiber: 11g; Sodium: 156mg

126.   Chicken and Pepperoni

Preparation Time: 4 minutes

Cooking Time: 4 hours

Serving: 5

Ingredients

- 3½ to 4 pounds meaty chicken pieces
- 1/8 teaspoon salt
- 1/8 teaspoon black pepper
- 2 ounces sliced turkey pepperoni
- ¼ cup sliced pitted ripe olives
- ½ cup reduced-sodium chicken broth
- 1 tablespoon tomato paste
- 1 teaspoon dried Italian seasoning, crushed
- ½ cup shredded part-skim mozzarella cheese (2 ounces)

Direction

1. Put chicken into a 3 1/2 to 5-qt. slow cooker. Sprinkle pepper and salt on the chicken. Slice pepperoni slices in half. Put olives and pepperoni into the slow cooker. In a small bowl, blend Italian seasoning, tomato paste and chicken broth together. Transfer the mixture into the slow cooker.

2. Cook with a cover for 3-3 1/2 hours on high.

3. Transfer the olives, pepperoni and chicken onto a serving platter with a slotted spoon. Discard the cooking liquid. Sprinkle cheese over the chicken. Use foil to loosely cover and allow to sit for 5 minutes to melt the cheese.

Nutrition: Calories 243 Carbs 1g Protein 41g Sugar: 11g; Fiber: 6g; Sodium: 372mg

127. Chicken and Sausage Gumbo

Preparation Time: 6 minutes

Cooking Time: 4 hours

Serving: 5

Ingredients

- 1/3 cup all-purpose flour
- 1 (14 ounce) can reduced-sodium chicken broth
- 2 cups chicken breast
- 8 ounces smoked turkey sausage links
- 2 cups sliced fresh okra
- 1 cup water
- 1 cup coarsely chopped onion
- 1 cup sweet pepper
- ½ cup sliced celery
- 4 cloves garlic, minced
- 1 teaspoon dried thyme
- ½ teaspoon ground black pepper
- ¼ teaspoon cayenne pepper
- 3 cups hot cooked brown rice

Direction

1. To make the roux: Cook the flour upon a medium heat in a heavy medium-sized saucepan, stirring periodically, for roughly 6 minutes or until the flour browns. Take off the heat and slightly cool, then slowly stir in the broth. Cook the roux until it bubbles and thickens up.

2. Pour the roux in a 3 1/2- or 4-quart slow cooker, then add in cayenne pepper, black pepper, thyme, garlic, celery, sweet pepper, onion, water, okra, sausage, and chicken.

3. Cook the soup covered on a high setting for 3 - 3 1/2 hours. Take the fat off the top and serve atop hot cooked brown rice.

Nutrition: Calories 230 Sugar 3g Protein 19g Carbs: 51g; Fiber: 9g; Sodium: 334mg

128. Chicken, Barley, and Leek Stew

Preparation Time: 10 minutes

Cooking Time: 3 hours

Serving: 2

Ingredients

- 1-pound chicken thighs
- 1 tablespoon olive oil
- 1 (49 ounce) can reduced-sodium chicken broth
- 1 cup regular barley (not quick-cooking)
- 2 medium leeks, halved lengthwise and sliced
- 2 medium carrots, thinly sliced
- 1½ teaspoons dried basil or Italian seasoning, crushed
- ¼ teaspoon cracked black pepper

Direction

1. In the big skillet, cook the chicken in hot oil till becoming brown on all sides. In the 4-5-qt. slow cooker, whisk the pepper, dried basil, carrots, leeks, barley, chicken broth and chicken.

2. Keep covered and cooked over high heat setting for 2: 2.5 hours or till the barley softens. As you wish, drizzle with the parsley or fresh basil prior to serving.

Nutrition: Calories 248 Fiber 6g Carbs 27g Protein: 15g; Sugar: 11g; Fiber: 9g; Sodium: 369mg

129. Cider Pork Stew

Preparation Time: 9 minutes

Cooking Time: 12 hours

Serving: 3

Ingredients

- 2 pounds pork shoulder roast
- 3 medium cubed potatoes
- 3 medium carrots
- 2 medium onions, sliced
- 1 cup coarsely chopped apple
- ½ cup coarsely chopped celery
- 3 tablespoons quick-cooking tapioca
- 2 cups apple juice
- 1 teaspoon salt
- 1 teaspoon caraway seeds
- ¼ teaspoon black pepper

Direction

1. Chop the meat into 1-in. cubes. In the 3.5- 5.5 qt. slow cooker, mix the tapioca, celery, apple, onions, carrots, potatoes and meat. Whisk in pepper, caraway seeds, salt and apple juice.

2. Keep covered and cook over low heat setting for 10-12 hours. If you want, use the celery leaves to decorate each of the servings.

Nutrition: Calories 244 Fiber 5g Carbs 33g Protein: 15g; Sugar: 11g; Fiber: 9g; Sodium: 396mg

130. Creamy Chicken Noodle Soup

Preparation Time: 7 minutes

Cooking Time: 8 hours

Serving: 4

Ingredients

- 1 (32 fluid ounce) container reduced-sodium chicken broth
- 3 cups water
- 2½ cups chopped cooked chicken
- 3 medium carrots, sliced
- 3 stalks celery

- 1½ cups sliced fresh mushrooms
- ¼ cup chopped onion
- 1½ teaspoons dried thyme, crushed
- ¾ teaspoon garlic-pepper seasoning
- 3 ounces reduced-fat cream cheese (Neufchâtel), cut up
- 2 cups dried egg noodles

Direction

1. Mix together the garlic-pepper seasoning, thyme, onion, mushrooms, celery, carrots, chicken, water and broth in a 5 to 6-quart slow cooker.

2. Put cover and let it cook for 6-8 hours on low-heat setting.

3. Increase to high-heat setting if you are using low-heat setting. Mix in the cream cheese until blended. Mix in uncooked noodles. Put cover and let it cook for an additional 20-30 minutes or just until the noodles become tender.

Nutrition: Calories 170 Sugar 3g Fiber 2g Protein: 15g; Carbs: 71g; Sodium: 275mg

131. Cuban Pulled Pork Sandwich

Preparation Time: 6 minutes

Cooking Time: 5 hours

Serving: 5

Ingredients

- 1 teaspoon dried oregano, crushed
- ¾ teaspoon ground cumin
- ½ teaspoon ground coriander
- ¼ teaspoon salt
- ¼ teaspoon black pepper
- ¼ teaspoon ground allspice
- 1 2 to 2½-pound boneless pork shoulder roast
- 1 tablespoon olive oil
- Nonstick cooking spray

- 2 cups sliced onions
- 2 green sweet peppers, cut into bite-size strips
- ½ to 1 fresh jalapeño pepper
- 4 cloves garlic, minced
- ¼ cup orange juice
- ¼ cup lime juice
- 6 heart-healthy wheat hamburger buns, toasted
- 2 tablespoons jalapeño mustard

Direction

1. Mix allspice, oregano, black pepper, cumin, salt, and coriander together in a small bowl. Press each side of the roast into the spice mixture. On medium-high heat, heat oil in a big non-stick pan; put in roast. Cook for 5mins until both sides of the roast is light brown, turn the roast one time.

2. Using a cooking spray, grease a 3 1/2 or 4qt slow cooker; arrange the garlic, onions, jalapeno, and green peppers in a layer. Pour in lime juice and orange juice. Slice the roast if needed to fit inside the cooker; put on top of the vegetables covered or 4 1/2-5hrs on high heat setting.

3. Move roast to a cutting board using a slotted spoon. Drain the cooking liquid and keep the jalapeno, green peppers, and onions. Shred the roast with 2 forks then place it back in the cooker. Remove fat from the liquid. Mix half cup of cooking liquid and reserved vegetables into the cooker. Pour in more cooking liquid if desired. Discard the remaining cooking liquid.

4. Slather mustard on rolls. Split the meat between the bottom roll halves. Add avocado on top if desired. Place the roll tops to sandwiches.

Nutrition: Calories 379 Carbs 32g Fiber 4g Protein: 15g; Sugar: 7g; Sodium: 318mg

Seafood Recipes

132.   Shrimp with Green Beans

Preparation Time: 10 minutes

Cooking Time: 2 Minutes

Servings: 4

Ingredients:

- ¾ pound fresh green beans, trimmed
- 1 pound medium frozen shrimp, peeled and deveined
- 2 tablespoons fresh lemon juice
- 2 tablespoons olive oil
- Salt and ground black pepper, as required

Directions:

1. Arrange a steamer trivet in the Instant Pot and pour cup of water.

2. Arrange the green beans on top of trivet in a single layer and top with shrimp.

3. Drizzle with oil and lemon juice.

4. Sprinkle with salt and black pepper.

5. Close the lid and place the pressure valve to "Seal" position.

6. Press "Steam" and just use the default time of 2 minutes.

7. Press "Cancel" and allow a "Natural" release.

8. Open the lid and serve.

Nutrition: Calories: 223, Fats: 1g, Carbs: 7.9g, Sugar: 1.4g, Proteins: 27.4g, Sodium: 322mg

133.   Crab Curry

Preparation Time: 10 minutes

Cooking Time: 20 Minutes

Servings: 2

Ingredients:

- 0.5lb chopped crab
- 1 thinly sliced red onion

- 0.5 cup chopped tomato
- 3tbsp curry paste
- 1tbsp oil or ghee

Directions:

1. Set the Instant Pot to sauté and add the onion, oil, and curry paste.
2. When the onion is soft, add the remaining ingredients and seal.
3. Cook on Stew for 20 minutes.
4. Release the pressure naturally.

Nutrition: Calories: 223, Fats: 1g, Carbs: 7.9g, Sugar: 1.4g, Proteins: 27.4g, Sodium: 322mg Fiber: 9g;

134.   Mixed Chowder

Preparation Time: 10 minutes

Cooking Time: 35 Minutes

Servings: 2

Ingredients:

- 1lb fish stew mix
- 2 cups white sauce
- 3tbsp old bay seasoning

Directions:

1. Mix all the ingredients in your Instant Pot.
2. Cook on Stew for 35 minutes.
3. Release the pressure naturally.

Nutrition: Calories: 320; Carbs: 9; Sugar: 2; Fat: 16; Protein: 4, Fiber: 9g; Sodium: 279mg

135.   Mussels in Tomato Sauce

Preparation Time: 10 minutes

Cooking Time: 3 Minutes

Servings: 4

Ingredients:

- 2 tomatoes, seeded and chopped finely
- 2 pounds mussels, scrubbed and de-bearded

- 1 cup low-sodium chicken broth
- 1 tablespoon fresh lemon juice
- 2 garlic cloves, minced

Directions:

1. In the pot of Instant Pot, place tomatoes, garlic, wine and bay leaf and stir to combine.
2. Arrange the mussels on top.
3. Close the lid and place the pressure valve to "Seal" position.
4. Press "Manual" and cook under "High Pressure" for about 3 minutes.
5. Press "Cancel" and carefully allow a "Quick" release.
6. Open the lid and serve hot.

Nutrition: Calories: 213, Fats: 25.2g, Carbs: 11g, Sugar: 1. Proteins: 28.2g, Fiber: 11g.

136.   Citrus Salmon

Preparation Time: 10 minutes

Cooking Time: 7 Minutes

Servings: 4

Ingredients:

- 4 (4-ounce) salmon fillets
- 1 cup low-sodium chicken broth
- 1 teaspoon fresh ginger, minced
- 2 teaspoons fresh orange zest, grated finely
- 3 tablespoons fresh orange juice
- 1 tablespoon olive oil
- Ground black pepper, as required

Directions:

1. In Instant Pot, add all ingredients and mix.
2. Close the lid and place the pressure valve to "Seal" position.
3. Press "Manual" and cook under "High Pressure" for about 7 minutes.

4. Press "Cancel" and allow a "Natural" release.

5. Open the lid and serve the salmon fillets with the topping of cooking sauce.

Nutrition: Calories: 190, Fats: 10.5g, Carbs: 1.8g, Sugar: 1g, Proteins: 22. Sodium: 68mg Fiber: 9g.

137.   Herbed Salmon

Preparation Time: 10 minutes

Cooking Time: 3 Minutes

Servings: 4

Ingredients:

- 4 (4-ounce) salmon fillets

- ¼ cup olive oil

- 2 tablespoons fresh lemon juice

- 1 garlic clove, minced

- ¼ teaspoon dried oregano

- Salt and ground black pepper, as required

- 4 fresh rosemary sprigs

- 4 lemon slices

Directions:

1. For dressing: in a large bowl, add oil, lemon juice, garlic, oregano, salt and black pepper and beat until well co combined.

2. Arrange a steamer trivet in the Instant Pot and pour 11/2 cups of water in Instant Pot.

3. Place the salmon fillets on top of trivet in a single layer and top with dressing.

4. Arrange 1 rosemary sprig and 1 lemon slice over each fillet.

5. Close the lid and place the pressure valve to "Seal" position.

6. Press "Steam" and just use the default time of 3 minutes.

7. Press "Cancel" and carefully allow a "Quick" release.

8. Open the lid and serve hot.

Nutrition: Calories: 262, Fats: 17g, Carbs: 0.7g, Sugar: 0.2g, Proteins: 22.1g, Sodium: 91mg Fiber: 9g;

138.   Salmon in Green Sauce

Preparation Time: 10 minutes

Cooking Time: 12 Minutes

Servings: 4

Ingredients:

- 4 (6-ounce) salmon fillets

- 1 avocado, peeled, pitted and chopped

- 1/2 cup fresh basil, chopped

- 3 garlic cloves, chopped

- 1 tablespoon fresh lemon zest, grated finely

Directions:

1. Grease a large piece of foil.

2. In a large bowl, add all ingredients except salmon and water and with a fork, mash completely.

3. Place fillets in the center of foil and top with avocado mixture evenly.

4. Fold the foil around fillets to seal them.

5. Arrange a steamer trivet in the Instant Pot and pour 1/2 cup of water.

6. Place the foil packet on top of trivet.

7. Close the lid and place the pressure valve to "Seal" position.

8. Press "Manual" and cook under "High Pressure" for about minutes.

9. Meanwhile, preheat the oven to broiler.

10. Press "Cancel" and allow a "Natural" release.

11. Open the lid and transfer the salmon fillets onto a broiler pan.

12. Broil for about 3-4 minutes.

13. Serve warm.

Nutrition: Calories: 333, Fats: 20.3g, Carbs: 5.5g, Sugar: 0.4g, Proteins: 34.2g, Sodium: 79mg; Fiber: 11g;

139.   Braised Shrimp

Preparation Time: 10 minutes

Cooking Time: 4 Minutes

Servings: 4

Ingredients:

- 1 pound frozen large shrimp, peeled and deveined
- 2 shallots, chopped
- ¾ cup low-sodium chicken broth
- 2 tablespoons fresh lemon juice
- 2 tablespoons olive oil
- 1 tablespoon garlic, crushed
- Ground black pepper, as required

Directions:

1. In the Instant Pot, place oil and press "Sauté". Now add the shallots and cook for about 2 minutes.
2. Add the garlic and cook for about 1 minute.
3. Press "Cancel" and stir in the shrimp, broth, lemon juice and black pepper.
4. Close the lid and place the pressure valve to "Seal" position.
5. Press "Manual" and cook under "High Pressure" for about 1 minute.
6. Press "Cancel" and carefully allow a "Quick" release.
7. Open the lid and serve hot.

Nutrition: Calories: 209, Fats: 9g, Carbs: 4.3g, Sugar: 0.2g, Proteins: 26.6g, Sodium: 293mg Fiber: 10g;

140.   Shrimp Coconut Curry

Preparation Time: 10 minutes

Cooking Time: 20 Minutes

Servings: 2

Ingredients:

- 0.5lb cooked shrimp
- 1 thinly sliced onion
- 1 cup coconut yogurt
- 3tbsp curry paste
- 1tbsp oil or ghee

Directions:

1. Set the Instant Pot to sauté and add the onion, oil, and curry paste.
2. When the onion is soft, add the remaining ingredients and seal.
3. Cook on Stew for 20 minutes.
4. Release the pressure naturally.

Nutrition: Calories: 380; Carbs: 13; Sugar: 4; Fat: 22; Protein: 40; Fiber: 9g; Sodium: 318mg

141.   Trout Bake

Preparation Time: 10 minutes

Cooking Time: 35 Minutes

Servings: 2

Ingredients:

- 1lb trout fillets, boneless
- 1lb chopped winter vegetables
- 1 cup low sodium fish broth
- 1tbsp mixed herbs
- sea salt as desired

Directions:

1. Mix all the ingredients except the broth in a foil pouch.
2. Place the pouch in the steamer basket your Instant Pot.
3. Pour the broth into the Instant Pot.
4. Cook on Steam for 35 minutes.
5. Release the pressure naturally.

Nutrition: Calories: 310; Carbs: 14; Sugar: 2; Fat: 12; Protein: 40; Fiber: 9g; Sodium: 288mg

142.   Sardine Curry

Preparation Time: 10 minutes

Cooking Time: 35 Minutes

Servings: 2

Ingredients:

- 5 tins of sardines in tomato
- 1lb chopped vegetables
- 1 cup low sodium fish broth
- 3tbsp curry paste

Directions:

1. Mix all the ingredients in your Instant Pot.
2. Cook on Stew for 35 minutes.
3. Release the pressure naturally.

Nutrition: Calories: 320; Carbs: 8; Sugar: 2; Fat: 16; Protein: 3g Fiber: 9g; sodium:284mg

143.   Swordfish Steak

Preparation Time: 10 minutes

Cooking Time: 35 Minutes

Servings: 2

Ingredients:

- 1lb swordfish steak, whole
- 1lb chopped Mediterranean vegetables
- 1 cup low sodium fish broth
- 2tbsp soy sauce

Directions:

1. Mix all the ingredients except the broth in a foil pouch.
2. Place the pouch in the steamer basket for your Instant Pot.
3. Pour the broth into the Instant Pot. Lower the steamer basket into the Instant Pot.
4. Cook on Steam for 35 minutes.
5. Release the pressure naturally.

Nutrition: Calories: 270; Carbs: 5; Sugar: 1; Fat: 10; Protein: 48; GL: 1

144.   Lemon Sole

Preparation Time: 10 minutes

Cooking Time: 5 Minutes

Servings: 2

Ingredients:

- 1lb sole fillets, boned and skinned
- 1 cup low sodium fish broth
- 2 shredded sweet onions
- juice of half a lemon
- 2tbsp dried cilantro

Directions:

1. Mix all the ingredients in your Instant Pot.
2. Cook on Stew for 5 minutes.
3. Release the pressure naturally.

Nutrition: Calories: 270; Carbs: 5; Sugar: 1; Fat: 10; Protein: 48; Fiber: 11g; Sodium: 329mg

145.   Lemony Salmon

Preparation Time: 10 minutes

Cooking Time: 3 Minutes

Servings: 3

Ingredients:

- 1 pound salmon fillet, cut into 3 pieces
- 3 teaspoons fresh dill, chopped
- 5 tablespoons fresh lemon juice, divided
- Salt and ground black pepper, as required

Directions:

1. Arrange a steamer trivet in Instant Pot and pour ¼ cup of lemon juice.
2. Season the salmon with salt and black pepper evenly.

3. Place the salmon pieces on top of trivet, skin side down and drizzle with remaining lemon juice.

4. Now, sprinkle the salmon pieces with dill evenly.

5. Close the lid and place the pressure valve to "Seal" position.

6. Press "Steam" and use the default time of 3 minutes.

7. Press "Cancel" and allow a "Natural" release.

8. Open the lid and serve hot.

Nutrition: Calories: 230; Carbs: Sugar: 1; Fat: 6; Protein: 46; Fiber: 16g; Sodium: 285mg

146.   Tuna Sweet corn Casserole

Preparation Time: 10 minutes

Cooking Time: 35 Minutes

Servings: 2

Ingredients:

- 3 small tins of tuna
- 0.5lb sweet corn kernels
- 1lb chopped vegetables
- 1 cup low sodium vegetable broth
- 2tbsp spicy seasoning

Directions:

1. Mix all the ingredients in your Instant Pot.

2. Cook on Stew for 35 minutes.

3. Release the pressure naturally.

Nutrition: Calories: 300; Carbs: 6; Sugar: 1; Fat: 9; Protein: 45 Fiber: 12g; Sodium: 287mg.

147.   Lemon Pepper Salmon

Preparation Time: 10 minutes

Cooking Time: 10 Minutes

Servings: 4

Ingredients:

- 3 tbsps. ghee or avocado oil

- 1 lb. skin-on salmon filet
- 1 julienned red bell pepper
- 1 julienned green zucchini
- 1 julienned carrot
- ¾ cup water
- A few sprigs of parsley, tarragon, dill, basil or a combination
- 1/2 sliced lemon
- 1/2 tsp. black pepper
- ¼ tsp. sea salt

Directions:

1. Add the water and the herbs into the bottom of the Instant Pot and put in a wire steamer rack making sure the handles extend upwards.

2. Place the salmon filet onto the wire rack, with the skin side facing down.

3. Drizzle the salmon with ghee, season with black pepper and salt, and top with the lemon slices.

4. Close and seal the Instant Pot, making sure the vent is turned to "Sealing".

5. Select the "Steam" setting and cook for 3 minutes.

6. While the salmon cooks, julienne the vegetables, and set aside.

7. Once done, quick release the pressure, and then press the "Keep Warm/Cancel" button.

8. Uncover and wearing oven mitts, carefully remove the steamer rack with the salmon.

9. Remove the herbs and discard them.

10. Add the vegetables to the pot and put the lid back on.

11. Select the "Sauté" function and cook for 1-2 minutes.

12. Serve the vegetables with salmon and add the remaining fat to the pot.

13. Pour a little of the sauce over the fish and vegetables if desired.

Nutrition: Calories 296, Carbs 8g, Fat 15 g, Protein 31 g, Fiber 12g, Sodium 284 mg

148. Baked Salmon with Garlic Parmesan Topping

Preparation time: 5 minutes,

Cooking time: 20 minutes,

Servings: 4

Ingredients:

- 1 lb. wild caught salmon filets
- 2 tbsp. margarine
- What you'll need from store cupboard:
- ¼ cup reduced fat parmesan cheese, grated
- ¼ cup light mayonnaise
- 2-3 cloves garlic, diced
- 2 tbsp. parsley
- Salt and pepper

Directions:

1. Heat oven to 350 and line a baking pan with parchment paper.
2. Place salmon on pan and season with salt and pepper.
3. In a medium skillet, over medium heat, melt butter. Add garlic and cook, stirring 1 minute.
4. Reduce heat to low and add remaining Ingredients. Stir until everything is melted and combined.
5. Spread evenly over salmon and bake 15 minutes for thawed fish or 20 for frozen. Salmon is done when it flakes easily with a fork. Serve.

Nutrition: Calories 408 Carbs 4g Protein 41g Fat 24g Sugar 1g Fiber 0g Sodium: 228mg

149. Blackened Shrimp

Preparation time: 5 minutes

Cooking time: 5 minutes

Servings: 4

Ingredients:

- 1 1/2 lbs. shrimp, peel & devein
- 4 lime wedges
- 4 tbsp. cilantro, chopped
- What you'll need from store cupboard:
- 4 cloves garlic, diced
- 1 tbsp. chili powder
- 1 tbsp. paprika
- 1 tbsp. olive oil
- 2 tsp. Splenda brown sugar
- 1 tsp. cumin
- 1 tsp. oregano
- 1 tsp. garlic powder
- 1 tsp. salt
- 1/2 tsp. pepper

Directions:

1. In a small bowl combine seasonings and Splenda brown sugar.
2. Heat oil in a skillet over med-high heat. Add shrimp, in a single layer, and cook 1-2 minutes per side.
3. Add seasonings, and cook, stirring, 30 seconds. Serve garnished with cilantro and a lime wedge.

Nutrition: Calories 252 Carbs 7g Protein 39g Fat 7g Sugar 2g Fiber 1g; Sodium: 396mg

150. Cajun Catfish

Preparation time: 5 minutes

Cooking time: 15 minutes

Servings: 4

Ingredients:

- 4 (8 oz.) catfish fillets
- What you'll need from store cupboard:
- 2 tbsp. olive oil
- 2 tsp. garlic salt
- 2 tsp. thyme
- 2 tsp. paprika
- 1/2 tsp. cayenne pepper
- 1/2 tsp. red hot sauce
- ¼ tsp. black pepper
- Nonstick cooking spray

Directions:

1. Heat oven to 450 degrees. Spray a 9x13-inch baking dish with cooking spray.
2. In a small bowl whisk together everything but catfish. Brush both sides of fillets, using all the spice mix.
3. Bake 10-13 minutes or until fish flakes easily with a fork. Serve.

Nutrition: Calories 366 Carbs 0g Protein 35g Fat 24g Sugar 0g Fiber 0g Sodium: 288mg

151.   Cajun Flounder & Tomatoes

Preparation time: 10 minutes

Cooking time: 15 minutes

Servings: 4

Ingredients:

- 4 flounder fillets
- 2 1/2 cups tomatoes, diced
- ¾ cup onion, diced
- ¾ cup green bell pepper, diced
- What you'll need from store cupboard:
- 2 cloves garlic, diced fine
- 1 tbsp. Cajun seasoning
- 1 tsp. olive oil

Directions:

1. Heat oil in a large skillet over med-high heat. Add onion and garlic and cook 2 minutes, or until soft. Add tomatoes, peppers and spices, and cook 2-3 minutes until tomatoes soften.
2. Lay fish over top. Cover, reduce heat to medium and cook, 5-8 minutes, or until fish flakes easily with a fork. Transfer fish to serving plates and top with sauce.

Nutrition: Calories 194 Carbs 8g Protein 32g Fat 3g Sugar 5g Fiber 2g Sodium: 227mg

152.   Cajun Shrimp & Roasted Vegetables

Preparation time: 5 minutes

Cooking time: 15 minutes

Servings: 4

Ingredients:

- 1 lb. large shrimp, peeled and deveined
- 2 zucchinis, sliced
- 2 yellow squash, sliced
- 1/2 bunch asparagus, cut into thirds
- 2 red bell pepper, cut into chunks
- What you'll need from store cupboard:
- 2 tbsp. olive oil
- 2 tbsp. Cajun Seasoning
- Salt & pepper, to taste

Directions:

1. Heat oven to 400 degrees.
2. Combine shrimp and vegetables in a large bowl. Add oil and seasoning and toss to coat.
3. Spread evenly in a large baking sheet and bake 15-20 minutes, or until vegetables are tender. Serve.

Nutrition: Calories 251 Carbs 13g Protein 30g Fat 9g Sugar 6g Fiber 4g Sodium: 257mg

153.   Cilantro Lime Grilled Shrimp

Preparation time: 5 minutes,

Cooking time: 5 minutes,

Servings: 6

Ingredients:

- 1 1/2 lbs. large shrimp raw, peeled, deveined with tails on

- Juice and zest of 1 lime

- 2 tbsp. fresh cilantro chopped

- What you'll need from store cupboard:

- ¼ cup olive oil

- 2 cloves garlic, diced fine

- 1 tsp. smoked paprika

- ¼ tsp. cumin

- 1/2 teaspoon salt

- ¼ tsp. cayenne pepper

Directions:

1. Place the shrimp in a large Ziploc bag.

2. Mix remaining Ingredients in a small bowl and pour over shrimp. Let marinate 20-30 minutes.

3. Heat up the grill. Skewer the shrimp and cook 2-3 minutes, per side, just until they turn pick. Be careful not to overcook them. Serve garnished with cilantro.

Nutrition: Calories 317 Carbs 4g Protein 39g Fat 15g Sugar 0g Fiber 0g Sodium: 396mg

154.   Crab Frittata

Preparation time: 10 minutes

Cooking time: 50 minutes

Servings: 4

Ingredients:

- 4 eggs

- 2 cups lump crabmeat

- 1 cup half-n-half

- 1 cup green onions, diced

- What you'll need from store cupboard:

- 1 cup reduced fat parmesan cheese, grated

- 1 tsp. salt

- 1 tsp. pepper

- 1 tsp. smoked paprika

- 1 tsp. Italian seasoning

- Nonstick cooking spray

Directions:

1. Heat oven to 350 degrees. Spray an 8-inch springform pan, or pie plate with cooking spray.

2. In a large bowl, whisk together the eggs and half-n-half. Add seasonings and parmesan cheese, stir to mix.

3. Stir in the onions and crab meat. Pour into prepared pan and bake 35-40 minutes, or eggs are set and top is lightly browned.

4. Let cool 10 minutes, then slice and serve warm or at room temperature.

Nutrition: Calories 276 Carbs 5g Protein 25g Fat 17g Sugar 1g Fiber 1g Sodium: 287mg

155. Brussels Sprouts

Preparation Time: 5 minutes

Cooking Time: 3 minutes

Servings: 5

Ingredients:

- 1 tsp. extra-virgin olive oil
- 1 lb. halved Brussels sprouts
- 3 tbsps. apple cider vinegar
- 3 tbsps. gluten-free tamari soy sauce
- 3 tbsps. chopped sun-dried tomatoes

Direction:

1. Select the "Sauté" function on your Instant Pot, add oil and allow the pot to get hot.
2. Cancel the "Sauté" function and add the Brussels sprouts.
3. Stir well and allow the sprouts to cook in the residual heat for 2-3 minutes.
4. Add the tamari soy sauce and vinegar, and then stir.
5. Cover the Instant Pot, sealing the pressure valve by pointing it to "Sealing."
6. Select the "Manual, High Pressure" setting and cook for 3 minutes.
7. Once the cook cycle is done, do a quick pressure release, and then stir in the chopped sun-dried tomatoes.
8. Serve immediately.

Nutrition: Calories 62 Carbs 10g Fat 1g Protein: 15g; Sugar: 11g; Fiber: 9g; Sodium: 396mg

156. Garlic and Herb Carrots

Preparation Time: 2 minutes

Cooking Time: 18 minutes

Servings: 3

Ingredients:

- 2 tbsps. butter
- 1 lb. baby carrots
- 1 cup water
- 1 tsp. fresh thyme or oregano
- 1 tsp. minced garlic
- Black pepper
- Coarse sea salt

Direction:

1. Fill water to the inner pot of the Instant Pot, and then put in a steamer basket.
2. .Layer the carrots into the steamer basket.
3. Close and seal the lid, with the pressure vent in the "Sealing" position.
4. Select the "Steam" setting and cook for 2 minutes on high pressure.
5. Quick release the pressure and then carefully remove the steamer basket with the steamed carrots, discarding the water.
6. Add butter to the inner pot of the Instant Pot and allow it to melt on the "Sauté" function.
7. Add garlic and sauté for 30 seconds, and then add the carrots. Mix well.
8. Stir in the fresh herbs, and cook for 2-3 minutes.
9. Season with salt and black pepper, and the transfer to a serving bowl.
10. .Serve warm and enjoy!

Nutrition: Calories 122 Carbs 12g Fat 7g Protein: 15g; Sugar: 10g; Fiber: 19g; Sodium: 322mg

157. Cilantro Lime Drumsticks

Preparation Time: 5 minutes

Cooking Time: 15 minutes

Servings: 6

Ingredients:

- 1 tbsp. olive oil

- 6 chicken drumsticks
- 4 minced garlic cloves
- ½ cup low-sodium chicken broth
- 1 tsp. cayenne pepper
- 1 tsp. crushed red peppers
- 1 tsp. fine sea salt
- Juice of 1 lime

To Serve:

- 2 tbsp. chopped cilantro
- Extra lime zest

Direction:

1. Pour olive oil to the Instant Pot and set it on the "Sauté" function.
2. Once the oil is hot adding the chicken drumsticks, and season them well.
3. Using tongs, stir the drumsticks and brown the drumsticks for 2 minutes per side.
4. Add the lime juice, fresh cilantro, and chicken broth to the pot.
5. Lock and seal the lid, turning the pressure valve to "Sealing."
6. Cook the drumsticks on the "Manual, High Pressure" setting for 9 minutes.
7. Once done let the pressure release naturally.
8. Carefully transfer the drumsticks to an aluminum-foiled baking sheet and broil them in the oven for 3-5 minutes until golden brown.
9. Serve warm, garnished with more cilantro and lime zest.

Nutrition: Calories 480 Carbs 3.3g Fat 29g Protein: 15g; Sugar: 13g; Fiber: 18g; Sodium: 320mg

158.   Eggplant Spread

Preparation Time: 5 minutes

Cooking Time: 18 minutes

Servings: 5

Ingredients:

- 4 tbsps. extra-virgin olive oil
- 2 lbs. eggplant
- 4 skin-on garlic cloves
- ½ cup water
- ¼ cup pitted black olives
- 3 sprigs fresh thyme
- Juice of 1 lemon
- 1 tbsp. tahini
- 1 tsp. sea salt
- Fresh extra-virgin olive oil

Direction:

1. Peel the eggplant in alternating stripes, leaving some areas with skin and some with no skin.
2. Slice into big chunks and layer at the bottom of your Instant Pot.
3. Add olive oil to the pot, and on the "Sauté" function, fry and caramelize the eggplant on one side, about 5 minutes.
4. Add in the garlic cloves with the skin on.
5. Flip over the eggplant and then add in the remaining uncooked eggplant chunks, salt, and water.
6. Close the lid, ensure the pressure release valve is set to "Sealing."
7. Cook for 5 minutes on the "Manual, High Pressure" setting.
8. Once done, carefully open the pot by quick releasing the pressure through the steam valve.
9. Discard most of the brown cooking liquid.

10. Remove the garlic cloves and peel them.
11. Add the lemon juice, tahini, cooked and fresh garlic cloves and pitted black olives to the pot.
12. Using a hand-held immersion blender, process all the ingredients until smooth.
13. Pour out the spread into a serving dish and season with fresh thyme, whole black olives and some extra-virgin olive oil, prior to serving.

Nutrition: Calories 155 Carbs 16.8g Fat 11.7g Protein: 27g; Sugar: 19g; Fiber: 28g; Sodium: 313mg

159.   Carrot Hummus

Preparation Time: 15 minutes

Cooking Time: 10 minutes

Servings: 2

Ingredients:

- 1 chopped carrot
- 2 oz. cooked chickpeas
- 1 tsp. lemon juice
- 1 tsp. tahini
- 1 tsp. fresh parsley

Direction:

1. Place the carrot and chickpeas in your Instant Pot.
2. Add a cup of water, seal, cook for 10 minutes on Stew.
3. Depressurize naturally. Blend with the remaining ingredients.

Nutrition: Calories 58 Carbs 8g Fat 2g Protein: 11g; Sugar: 15g; Fiber: 12g; Sodium: 372mg

160.   Vegetable Rice Pilaf

Preparation Time: 5 minutes

Cooking Time: 25 minutes

Servings: 6

Ingredients:

- 1 tablespoon olive oil
- ½ medium yellow onion, diced
- 1 cup uncooked long-grain brown rice
- 2 cloves minced garlic
- ½ teaspoon dried basil
- Salt and pepper
- 2 cups fat-free chicken broth
- 1 cup frozen mixed veggies

Direction:

1. Cook oil in a large skillet over medium heat.
2. Add the onion and sauté for 3 minutes until translucent.
3. Stir in the rice and cook until lightly toasted.
4. Add the garlic, basil, salt, and pepper then stir to combined.
5. Stir in the chicken broth then bring to a boil.
6. Decrease heat and simmer, covered, for 10 minutes.
7. Stir in the frozen veggies then cover and cook for another 10 minutes until heated through. Serve hot.

Nutrition: Calories 90 Carbs 12.6g Protein: 12.5g; Sugar: 14.1g; Fiber: 9.6g; Sodium: 321.3mg

161.   Curry Roasted Cauliflower Florets

Preparation Time: 5 minutes

Cooking Time: 25 minutes

Servings: 6

Ingredients:

- 8 cups cauliflower florets
- 2 tablespoons olive oil
- 1 teaspoon curry powder

- ½ teaspoon garlic powder
- Salt and pepper

Direction:

1. Prep the oven to 425°F and line a baking sheet with foil.
2. Toss the cauliflower with the olive oil and spread on the baking sheet.
3. Sprinkle with curry powder, garlic powder, salt, and pepper.
4. Roast for 25 minutes or until just tender. Serve hot.

Nutrition: Calories 75 Carbs 7.4g Fiber 3.5g Protein: 15g; Sugar: 11g; Fiber: 9g; Sodium: 396mg

162. Mushroom Barley Risotto

Preparation Time: 5 minutes

Cooking Time: 25 minutes

Servings: 8

Ingredients:

- 4 cups fat-free beef broth
- 2 tablespoons olive oil
- 1 small onion, diced well
- 2 cloves minced garlic
- 8 ounces thinly sliced mushrooms
- ¼ tsp dried thyme
- Salt and pepper
- 1 cup pearled barley
- ½ cup dry white wine

Direction:

1. Heat the beef broth in a medium saucepan and keep it warm.
2. Heat the oil in a large, deep skillet over medium heat.
3. Add the onions and garlic and sauté for 2 minutes then stir in the mushrooms and thyme.

4. Season with salt and pepper and sauté for 2 minutes more.
5. Add the barley and sauté for 1 minute then pour in the wine.
6. Ladle about ½ cup of beef broth into the skillet and stir well to combine.
7. Cook until most of the broth has been absorbed then add another ladle.
8. Repeat until you have used all of the broth and the barley is cooked to al dente.
9. Season and serve hot.

Nutrition: Calories 155 Carbs 21.9g Fiber 4.4g Protein: 15g; Sugar: 11g; Fiber:11.2g; Sodium: 396mg

163. Lemon Garlic Green Beans

Preparation time: 5 minutes

Cooking Time: 10 minutes

Servings: 6

Ingredients:

- 1 1/2 pounds green beans, trimmed
- 2 tablespoons olive oil
- 1 tablespoon fresh lemon juice
- 2 cloves minced garlic
- Salt and pepper

Directions:

1. Fill a large bowl with ice water and set aside.
2. Bring a pot of salted water to boil then add the green beans.
3. Cook for 3 minutes then drain and immediately place in the ice water.
4. Cool the beans completely then drain them well.
5. Heat the oil in a large skillet over medium-high heat.
6. Add the green beans, tossing to coat, then add the lemon juice, garlic, salt, and pepper.

7. Sauté for 3 minutes until the beans are tender-crisp then serve hot.

Nutrition: Calories 75, Fat 4.8g, Carbs 8.5g, Protein 2.1g, Sugar 1.7g, Fiber 3.9g, Sodium 7mg

164. Brown Rice & Lentil Salad

Preparation time: 10 minutes

Cooking Time: 10 minutes

Servings: 4

Ingredients:

- 1 cup water
- 1/2 cup instant brown rice
- 2 tablespoons olive oil
- 2 tablespoons red wine vinegar
- 1 tablespoon Dijon mustard
- 1 tablespoon minced onion
- 1/2 teaspoon paprika
- Salt and pepper
- 1 (15-ounce) can brown lentils, rinsed and drained
- 1 medium carrot, shredded
- 2 tablespoons fresh chopped parsley

Directions:

1. Stir together the water and instant brown rice in a medium saucepan.
2. Bring to a boil then simmer for 10 minutes, covered.
3. Remove from heat and set aside while you prepare the salad.
4. Whisk together the olive oil, vinegar, Dijon mustard, onion, paprika, salt, and pepper in a medium bowl.
5. Toss in the cooked rice, lentils, carrots, and parsley.
6. Adjust seasoning to taste then stir well and serve warm.

Nutrition: Calories 145, Fat 7.7g, Carbs 13.1g, Protein 6g, Sugar 1g, Fiber 2.2g, Sodium 57mg

165. Mashed Butternut Squash

Preparation time: 5 minutes

Cooking Time: 25 minutes

Servings: 6

Ingredients:

- 3 pounds whole butternut squash (about 2 medium)
- 2 tablespoons olive oil
- Salt and pepper

Directions:

1. Preheat the oven to 400F and line a baking sheet with parchment.
2. Cut the squash in half and remove the seeds.
3. Cut the squash into cubes and toss with oil then spread on the baking sheet.
4. Roast for 25 minutes until tender then place in a food processor.
5. Blend smooth then season with salt and pepper to taste.

Nutrition: Calories 90, Fat 4.8g, Carbs 12.3g, Protein 1.1g, Sugar 2.3g, Fiber 2.1g, Sodium 4mg

166. Cilantro Lime Quinoa

Preparation time: 5 minutes

Cooking Time: 25 minutes

Servings: 6

Ingredients:

- 1 cup uncooked quinoa
- 1 tablespoon olive oil
- 1 medium yellow onion, diced
- 2 cloves minced garlic
- 1 (4-ounce) can diced green chiles, drained
- 1 1/2 cups fat-free chicken broth
- ¾ cup fresh chopped cilantro
- 1/2 cup sliced green onion

- 2 tablespoons lime juice
- Salt and pepper

Directions:

1. Rinse the quinoa thoroughly in cool water using a fine mesh sieve.
2. Heat the oil in a large saucepan over medium heat.
3. Add the onion and sauté for 2 minutes then stir in the chile and garlic.
4. Cook for 1 minute then stir in the quinoa and chicken broth.
5. Bring to a boil then reduce heat and simmer, covered, until the quinoa absorbs the liquid: about 20 to 25 minutes.
6. Remove from heat then stir in the cilantro, green onions, and lime juice.
7. Season with salt and pepper to taste and serve hot.

Nutrition: Calories 150, Fat 4.1g, Carbs 22.5g, Protein 6g, Sugar 1.7g, Fiber 2.7g, Sodium 179mg

167.   Oven-Roasted Veggies

Preparation time: 5 minutes

Cooking Time: 25 minutes

Servings: 6

Ingredients:

- 1 pound cauliflower florets
- 1/2 pound broccoli florets
- 1 large yellow onion, cut into chunks
- 1 large red pepper, cored and chopped
- 2 medium carrots, peeled and sliced
- 2 tablespoons olive oil
- 2 tablespoons apple cider vinegar
- Salt and pepper

Directions:

1. Preheat the oven to 425F and line a large rimmed baking sheet with parchment.
2. Spread the veggies on the baking sheet and drizzle with oil and vinegar.
3. Toss well and season with salt and pepper.
4. Spread the veggies in a single layer then roast for 20 to 25 minutes, stirring every 10 minutes, until tender.
5. Adjust seasoning to taste and serve hot.

Nutrition: Calories 100, Fat 5g, Carbs 12.4g, Protein 3.2g, Sugar 5.5g, Fiber 4.2g, Sodium 51mg

168.   Parsley Tabbouleh

Preparation time: 5 minutes

Cooking Time: 25 minutes

Servings: 6

Ingredients:

- 1 cup water
- 1/2 cup bulgur
- ¼ cup fresh lemon juice
- 2 tablespoons olive oil
- 2 cloves minced garlic
- Salt and pepper
- 2 cups fresh chopped parsley
- 2 medium tomatoes, died
- 1 small cucumber, diced
- ¼ cup fresh chopped mint

Directions:

1. Bring the water and bulgur to a boil in a small saucepan then remove from heat.
2. Cover and let stand until the water is fully absorbed, about 25 minutes.

3. Meanwhile, whisk together the lemon juice, olive oil, garlic, salt, and pepper in a medium bowl.

4. Toss in the cooked bulgur along with the parsley, tomatoes, cucumber, and mint.

5. Season with salt and pepper to taste and serve.

Nutrition: Calories 110, Fat 5.3g, Carbs 14.4g, Protein 3g, Sugar 2.4g, Fiber 3.9g, Sodium 21mg

169.   Garlic Sautéed Spinach

Preparation time: 5 minutes

Cooking Time: 10 minutes

Servings: 4

Ingredients:

- 1 1/2 tablespoons olive oil
- 4 cloves minced garlic
- 6 cups fresh baby spinach
- Salt and pepper

Directions:

1. Heat the oil in a large skillet over medium-high heat.

2. Add the garlic and cook for 1 minute.

3. Stir in the spinach and season with salt and pepper.

4. Sauté for 1 to 2 minutes until just wilted. Serve hot.

Nutrition: Calories 60, Fat 5.5g, Carbs 2.6g, Protein 1.5g, Sugar 0.2g, Fiber 1.1g, Sodium 36mg

170.   French Lentils

Preparation time: 5 minutes

Cooking Time: 25 minutes

Servings: 10

Ingredients:

- 2 tablespoons olive oil
- 1 medium onion, diced
- 1 medium carrot, peeled and diced
- 2 cloves minced garlic
- 5 1/2 cups water
- 2 ¼ cups French lentils, rinsed and drained
- 1 teaspoon dried thyme
- 2 small bay leaves
- Salt and pepper

Directions:

1. Heat the oil in a large saucepan over medium heat.

2. Add the onions, carrot, and garlic and sauté for 3 minutes.

3. Stir in the water, lentils, thyme, and bay leaves: season with salt.

4. Bring to a boil then reduce to a simmer and cook until tender, about 20 minutes.

5. Drain any excess water and adjust seasoning to taste. Serve hot.

Nutrition: Calories 185, Fat 3.3g, Carbs 27.9g, Protein 11.4g, Sugar 1.7g, Fiber 13.7g, Sodium 11mg

171.   Grain-Free Berry Cobbler

Preparation time: 5 minutes

Cooking Time: 25 minutes

Servings: 10

Ingredients:

- 4 cups fresh mixed berries
- 1/2 cup ground flaxseed
- ¼ cup almond meal
- ¼ cup unsweetened shredded coconut
- 1/2 tablespoon baking powder
- 1 teaspoon ground cinnamon
- ¼ teaspoon salt
- Powdered stevia, to taste

- 6 tablespoons coconut oil

Directions:

1. Preheat the oven to 375F and lightly grease a 10-inch cast-iron skillet.
2. Spread the berries on the bottom of the skillet.
3. Whisk together the dry ingredients in a mixing bowl.
4. Cut in the coconut oil using a fork to create a crumbled mixture.
5. Spread the crumble over the berries and bake for 25 minutes until hot and bubbling.
6. Cool the cobbler for 5 to 10 minutes before serving.

Nutrition: Calories 215 Fat 16.8g, Carbs 13.1g, Protein 3.7g, Sugar 5.3g, Fiber 6.4g, Sodium 61mg

172.   Coffee-Steamed Carrots

Preparation Time: 10 minutes

Cooking Time: 3 minutes

Servings: 4

Ingredients:

- 1 cup brewed coffee
- 1 teaspoon light brown sugar
- ½ teaspoon kosher salt
- Freshly ground black pepper
- 1-pound baby carrots
- Chopped fresh parsley
- 1 teaspoon grated lemon zest

Directions:

1. Pour the coffee into the electric pressure cooker. Stir in the brown sugar, salt, and pepper. Add the carrots.
2. Close the pressure cooker. Set to sealing.
3. Cook on high pressure for minutes.
4. Once complete, click Cancel and quick release the pressure.

5. Once the pin drops, open and remove the lid.
6. Using a slotted spoon, portion carrots to a serving bowl. Topped with the parsley and lemon zest, and serve.

Nutrition: Calories: 48 Carbs: 11g Protein: 3g Sugar: 11g; Fiber: 10g; Sodium: 318mg

173.   Rosemary Potatoes

Preparation Time: 5 minutes

Cooking Time: 25 minutes

Servings: 2

Ingredients:

- 1lb red potatoes
- 1 cup vegetable stock
- 2tbsp olive oil
- 2tbsp rosemary sprigs

Directions:

1. Situate potatoes in the steamer basket and add the stock into the Instant Pot.
2. Steam the potatoes in your Instant Pot for 15 minutes.
3. Depressurize and pour away the remaining stock.
4. Set to sauté and add the oil, rosemary, and potatoes.
5. Cook until brown.

Nutrition: Calories 171 Carbs 21g Protein 6.8g Sugar: 11g; Fiber: 9g; Sodium: 396mg

174.   Vegetable Salad

Preparation time: 10 minutes

Cooking time: 0 minutes

Servings: 1-2

Ingredients:

- 4 cups each of raw spinach and romaine lettuce
- 2 cups each of cherry tomatoes, sliced cucumber, chopped baby carrots and

chopped red, orange and yellow bell pepper

- 1 cup each of chopped broccoli, sliced yellow squash, zucchini and cauliflower.

Directions:

1. Wash all these vegetables.

2. Mix in a large mixing bowl and top off with a non-fat or low-fat dressing of your choice.

Nutrition: Calories: 48 Carbs: 11g Protein: 3g Sugar: 11g; Fiber: 10g; Sodium: 318mg

Dessert Recipes

175. Peanut Butter Cups

Preparation Time: 5 minutes

Cooking Time: 10 minutes

Servings: 4

Ingredients:

- 1 packet plain gelatin
- ¼ cup sugar substitute
- 2 cups nonfat cream
- ½ teaspoon vanilla
- ¼ cup low-fat peanut butter
- 2 tablespoons unsalted peanuts, chopped

Directions:

1. Mix gelatin, sugar substitute and cream in a pan.
2. Let sit for 5 minutes.
3. Place over medium heat and cook until gelatin has been dissolved.
4. Stir in vanilla and peanut butter.
5. Pour into custard cups. Chill for 3 hours.
6. Top with the peanuts and serve.

Nutrition: 171 Calories 21g Carbohydrate 6.8g Protein

176. Fruit Pizza

Preparation Time: 5 minutes

Cooking Time: 10 minutes

Servings: 4

Ingredients:

- 1 teaspoon maple syrup
- ¼ teaspoon vanilla extract
- ½ cup coconut milk yogurt
- 2 round slices watermelon
- ½ cup blackberries, sliced
- ½ cup strawberries, sliced
- 2 tablespoons coconut flakes (unsweetened)

Directions:

1. Mix maple syrup, vanilla and yogurt in a bowl.

2. Spread the mixture on top of the watermelon slice.

3. Top with the berries and coconut flakes.

Nutrition: Calories 70 Carbs 14.6g Protein 1.2g Sugar: 13.2g; Fiber: 9.4g; Sodium: 331mg

177. Choco Peppermint Cake

Preparation Time: 5 minutes

Cooking Time: 10 minutes

Servings: 4

Ingredients:

- Cooking spray
- 1/3 cup oil
- 15 oz. package chocolate cake mix
- 3 eggs, beaten
- 1 cup water
- ¼ teaspoon peppermint extract

Directions:

1. Spray slow cooker with oil.

2. Mix all the ingredients in a bowl.

3. Use an electric mixer on medium speed setting to mix ingredients for 2 minutes.

4. Pour mixture into the slow cooker.

5. Cover the pot and cook on low for 3 hours.

6. Let cool before slicing and serving.

Nutrition: Calories 102 Carbs 27g Protein 3.8g Sugar: 11g; Fiber: 9g; Sodium: 336mg

178. Roasted Plums

Preparation Time: 5 minutes

Cooking Time: 10 minutes

Servings: 4

Ingredients:

- Cooking spray
- 6 plums, sliced
- ½ cup pineapple juice (unsweetened)
- 1 tablespoon brown sugar
- 2 tablespoons brown sugar
- ¼ teaspoon ground cardamom
- ½ teaspoon ground cinnamon
- 1/8 teaspoon ground cumin

Directions:

1. Combine all the ingredients in a baking pan.

2. Roast in the oven at 450 degrees F for 20 minutes.

Nutrition: Calories 102 Carbs 18.7g Protein 2g Sugar: 11g; Sodium: 396mg Fiber: 9g;

179. Flourless Chocolate Cake

Preparation Time: 10 minutes

Cooking Time: 45 minutes

Servings: 6

Ingredients:

- ½ Cup of stevia

- 12 Ounces of unsweetened baking chocolate
- 2/3 Cup of ghee
- 1/3 Cup of warm water
- ¼ Teaspoon of salt
- 4 Large pastured eggs
- 2 Cups of boiling water

Directions:

1. Line the bottom of a 9-inch pan of a spring form with a parchment paper.

2. Heat the water in a small pot; then add the salt and the stevia over the water until wait until the mixture becomes completely dissolved.

3. Melt the baking chocolate into a double boiler or simply microwave it for about 30 seconds.

4. Mix the melted chocolate and the butter in a large bowl with an electric mixer.

5. Beat in your hot mixture; then crack in the egg and whisk after adding each of the eggs.

6. Pour the obtained mixture into your prepared spring form tray.

7. Wrap the spring form tray with a foil paper.

8. Place the spring form tray in a large cake tray and add boiling water right to the outside; make sure the depth doesn't exceed 1 inch.

9. Bake the cake into the water bath for about 45 minutes at a temperature of about 350 F.

10. Remove the tray from the boiling water and transfer to a wire to cool.

11. Let the cake chill for an overnight in the refrigerator.

Nutrition: Calories 295 Carbs 6g Fiber 4g Sodium: 319mg Protein: 15g; Sugar: 11g;

180.   Lava Cake

Preparation Time: 10 minutes

Cooking Time: 10 minutes

Servings: 2

Ingredients:

- 2 Oz of dark chocolate; you should at least use chocolate of 85% cocoa solids
- 1 Tablespoon of super-fine almond flour
- 2 Oz of unsalted almond butter
- 2 Large eggs

Directions:

1.   Heat your oven to a temperature of about 350 Fahrenheit.

2.   Grease 2 heat proof ramekins with almond butter.

3.   Now, melt the chocolate and the almond butter and stir very well.

4.   Beat the eggs very well with a mixer.

5.   Add the eggs to the chocolate and the butter mixture and mix very well with almond flour and the swerve; then stir.

6.   Pour the dough into 2 ramekins.

7.   Bake for about 9 to 10 minutes.

8.   Turn the cakes over plates and serve with pomegranate seeds!

Nutrition: Calories 459 Carbs 3.5g Fiber 0.8g Protein: 15g; Sugar: 11g; Sodium: 273mg

181.   Pretzels

Preparation Time: 10 minutes

Cooking Time: 20 minutes

Servings: 8

Ingredients:

- 1 and ½ cups of pre-shredded mozzarella
- 2 Tablespoons of full fat cream cheese
- 1 Large egg

- ¾ Cup of almond flour+ 2 tablespoons of ground almonds or almond meal
- ½ Teaspoon of baking powder
- 1 Pinch of coarse sea salt

Directions:

1.   Heat your oven to a temperature of about 180 C/356 F.

2.   Melt the cream cheese and the mozzarella cheese and stir over a low heat until the cheeses are perfectly melted.

3.   If you choose to microwave the cheese, just do that for about 1 minute no more and if you want to do it on the stove, turn off the heat as soon as the cheese is completely melted.

4.   Add the large egg to the prepared warm dough; then stir until your ingredients are very well combined. If the egg is cold; you will need to heat it gently.

5.   Add in the ground almonds or the almond flour and the baking powder and stir until your ingredients are very well combined.

6.   Take one pinch of the dough of cheese and toll it or stretch it in your hands until it is about 18 to 20 cm of length; if your dough is sticky, you can oil your hands to avoid that.

7.   Now, form pretzels from the cheese dough and nicely shape it; then place it over a baking sheet.

8.   Sprinkle with a little bit of salt and bake for about 17 minutes.

Nutrition: Calories 113 Carbs 2.5g Fiber 0.8g Protein: 11g; Sugar: 12g; Sodium: 314mg

182.   Cheesy Taco Bites

Preparation Time: 5 minutes

Cooking Time: 10minutes

Serving: 12

Ingredients

- 2 Cups of Packaged Shredded Cheddar Cheese
- 2 Tablespoon of Chili Powder
- 2 Tablespoons of Cumin

- 1 Teaspoon of Salt
- 8 Teaspoons of coconut cream for garnishing
- Use Pico de Gallo for garnishing as well

Directions:

1. Preheat your oven to a temperature of about 350 F.

2. Over a baking sheet lined with a parchment paper, place 1 tablespoon piles of cheese and make sure to a space of 2 inches between each.

3. Place the baking sheet in your oven and bake for about 5 minutes.

4. Remove from the oven and let the cheese cool down for about 1 minute; then carefully lift up and press each into the cups of a mini muffin tin.

5. Make sure to press the edges of the cheese to form the shape of muffins mini.

6. Let the cheese cool completely; then remove it.

7. While you continue to bake the cheese and create your cups.

8. Fill the cheese cups with the coconut cream, then top with the Pico de Gallo.

Nutrition: Calories 73 Carbs 3g Protein 4g Sugar: 11g; Fiber: 9g; Sodium: 237mg

183. Nut Squares

Preparation Time: 30 minutes

Cooking Time: 10 minutes

Serving: 10

Ingredients:

- 2 Cups of almonds, pumpkin seeds, sunflower seeds and walnuts
- ½ Cup of desiccated coconut
- 1 Tablespoon of chia seeds
- ¼ Teaspoon of salt
- 2 Tablespoons of coconut oil
- 1 Teaspoon of vanilla extract

- 3 Tablespoons of almond or peanut butter
- 1/3 Cup of Sukrin Gold Fiber Syrup

Directions:

1. Line a square baking tin with a baking paper; then lightly grease it with cooking spray

2. Chop all the nuts roughly; then slightly grease it too, you can also leave them as whole

3. Mix the nuts in a large bowl; then combine them in a large bowl with the coconut, the chia seeds and the salt

4. In a microwave-proof bowl; add the coconut oil; then add the vanilla, the coconut butter or oil, the almond butter and the fiber syrup and microwave the mixture for about 30 seconds

5. Stir your ingredients together very well; then pour the melted mixture right on top of the nuts

6. Press the mixture into your prepared baking tin with the help of the back of a measuring cup and push very well

7. Freeze your treat for about 1 hour before cutting it

8. Cut your frozen nut batter into small cubes or squares of the same size

Nutrition: Calories 268 Carbs 14g Fiber 1g Protein: 18g; Sugar: 11g; Sodium: 329mg

184. Pumpkin & Banana Ice Cream

Preparation Time: 5 minutes

Cooking Time: 10 minutes

Servings: 4

Ingredients:

- 15 oz. pumpkin puree
- 4 bananas, sliced and frozen
- 1 teaspoon pumpkin pie spice
- Chopped pecans

Directions:

1. Add pumpkin puree, bananas and pumpkin pie spice in a food processor.

2. Pulse until smooth.

3. Chill in the refrigerator.

4. Garnish with pecans.

Nutrition: Calories 71 Carbs 18g Protein 1.2g Sugar: 11g; Fiber: 9g; Sodium: 396mg

185. Brulee Oranges

Preparation Time: 5 minutes

Cooking Time: 10 minutes

Servings: 4

Ingredients:

- 4 oranges, sliced into segments
- 1 teaspoon ground cardamom
- 6 teaspoons brown sugar
- 1 cup nonfat Greek yogurt

Directions:

1. Preheat your broiler.

2. Arrange orange slices in a baking pan.

3. In a bowl, mix the cardamom and sugar.

4. Sprinkle mixture on top of the oranges. Broil for 5 minutes.

5. Serve oranges with yogurt.

Nutrition: Calories 168 Carbs 26.9g Protein 6.8g Sugar: 13g; Fiber: 19g; Sodium: 221mg

186. Frozen Lemon & Blueberry

Preparation Time: 5 minutes

Cooking Time: 10 minutes

Servings: 4

Ingredients:

- 6 cup fresh blueberries
- 8 sprigs fresh thyme
- ¾ cup light brown sugar
- 1 teaspoon lemon zest
- ¼ cup lemon juice
- 2 cups water

Directions:

1. Add blueberries, thyme and sugar in a pan over medium heat.

2. Cook for 6 to 8 minutes.

3. Transfer mixture to a blender.

4. Remove thyme sprigs.

5. Stir in the remaining ingredients.

6. Pulse until smooth.

7. Strain mixture and freeze for 1 hour.

Nutrition: Calories 78 Carbs 20g Protein 3g Sugar: 21g; Fiber: 12g; Sodium: 391mg

187. Peanut Butter Choco Chip Cookies

Preparation Time: 5 minutes

Cooking Time: 10 minutes

Servings: 4

Ingredients:

- 1 egg
- ½ cup light brown sugar
- 1 cup natural unsweetened peanut butter
- Pinch salt
- ¼ cup dark chocolate chips

Directions:

1. Preheat your oven to 375 degrees F.

2. Mix egg, sugar, peanut butter, salt and chocolate chips in a bowl.

3. Form into cookies and place in a baking pan.

4. Bake the cookie for 10 minutes.

5. Let cool before serving.

Nutrition: Calories 159 Carbs 12g Protein 4.3g Sugar: 11g; Fiber: 9g; Sodium: 313mg

188. Watermelon Sherbet

Preparation Time: 5 minutes

Cooking Time: 3 minutes

Servings: 4

Ingredients:

- 6 cups watermelon, sliced into cubes
- 14 oz. almond milk
- 1 tablespoon honey
- ¼ cup lime juice
- Salt to taste

Directions:

1. Freeze watermelon for 4 hours.
2. Add frozen watermelon and other ingredients in a blender.
3. Blend until smooth.
4. Transfer to a container with seal.
5. Seal and freeze for 4 hours.

Nutrition: 132 Calories 24.5g Carbohydrate 3.1g Protein

189. Strawberry & Mango Ice Cream

Preparation Time: 5 minutes

Cooking Time: 10 minutes

Servings: 4

Ingredients:

- 8 oz. strawberries, sliced
- 12 oz. mango, sliced into cubes
- 1 tablespoon lime juice

Directions:

1. Add all ingredients in a food processor.
2. Pulse for 2 minutes.
3. Chill before serving.

Nutrition: Calories 70 Carbs 17.4g Protein 11g; Sugar: 12.1g Fiber: 15g; Sodium: 292mg

190. Sparkling Fruit Drink

Preparation Time: 5 minutes

Cooking Time: 10 minutes

Servings: 4

Ingredients:

- 8 oz. unsweetened grape juice
- 8 oz. unsweetened apple juice
- 8 oz. unsweetened orange juice
- 1 qt. homemade ginger ale
- Ice

Directions:

1.   1.Makes 7 servings. Mix first 4 ingredients together in a pitcher. Stir in ice cubes and 9 ounces of the beverage to each glass. Serve immediately.

Nutrition: Calories 60 Protein 1.1g Carbs: 71g; Sodium: 396mg Sugar: 11g; Fiber: 9g;

191. Tiramisu Shots

Preparation Time: 5 minutes

Cooking Time: 10 minutes

Servings: 4

Ingredients:

- 1 pack silken tofu
- 1 oz. dark chocolate, finely chopped
- ¼ cup sugar substitute
- 1 teaspoon lemon juice
- ¼ cup brewed espresso
- Pinch salt
- 24 slices angel food cake
- Cocoa powder (unsweetened)

Directions:

1.   Add tofu, chocolate, sugar substitute, lemon juice, espresso and salt in a food processor.
2.   Pulse until smooth.

3.   Add angel food cake pieces into shot glasses.

4.   Drizzle with the cocoa powder.

5.   Pour the tofu mixture on top.

6.   Top with the remaining angel food cake pieces.

7.   Chill for 30 minutes and serve.

Nutrition: Calories 75 Carbs 12g Protein 2.9g Sugar: 9g; Fiber: 18g; Sodium: 272mg

192.   Ice Cream Brownie Cake

Preparation Time: 5 minutes

Cooking Time: 10 minutes

Servings: 4

Ingredients:

- Cooking spray
- 12 oz. no-sugar brownie mix
- ¼ cup oil
- 2 egg whites
- 3 tablespoons water
- 2 cups sugar-free ice cream

Directions:

1.   Preheat your oven to 325 degrees F.

2.   Spray your baking pan with oil.

3.   Mix brownie mix, oil, egg whites and water in a bowl.

4.   Pour into the baking pan.

5.   Bake for 25 minutes.

6.   Let cool.

7.   Freeze brownie for 2 hours.

8.   Spread ice cream over the brownie.

9.   Freeze for 8 hours.

Nutrition: Calories 198 Carbs 33g Protein 3g Sugar: 11g; Fiber: 9g; Sodium: 256mg

193.   Berry Sorbet

Preparation time: 10 minutes

Cooking time: 20 minutes

Servings: 6

Ingredients:

- Water, 2 c
- Blend strawberries, 2 c
- Spelt Flour, 1.5 tsp.
- Date sugar,.5 c

Directions:

1.   Add the water into a large pot and let the water begin to warm. Add the flour and date sugar and stir until dissolved. Allow this mixture to start boiling and continue to cook for around ten minutes. It should have started to thicken. Take off the heat and set to the side to cool.

2.   Once the syrup has cooled off, add in the strawberries, and stir well to combine.

3.   Pour into a container that is freezer safe and put it into the freezer until frozen.

4.   Take sorbet out of the freezer, cut into chunks, and put it either into a blender or a food processor. Hit the pulse button until the mixture is creamy.

5.   Pour this into the same freezer-safe container and put it back into the freezer for four hours.

Nutrition: Calories: 99 Carbs: 8 g Protein: 15g; Sugar: 11g; Fiber: 9g; Sodium: 396mg

194.   Quinoa Porridge

Preparation time: 5 minutes

Cooking time: 15 minutes

Servings: 04

Ingredients:

- Zest of one lime
- Coconut milk,.5 c
- Cloves,.5 tsp.
- Ground ginger, 1.5 tsp.
- Spring water, 2 c
- Quinoa, 1 c

- Grated apple, 1

Directions:

1.   Cook the quinoa. Follow the instructions on the package. When the quinoa has been cooked, drain well. Place it back into the pot and stir in spices.

2.   Add coconut milk and stir well to combine.

3.   Grate the apple now and stir well.

4.   Divide equally into bowls and add the lime zest on top. Sprinkle with nuts and seeds of choice.

Nutrition: Calories: 180 Fat: 3 g Carbs: 40 g Protein: 10 g Sugar: 10g; Fiber: 19g; Sodium: 322mg

195.   Apple Quinoa

Preparation time: 15 minutes

Cooking time: 30 minutes

Servings: 04

Ingredients:

- Coconut oil, 1 tbsp.
- Ginger
- Key lime.5
- Apple, 1
- Quinoa,.5 c
- Optional toppings
- Seeds
- Nuts
- Berries

Directions:

1.   Fix the quinoa according to the instructions on the package. When you are getting close to the end of the **Cooking time,** grate in the apple and cook for 30 seconds.

2.   Zest the lime into the quinoa and squeeze the juice in. Stir in the coconut oil.

3.   Divide evenly into bowls and sprinkle with some ginger.

4.   You can add in some berries, nuts, and seeds right before you eat.

Nutrition: Calories: 146 Fiber: 2.3 g Fat: 8.3 g Protein: 17g; Carbs: 71g; Sugar: 13g; Sodium: 381mg

196.   Kamut Porridge

Preparation time: 10 minutes

Cooking time: 25 minutes

Servings: 04

Ingredients:

- Agave syrup, 4 tbsp.
- Coconut oil, 1 tbsp.
- Sea salt,.5 tsp.
- Coconut milk, 3.75 c
- Kamut berries, 1 c
- Optional toppings
- Berries
- Coconut chips
- Ground nutmeg
- Ground cloves

Directions:

1.   You need to "crack" the Kamut berries. You can try this by placing the berries into a food processor and pulsing until you have 1.25 cups of Kamut.

2.   Place the cracked Kamut in a pot with salt and coconut milk. Give it a good stir in order to combine everything. Allow this mixture to come to a full rolling boil and then turn the heat down until the mixture is simmering. Stir every now and then until the Kamut has thickened to your likeness. This normally takes about ten minutes.

3.   Take off heat, stir in agave syrup and coconut oil.

4.   Garnish with toppings of choice and enjoy.

Nutrition: Calories: 114 Protein: 5 g Fat: 8.3 g Carbs: 24g Fiber: 4 g: 11g; Sodium: 383mg

197. Hot Kamut With Peaches, Walnuts, And Coconut

Preparation time: 10 minutes

Cooking time: 35 minutes

Servings: 04

Ingredients:

- Toasted coconut, 4 tbsp.
- Toasted and chopped walnuts,.5 c
- Chopped dried peaches, 8
- Coconut milk, 3 c
- Kamut cereal, 1 c

Directions:

1. Mix the coconut milk into a saucepan and allow it to warm up. When it begins simmering, add in the Kamut. Let this cook about 15 minutes, while stirring every now and then.

2. When done, divide evenly into bowls and top with the toasted coconut, walnuts, and peaches.

3. You could even go one more and add some fresh berries.

Nutrition: Calories: 156 Protein: 5.8 g Fat: 7.5 g Carbs: 25 g Fiber: 6 g Sugar: 11g; Sodium: 396mg

198. Overnight "Oats"

Preparation time: 5 minutes

Cooking time: 0 minutes

Servings: 04

Ingredients:

- Berry of choice,.5 c
- Walnut butter,.5 tbsp.
- Burro banana,.5
- Ginger,.5 tsp.
- Coconut milk,.5 c
- Hemp seeds,.5 c

Directions:

1. Put the hemp seeds, salt, and coconut milk into a glass jar. Mix well.

2. Place the lid on the jar then put in the refrigerator to sit overnight.

3. The next morning, add the ginger, berries, and banana. Stir well and enjoy.

Nutrition: Calories: 139 Fat: 4.1 g Protein: 9 g Sugar: 7 g Carbs: 15g Fiber: 12g; Sodium: 283mg

199. Blueberry Cupcakes

Preparation time: 15 minutes

Cooking time: 40 minutes

Servings: 04

Ingredients:

- Grapeseed oil
- Sea salt,.5 tsp.
- Sea moss gel,.25 c
- Agave,.3 c
- Blueberries,.5 c
- Teff flour,.75 c
- Spelt flour,.75 c
- Coconut milk, 1 c

Directions:

1. Warm your oven to 365. Place paper liners into a muffin tin.

2. Place sea moss gel, sea salt, agave, flour, and milk in large bowl. Mix well to combine. Gently fold in blueberries.

3. Gently pour batter into paper liners. Place in oven and bake 30 minutes.

4. They are done if they have turned a nice golden color, and they spring back when you touch them.

Nutrition: Calories: 85 Fat: 0.7 g Carbs: 12 g Protein: 1.4 g Fiber: 5 g Sugar: 11g; Sodium: 686mg

Chapter 6: Meal Plan

28 DAYS	BREAKFAST	LUNCH	DINNER
Day 1	Bacon and Chicken Garlic Wrap	Cauliflower Rice with Chicken	Cauliflower Mac & Cheese
Day 2	Salty Macadamia Chocolate Smoothie	Turkey with Fried Eggs	Easy Egg Salad
Day 3	Buckwheat grouts breakfast bowl	Sweet Potato, Kale, and White Bean Stew	Baked Chicken Legs
Day 4	Peach muesli bake	Slow Cooker Two-Bean Sloppy Joes	Creamed Spinach
Day 5	Steel-cut oatmeal bowl with fruit and nuts	Lighter Eggplant Parmesan	Stuffed Mushrooms
Day 6	Whole-grain dutch baby pancake	Coconut-Lentil Curry	Vegetable Soup
Day 7	Mushroom, zucchini, and onion frittata	Stuffed Portobello with Cheese	Pork Chop Diane
Day 8	Berry-oat breakfast bars	Lighter Shrimp Scampi	Autumn Pork Chops with Red Cabbage and Apples
Day 9	Spinach and cheese quiche	Maple-Mustard Salmon	Chipotle Chili Pork Chops
Day 10	Spicy Jalapeno Popper Deviled Eggs	Chicken Salad with Grapes and Pecans	Orange-Marinated Pork Tenderloin
Day 11	Blueberry breakfast cake	Roasted Vegetables	Homestyle Herb Meatballs
Day 12	Lovely Porridge	Millet Pilaf	Lime-Parsley Lamb Cutlets
Day 13	Basil and Tomato Baked Eggs	Sweet and Sour Onions	Mediterranean Steak Sandwiches
Day 14	Whole-grain pancakes	Sautéed Apples and Onions	Roasted Beef with Peppercorn Sauce
Day 15	Whole-grain breakfast cookies	Zucchini Noodles with Portabella Mushrooms	Coffee-and-Herb-Marinated Steak
Day 16	Cinnamon and Coconut Porridge	Grilled Tempeh with Pineapple	Traditional Beef Stroganoff

Day 17	An Omelet of Swiss chard	Courgettes In Cider Sauce	Chicken and Roasted Vegetable Wraps
Day 18	Cheesy Low-Carb Omelet	Baked Mixed Mushrooms	Spicy Chicken Cacciatore
Day 19	Yogurt and Kale Smoothie	Spiced Okra	Scallion Sandwich
Day 20	Grilled Chicken Platter	Lemony Salmon Burgers	Lean Lamb and Turkey Meatballs with Yogurt
Day 21	Parsley Chicken Breast	Caprese Turkey Burgers	Air Fried Section and Tomato
Day 22	Mustard Chicken	Pasta Salad	Cheesy Salmon Fillets
Day 23	Balsamic Chicken	Chicken, Strawberry, And Avocado Salad	Salmon with Asparagus
Day 24	Greek Chicken Breast	Lemon-Thyme Eggs	Shrimp in Garlic Butter
Day 25	Chipotle Lettuce Chicken	Spinach Salad with Bacon	Cobb Salad
Day 26	Stylish Chicken-Bacon Wrap	Pea and Collards Soup	Seared Tuna Steak
Day 27	Healthy Cottage Cheese Pancakes	Spanish Stew	Beef Chili
Day 28	Avocado Lemon Toast	Creamy Taco Soup	Greek Broccoli Salad

Conclusion

Diabetes is a life-threatening disease caused by a lack of insulin. Insulin is a hormone that is required for the body's healthy functioning. The cells in a person's body do not respond to insulin effectively when they acquire diabetes. As a result, the cells does not get the energy and nutrients they require, and they begin to die.

Being diagnosed with diabetes will bring some major changes in your lifestyle. From the time you are diagnosed with it, it would always be a constant battle with food. You need to become a lot more careful with your food choices and the quantity that you ate. Every meal will feel like a major effort. You will be planning every day for the whole week, well in advance. Depending upon the type of food you ate, you have to keep checking your blood sugar levels. You may get used to taking long breaks between meals and staying away from snacks between dinner and breakfast.

Food would be treated as a bomb like it can go off at any time. According to an old saying, "When the body gets too hot, then your body heads straight to the kitchen."

Managing diabetes can be a very, very stressful ordeal. There will be many times that you will mark your glucose levels down on a piece of paper like you are plotting graph lines or something. You will mix your insulin shots up and then stress about whether or not you are giving yourself the right dosage. You will always be over-cautious because it involves a LOT of math and a really fine margin of error. But now, those days are gone!

With the help of technology and books, you can stock your kitchen with the right foods, like meal plans, diabetic friendly dishes, etc. You can also get an app that will even do the work for you. You can also people-watch on the internet and find the know-how to cook and eat right; you will always be a few meals away from certain disasters, like a plummeting blood sugar level. Always carry some sugar in your pocket. You won't have to experience the pangs of hunger but if you are unlucky, you will have to ration your food and bring along some simple low-calorie snacks with you.

This is the future of diabetes.

As you've reached the end of this book, you have gained complete control of your diabetes and this is where your expedition towards a better, healthier life starts. I hope I was able to inculcate some knowledge into you and make this adventure a little bit less of a struggle.

I would like to remind you that you're not alone in having to manage this disease and that nearly 85% of the new cases are 20 years old or younger.

Regardless of the length or seriousness of your diabetes, it can be managed! Take the information presented here and start with it!

Preparation is key to having a healthier and happier life.

It's helpful to remember that every tool at your disposal can help in some way.

Recipe index

Zucchini Noodles with Portabella
Mushrooms, 191

Zucchini Pizza, 92

Manufactured by Amazon.ca
Bolton, ON